FAITHFUL

PORTRAITS OF INTERNATIONAL SOCIAL WORK NOTABLES

ANGELS

James O. Billups, Editor

FAITHFUL

PORTRAITS OF INTERNATIONAL SOCIAL WORK NOTABLES

ANGELS

James O. Billups, Editor

NASW PRESS

National Association of Social Workers
Washington, DC

Terry Mizrahi, MSW, PhD, *President*
Elizabeth J. Clark, PhD, ACSW, MPH, *Executive Director*

CHERYL Y. BRADLEY, *Director, Member Services and Publications*
PAULA L. DELO, *Executive Editor*
SUSAN FISHER, *Staff Editor*
STEPH SELICE, *Senior Editor*
WILLIAM F. SCHROEDER, *Staff Editor*
JANUARY LAYMAN-WOOD, *Acquisitions Editor*
CHRISTINA BROMLEY, *Editorial Assistant*
ANNE R. GRANT, *Copy Editor*
NATALIE HOLMES, *Copy Editor*
LEONARD S. ROSENBAUM, *Proofreader and Indexer*

Cover and interior design by Metadog Design Group, Washington, DC
Printed and bound by Victor Graphics, Inc., Baltimore, MD

© 2002 by the NASW Press

LIBRARY OF CONGRESS CATALOGING-IN-PUBLICATION DATA

Faithful angels : portraits of international social work notables / James O. Billups, editor.
  p. cm.
  Includes index.
  ISBN 0-87101-314-2
  1. Social workers—Interviews. 2. Social service—History—20th Century. I.
  Billups, James O.

  HV27 .F35 2002
  361.7'3'0922—dc21

                                                            2001059095

TABLE OF CONTENTS

DEDICATION

This book is dedicated to the "faithful angels" represented here, other "faithful angels" not represented, and those in the process of becoming "faithful angels," all of whom illustrate through their life stories the laudable purposes and goals of social work, including concern for both private troubles and public issues, personal service, and social change.
James O. Billups

IN MEMORY OF
JAMES O. BILLUPS, DSW
1930–1999

J im Billups died suddenly on November 3, 1999, at age 69. Over the years in which he worked so diligently on *Faithful Angels*, Jim's greatest concern was that the book be a worthy tribute to the interviewees whom he admired so much and to the profession they loved. His loss is deeply felt by all who knew him.

This book is left as a tribute to an exceptional person and to the challenging and rewarding lifework he and others chose. Those of us who came to know Jim during the production of *Faithful Angels* considered him to be among the warmest, smartest, and most caring professionals we had ever known. The rare combination of honesty, wit, kindness, and talent that characterized him also shines through in this book, as does his affection for the 15 "angels" and his respect for their achievements.

Jim was highly regarded by his colleagues in NASW, of which he was a member since the early 1950s, and at The Ohio State University, where he was on the faculty for more than 30 years. But his greatest impact was probably felt in his deep commitment to international social work and the universality of what he believed his profession had to offer. Through his two terms as president of the Inter–University Consortium for International Social Development (IUCISD), his consulting work, his many publications, and his presentations and speeches all over the world, Jim dedicated himself to promoting peace and social justice through international social work and through the comradeship he shared with so many people. He was himself a faithful angel and a blessing to know and work with, and we miss him.

The Staff at NASW Press

PREFACE

T his book has come into being thanks to several inspirational events over the course of more than 30 years. Among the most memorable was studying the lives of early social work pioneers during my doctoral study at the George Warren Brown School of Social Work, Washington University in St. Louis. At that time, the mid-1960s, I had several engaging discussions about these pioneers with Professors Ralph and Muriel Pumphrey, based in large part on their widely acclaimed book, *The Heritage of American Social Work: Readings in its Philosophical and Institutional Development.*

Ralph Pumphrey was coordinating the writing of biographical sketches of nearly 100 deceased North American social workers who had made distinguished contributions to social work development or social welfare organization over the previous 100 years. I was invited to research and write up a small number of the sketches, all of which were to appear in the 1965 edition of *Encyclopedia of Social Work.*

One of the most unforgettable characters I met through the literature was Mary Eliza McDowell (1854–1936), who was director of the University of Chicago Settlement House for 40 years. I was fascinated to discover that she had earned several affectionate nicknames as a result of battles she had fought successfully on behalf of her settlement house neighbors and others. She was known at various stages of her career as the Victorious Garbage Lady, the Duchess of Bubbly Creek, Fighting Mary, the Angel of the Stockyards, the Social Politician, and One of the World's Best Neighbors. Similarly, Owen R. Lovejoy (1866–1961), an early child welfare advocate, had been described as that 'brave champion of good causes" and as one of the "unsung heroes of social work."

In summation, my meetings with the Pumphreys—and by extension my meetings through the literature with some of the profession's pioneers—were a welcome, largely unexpected, source of professional inspiration.

As the years went by, I became increasingly aware of other, more recent, inspirational social workers from many parts of the world. Like the early professional pioneers, they were making noteworthy contributions both to the profession and to human well-being. There were many opportunities for my path to cross with those individuals who were taking highly creative and often courageous actions, providing the profession with extraordinary leadership and exemplary practice in our own time. I was also encountering still other exemplary social workers by indirect means, either through their work in the professional literature or through public recognitions they had received from organizations that I respected.

Somewhat disconcertingly, I was increasingly aware that relatively few of my contemporaries seemed to know of these colleagues or the examples they were setting. Unlike the well-documented accounts of early national and international social work pioneers like Jane Addams, Stanton Coit, Frances Perkins, and Harry Hopkins, the professional contributions of more recent social workers have gone largely unrecorded. There were, of course, exceptions, such as the biographies of Whitney Young (1921–1971), social work champion of civil rights in the 1960s and adviser to American presidents John F. Kennedy and Lyndon B. Johnson. Nevertheless, detailed biographical history of the modern social worker of note was the exception rather than the rule. I saw a recognizable need to rectify this imbalance. However, even with my widening familiarity with some of today's social work leaders from around the world, I had no clear way to go about addressing the problem.

Then, almost 30 years after my initial study of the early pioneers of the modern–day profession, a fortuitous event took place. In 1995, I was invited to serve with Roland Meinert as guest co-editor of a special international issue of a new journal, *Reflections: Narratives of Professional Helping*. The journal's editor-in-chief, Sonia Abels, suggested that for this special issue I interview Dr. Katherine Kendall, who has held national and international social work leadership positions with great distinction during the second half of this century.

The interview was conducted and published. I found it highly inspirational, as well as unusually informative. However, because of the unflagging devotion and contributions of Katherine Kendall to the profession, it was soon out of date. I thought it deserved to be further developed. Moreover, the more I thought about it, the more I realized that the interview procedure might serve as the vehicle for capturing and collecting the reflections not only of this one remarkable individual but of a group of distinguished social workers around the world who have made noteworthy achievements in the past 50 or so years. My thought was that publishing such a collection might help fill the gap in the historical record of social work; as Ralph Waldo Emerson said, "There is no proper history, only biography."

My aim in collecting and preserving the life histories of key international figures in the social work profession has been to tap the hard-won wisdom, insights, and expertise they have gained—to learn why, when, where, and especially how these individuals have used their vision, knowledge, and skill to advance social work, social development, and human realization.

Six social workers with expertise in international social work and a ready familiarity with notable social workers from around the globe became the advisery panel for the work. They were asked to use a "reputational" model, employing three criteria to identify members of the profession that they rated most highly. The first and most important criterion was that individuals nominated must have made exceptional professional contributions to social work and to people's well-being in their own country *and beyond* during a major part of the second half of the twentieth century. Notables meeting this criterion, it turned out, were generally well known by the reputations they had gained through the philosophies they espoused, the professional responsibilities they assumed, the initiatives they undertook, and the public recognitions they received. Second, the nominees were to have reached retirement age in their own societies by the time of the interview. Third, the nominees were to have formally retired from their principal full-time professional positions (although not necessarily from all facets of their career activity) by the time the interviews were completed.

Nearly 40 names were submitted. Based on those individuals who were nominated with greatest frequency, the pool of candidates was narrowed to 15. This group came from all continents and was almost evenly divided by country of residence and location of principal professional practice, between countries generally identified as the Global South and the Global North.

The 15 were invited to be interviewed. Each agreed. All provided the requested professional résumé and most volunteered other documentary materials that they deemed might be helpful as background information.

On the strength of the documents provided to me, I first sent to each participant an individualized set of core questions, though the questions all followed a somewhat similar format. Each had the opportunity to individualize further the shape and direction of the interview by suggesting modifications to the questions, either before or during the interviews.

In most cases the interviews were conducted in the home country of the interview participant. Each interview usually took place in three or four sittings over two to three days, producing four to seven hours of audio tapes. The idea was to approach these recognized leaders person-to-person in a way that would allow them to share as freely and fully as possible their professional perspectives, concerns, approaches, and reflections on their major lifework.

After each interview, a transcript was returned to the participant to review for accuracy. All transcribed interviews were put through three or more revisions, until each of us agreed that the manuscript was ready for the publisher.

This book counterpoises the major theme of Harry Specht and Mark Courtney in *Unfaithful Angels: How Social Work Has Abandoned its Mission* (1994). Specht and Courtney pointed to many members of the profession in the USA (and perhaps implicitly in other parts of the world) who had become "unfaithful angels," forsaking the larger purposes of social work in their rush to practice "individual repair" through popular psychotherapies. The social work professionals featured here make clear—through their key values, career commitments, professional pursuits, experiences and reflections—that social work is not without its *faithful* angels.

As their stories unfold, the international notables whose lives are depicted in this book demonstrate that social workers can do more, and indeed are expected to do more, than practice within orientations that are primarily associated with disciplines other than social work (e.g., psychotherapy). Neither are social workers expected to limit their professional practice exclusively to the smallest of social systems and social structures.

The faithful angels have a broad vision and a wide repertoire of practice approaches that all remain integral parts of social work. They have engaged themselves in inventive interventions that may include but go well beyond conventional micro-oriented practices. Each of them has worked with groups and organizations through community and social development, social policy formulation, and social action, as well as other endeavors aimed at bringing about needed social change.

In their own words, these faithful angels tell about exceptional activism, often taking risks in out-of-the-ordinary but critically important fields of practice. They have been creative in multiple capacities: human rights advocate in behalf of national liberation; organizer of refugee camps; initiator of credit and loan services to women's micro-enterprises; trainer of military peacekeepers; leader, consultant, or adviser to a far-ranging array of organizations, from slum youth groups to the United Nations; social program initiator and educator in times of war, dictatorship, and revolution; organizer of relief and rehabilitation services; and social agent to help prevent marginalization of distressed populations.

The foreword written by Clarke Chambers previews in a concise but illuminating fashion what the reader may expect to find. In addition, an introductory biographical sketch precedes each interview, and each interview is complemented by a captioned photograph of each featured angel.

These are all useful features. Yet the preeminent feature of this volume is the manner in which each metaphorical angel shares freely and fully his or her story with all who care to learn about, and to profit from, the adventurous and rewarding lifework that social work offers its adherents.

James O. Billups

FOREWORD

T o some critics in the United States, social work in recent decades appeared to be an "unloved profession," feared by clients, suspected of the subversion of long-held American values by taxpaying citizens, and judged by many with a wary and skeptical eye.

These transcripts of oral interviews with social work leaders from regions scattered around this shrinking globe provide other perspectives: Persons engaged in the delivery of human services and the shaping of policies and programs for public well-being constitute a cadre of persons dedicated to making their corner of the world a better place. In this volume, full of stories told in their own words, social workers emerge as part of a many-splendored profession, differing in style and practice according to local or national customs and mores but ultimately united on basic principles and values.

From 13 nations, 15 individuals diverse in family circumstances (some privileged, many pressed to survive), eight women and seven men, reflect on the varied circumstances in their lives. Each narrative has its own authentic integrity. Educated in schools of wide variety and quality, these professionals followed life courses influenced as often by chance as by design. Eventually, all of them, after diverse career experiences, engaged their talents and energies in international enterprises that carried them far beyond their native provinces.

Some enjoyed what we might label "nonlinear" careers, advancing logically from one setting to another, from modest beginnings to major responsibilities. The more usual pattern of career, however, seems to have consisted of unforeseen zigs and zags with little discernable formal logic. The men among these 15 more often pursued the former more formal line; the women more often veered from one opportunity to another, their diverse paths often responding to claims of extended family. Whatever the path, it is clear that family played a crucial role in every case, and one finds in these accounts a moving affirmation of the centrality of family in human affairs.

In the midst of such widely (I am tempted to write *wildly*) varied circumstances and experiences, what commonalities emerge? Are there recurring themes hidden in these spoken autobiographical reports? There are none, I suspect, that cover all 15, but some that occur often enough to justify cautious generalizations.

First let me dwell briefly on some of the differences in the family backgrounds of the participants in this heroic enterprise. James Billups, with abounding energy and uncommon common sense, set out to record the life experiences of notable leaders selected from different nooks of the world. The diversity proved wider than perhaps even he could have guessed:

- Jona Rosenfeld came from a well-to-do Jewish family of Zionist visions in southern Germany, a family that had the resources, the will, and the wit to escape Nazism in the early 1930s by immigrating to Haifa.
- Seno Cornely, oldest of a family of nine boys and four girls, enjoyed the security (and hard labor) of a small farm in Brazil.
- Armaity Desai's parents were both professionals in India's social work system.
- Sattareh Farman-Farmaian's father claimed royal status and substantial wealth; 36 children born of eight wives all received a university education.
- Gloria Abate, daughter of an Italian immigrant to Peru, a self-made man of some success, was encouraged by her father in independent and self-reliant habits.
- Richard Splane, youngest of six children, came from the solid working class of rural Canada.
- Angelina C. Almanzor was born into an affluent business family in the Philippines whose substance was devastated by Japanese occupation in World War II, in which she lost her husband.
- In Australia, John Lawrence's father was a banker whose three children became academics.
- Aida Gindy's family (she was the youngest of five children) was soundly established and all the children followed a family tradition of service to the community.
- Herman Stein, born into a lower-middle-class immigrant family in New York, made his way up and out through the city's open educational system.
- Katherine Kendall, the other United States citizen in this anthology, had the resources and family encouragement for higher education.
- The Swedish Harriet Jakobsson, as a youth, had hoped to become a medical doctor but was persuaded by her prudent father to take up social work as a profession appropriate for girls.
- Meher Nanavatty came from an upper-middle-class family. As such, he says, "I was torn between a pro-British atmosphere at home and an [Indian] nationalist influence at school."
- Robin Huws Jones was reared by his father, "a very financially poor draper"; he spoke his native Welsh, only learning English at age six.
- Esinet Mapondera of Zimbabwe came from one of the poorest families; her husband was imprisoned for his activism as a leader of the African Mine Workers Union.

Clearly, no pattern emerges from these diverse family backgrounds that reflected all sorts and conditions of human kind.

Whether formally instructed or self-taught, all were drawn to an eclectic set of studies and intellectual interests usually centered on the liberal arts, including a firm grounding in humanistic and social scientific disciplines. One can detect a recurring and persisting excitement with the study of history, literature, philosophy, languages, the arts, economics, political science, and anthropology, as well as sociology and social theory. Two of the 15 wrote historical dissertations for their doctoral degrees. It is tempting to speculate that this wide-ranging intellectual curiosity, shared so broadly although experienced in different educational settings, was an important source in their later careers of a responsive versatility, a capacity to move easily through different institutions and agencies, a skill at innovating programs and policies, and, among the educators, an eagerness to initiate programs of professional study that were interdisciplinary.

In short, they were versatile and nimble in all affairs. They went from one agency to another and, later in their careers, skipped from one region of the world to another. Schooling and self-study, direct experience and practice, and working with others in international agencies all enlarged their capacity to be open to new ideas, new cultures, and new modes of practice. They were quick to perceive the interrelationships among issues of education, health, safety, and security—all linked to humane well-being. Intuitively, each found a way always to be involved, committed totally, to borrow a French term, to be *engagé*. They moved between private and public spheres, between school and practice, between neighborhood, regional, and international settings.

All of the 15 were introduced to human service as volunteers: in churches, scouting, YMCA and YWCA, YMHA, Red Cross, disaster work, youth camping, and work with the young in urban slums. Some taught in elementary or secondary schools on their way to social work.

The lifelong habit of reaching out and learning new ways stood them in good stead: Angelina Almanzor built and sold sound, affordable housing for profit. Mapondera kept her family going even while pursuing her professional career by selling her own garden produce in local markets. These international leaders were nimble; they made do and were open to the world, as to the neighborhood.

Most striking of all, they all seemed to find their unique way toward community development as their chief mode of practice, although many received their graduate degrees in American or British schools where casework, sometimes enriched by studies in social policy, was the long suit. Esinet Mapondera articulated that emphasis on grassroots self-help programs that involved teamwork and participation of those in special need. "Social ills stem from poverty," she asserts simply. "Policy had to address abroad social and economic needs of the people." In seeking fundamental social change, one has to begin where people are. First things are first: literacy and educational opportunities for women, the creation of cooperative economic enterprises, access to credit, provision of vocational skills to enhance work and income. The basic principle of successful social work is to enable persons to help themselves.

Harriet Jakobsson echoes those sentiments: "What we must do is support [the people] in doing so." Jona Rosenfeld hopes that school faculties will always be politically involved, that professionals will seek to be partners with those whose needs are to be served. Seno Cornely agrees: Field placements for students ideally should emphasize community settings. He urges the study of consequences that arise from the concentration of wealth—"massive misery and its social-political causes." Social workers, in that view, share daily life with people in need and seek collective solutions towards empowerment. In the classroom, Gloria Abate sought to encourage students to be participants in their own education. Robin Huws Jones asserted that the reform of social policy comes best from practitioners who know first-hand how "unnecessarily complex, patchy, and inadequate" programs of service delivery can become. And it is he who suggested that issues of environmental degradation fall logically within the agenda for action of social work.

Angelina Almanzor, as a young woman during the Japanese occupation of her homeland, earned her spurs working for the underground carrying food and smuggling information into prisoner of war camps. Later, she provided leadership to community groups seeking to solve community problems—poverty, drug use, child abuse, single parenthood—and moved from community action to social development. "Often violations of human rights come about as a result of the competitive pursuit of economic goals with a free market economy." Farm laborers, for example, must achieve the right to receive adequate compensation for work done and for basic medical care, the right to participation, the right to be heard on all of their problems.

Katherine Kendall, for her part, remained true to America's pioneer generation of social workers by seeking to change social and economic conditions that led to poverty and injustice, and to focus on community renewal. Meher Nanavatty shaped similar community–based learning and teaching that involved civic education, adult literacy, and political empowerment.

Sattareh Farman-Farmaian moved for the creation of community centers as staging areas for family planning, hygiene, nutrition, day care, literacy, and vocational training. And from Katherine Kendall, we have the admonition: "We must do a lot more thinking about community, not in the sense of community organization, but rather community renewal . . . and thus get back to the feeling that ours is a compassionate society."

Recorded in these interviews is the remarkable partnership among equals that developed in international social work between professional women and men working together, often under impossibly difficult and even dangerous conditions. In all the interviews, there is no sense of that gender hierarchy that infused so many other professions in that era. No wonder that there is also reflected in the transcripts a desire and a mission to empower the powerless that are so often the poor, especially poor women, and other disadvantaged groups in society. Evidenced throughout the conversations, then, is social work's ultimate commitment to participatory democracy, social justice, and human rights.

In the lives of such women and men, we may all find guidance and courage.

Clarke Chambers

ACKNOWLEDGMENTS

Grateful recognition is extended to the many people who have contributed so generously to making this book a reality. First and foremost, heartfelt appreciation goes to the 15 "faithful angels" whose interviews appear here. Each of them has given unstintingly of time and energy (as well as good measures of hospitality) in sharing so freely and fully their life stories. In doing their parts to complete the collective effort, the "angels" also provided abundant supplies of patience as they read and revised multiple versions of their typewritten audiotape transcripts in order to assure accuracy.

A special recognition goes to Clarke Chambers, an "angel" in his own right, who read drafts of each of the various interview transcripts in order to write the foreword to the book. He went further, providing much appreciated ongoing support throughout the project with his encouraging communications and with most helpful editorial suggestions.

The difficult task of transcribing the audiotapes was accomplished by a group of dedicated typists representing town and gown, including Carol Jiang from the Columbus, Ohio community and Catherine Kay of The Ohio State University Technological Services. Each had to struggle with audiotapes in need of audio enhancement. The Ohio State University student assistants available through the federal work-study program—Carlissa Allen, Monika Cooley, Annette Johnson, and Tarneisha Stimage—also served as able assistants with various drafts of the interview transcripts. Special and timely computer-related technical support was provided by Fred Felter, manager of the public computing sites of The Ohio State University, and Richard Ison, student programmer at The Ohio State University College of Social Work.

Helene Bache and Deborah Merritt, two of The Ohio State University College of Social Work secretaries, literally came to the rescue on more than one occasion. Meeting deadlines at critical points in the preparation of the book proposal and the final publisher–ready manuscript would not have been possible without their delightful poise and skillfulness.

Many other necessary infrastructure supports and services (too often taken for granted, but vitally necessary to the preparation of the final manuscript) were clearly evident and much appreciated. These were provided through the office of Tony Tripodi, dean of the College of Social Work of The Ohio State University.

GLORIA ABATE

Born in 1924, Gloria Abate graduated in 1945 from what was at the time the only school of social work in Peru. She worked first for the Ministry of Education Institute for Psychosocial Studies for Exceptional Children and then for the Ministry of Health Department of Maternal and Child Care. From 1946 to 1949, returning to the school of social work from which she graduated, she served as field supervisor and classroom instructor. In 1951, she earned an MSW from the Columbia University School of Social Work. After a year at the Institute of Social Studies, The Hague, she also earned a diploma in social welfare policy.

In 1952, Ms. Abate returned to Peru to work for the Public Board for Assistance to Newspaper, Magazine and Lottery Street Vendors, analyzing the socioeconomic realities of these individuals and their families. From 1952-1956, she directed the Department of Social Development at the Board of Public Works in Callao, and from 1956 to 1967 she was dean of the School of Social Work in Lima. During her tenure, the school made considerable strides, including university affiliation. She also served as president of the Peruvian Association of Social Workers and short-term adviser to Latin American professional associations, the United Nations, and UNICEF, and was a visiting scholar at Columbia University and the University of Pittsburgh for a year each in the late 1960s. Afterward, she became a consultant to the Pan American Health Organization (1970–1979), serving as PAHO/WHO Regional Adviser in Health and Social Welfare and then as Social Affairs Officer for the UN Center for Social Development and Humanitarian Affairs. She has received various professional awards.

Since retiring from social work and moving to Guayaquil, Ecuador, Ms. Abate has managed a full-color Sunday newspaper magazine, a real estate corporation and related businesses, and the Cultural Center for the Promotion of Art and Cultural Activities.

BILLUPS: *Could you please tell us about your childhood influences, including your schoolgirl experiences, in Peru?*

ABATE: I was born in Lima and was the second daughter, seven years younger than my sister. I also had a younger brother and sister. After two years of preschool, I could read and write.

My mother was a practical woman, the Sancho Panza of the family. She collected the rents, raised poultry, collected eggs, got the water from a well behind our home. My maternal grandparents lived with us, and other extended family visited regularly. Men, women, and kids all had their chores.

My Italian grandparents, particularly my grandmother, who lived with us until she died at 97, influenced my early life.

My father was born in southern Italy. In his boyhood he migrated to Panama, where his father became a prosperous businessman. When my father was about 18, he settled in Lima, though he traveled extensively throughout Peru, Bolivia, Chile, and Venezuela. He was a loving father with a good sense of humor. He shared with us the love for nature, raising a variety of animals—some for family consumption, others for company and amusement.

What influenced you to pursue social work education?

ABATE: I attended a public secondary school. There I was granted the first of many scholarships. My parents, who believed their daughters should marry early and did not encourage studies, had to accept that I would pursue a different way of living.

I was interested in history, because of the richness of ancient Peruvian civilization. By the time I was finishing high school at age 17, my interests switched to the present, to the people.

At the invitation of a former high school teacher, I applied for entry to the Peruvian School of Social Work. I passed the entry exams, and I was granted a free education.

Tell us something about your social work education in Peru.

Some of the subject matter didn't have any relevance to the profession. We had infirmary, religion, home economics, nutrition, pathology, psychology (but not dynamic psychology), and some study of Peruvian legislation. All the teachers were doctors, lawyers, and nurses, except for one social worker, who lectured us on social casework. That was the only practice known at the time in Peru.

I never had my student fieldwork supervised by a social worker. I was assigned to a general hospital and a psychiatric hospital, and I learned a lot from being close to the doctors. But the supervisors of social work practice in these hospitals didn't have any guidelines from the school as to what to do with the students, so they left us free to do whatever we thought necessary. The school didn't ask for any reports from the field instruction supervisors.

We started with some 80 students in my class in 1943, and we finished with 13 two years later. When they were about to leave the school, students questioned ,"What am I going to do? I don't even know what I am supposed to do. I don't know what my work is." There was no clear identity for the profession. They were mostly young women recruited primarily from the upper classes. They were good people, but they didn't know how to practice professionally, and most had never worked.

The 1936 law that created the first school of social work assured employment for graduates with a clear mandate, which is still valid: All private companies in industry and business with 300 or more employees were required to hire at least one social worker.

In the initial years, 1938–1942, the school had followed European educational models, mostly adopted from Belgium, Germany, and active Roman Catholic organizations.

In my field practice in a psychiatric hospital for a year, I was shocked by the lack of respect for mentally ill people. Nobody bothered to explain the nature of the treatment to the patients. The physicians believed that people with mental illnesses did not feel pain, but the terror I saw in their eyes proved the contrary. I soon realized that human rights were being ignored, at the least, if not denied, and that the underprivileged did not have anyone to speak for them. I worked with the families, giving some support, some interpretation of what their relatives were experiencing.

Despite the doubts that students had about the profession as a result of their undergraduate social work education, you were quickly employed by the government, weren't you?

ABATE: Yes. I worked with two government ministries after graduation. The first was the Institute for Psychosocial Studies of Exceptional Children within the Ministry of Education, where I was part of an interdisciplinary team including psychologists, special educators, medical doctors, psychiatrists, and others, working on diagnosis and treatment of problems interfering with learning. The students were referred by the public school system. The director of the Institute was a psychiatrist who had been my professor at the School of Social Work, and he had requested my services. My contribution was the study of the social and family environments. Though I was the youngest member of the team, my reports were well-accepted.

Later, within the Ministry of Public Health, I was assigned to the Department of Maternal and Child Care. Though a few social workers were in charge of substitute home placement or foster care, I was appointed to the legal section in charge of locating deserting fathers to secure voluntary agreements to support their children. When voluntary agreements failed, lawyers and judges intervened to request employers to retain the money. But the bureaucratic system was slow, and the women, once they got a favorable verdict, had to collect the allowances in places far from their homes. They had to leave their children unattended or else carry them along. If they were working, they had to ask for time off. It was really an inconvenience for them. So I didn't pay attention exclusively to the legal or the economic aspects of these situations. We organized courses for these women and engaged volunteers to teach them skills to increase their incomes, and we gave them information on raising children. Through small gatherings we tried to reinforce values and help these women to develop a sense of self-esteem.

Almost immediately following your undergraduate studies, you also began teaching part-time at the School of Social Work. Were there any problems in making the change to faculty member so soon after having been a student?

ABATE: Well, let me say that sharing and communication have been part of my entire life. When I was a girl I would pretend I was a teacher; my students were my younger siblings and my friends. So let us say that I had a vocation for teaching, and I felt gratified when I realized that my messages were understood.

Of course, teaching at the school had its difficulties. I was asked to teach students who were more or less my age. I did not have any preparation, any training on educational methodologies—but neither did the other professors, who were lawyers, medical doctors, psychologists, and who were very knowledgeable, and who delivered lectures to a silent group as sort of a continuation of the secondary school system.

As a student, I had not liked the instruction we were given, either the content or the ways it was communicated. So I decided to try new ways of teaching. The students became active participants. To demonstrate that observation is not always as accurate as it should be for a proper diagnosis, for instance, the students were assigned in pairs to watch a situation for 15 minutes—to observe and report. Some went to markets, to observe the fruit vendors. Some others went to the streets. Although the observations were made in pairs, students were asked to write individual reports. The findings were a surprise to them: They had seen the same situation, but the reports were quite different. That was a way to demonstrate that subjective elements had to be taken into account to produce relevant material. Personal biases had to be recognized.

Sometimes an interview was carried out in the classroom in front of the students. Interviews between a social worker and a client were tape recorded. The students were to write about their observations of the interviews. With the help of notes and questions that I wrote in the margins of their exercises, they realized that often the important data were not there. In this way, I was introducing the students to the importance of making good observations and writing precise reports. This explicit participation of the students made them feel comfortable and relaxed enough to learn readily.

Since we didn't have enough reading materials, and many of those we had were in English, I translated into Spanish whatever books on case materials were available in our small library. When the time for final exams came, the exams were based on these practical cases. Students were asked to work individually, but they were allowed to consult their notes and books. They could even leave the room and go to the library if they wanted. I wrote comments on the good parts, on the bad parts, and the students learned that what they answered wasn't all that mattered, but also how they presented their thinking.

Most of my early teaching experience was based on intuition, imagination, and also on my rejection of the traditional ways of teaching through lectures. Maybe it was from my experience in working with prestigious psychiatrists where I learned the importance of teamwork, of meetings, and of having enough materials for teaching. These ways of teaching (I don't know where I got them) gave me an advantage, and the students and I enjoyed the experiences.

You began teaching part-time and soon received a full-time appointment?

ABATE: Yes. The School of Social Work badly needed fieldwork supervisors and also teachers of social work practice. With my experience, they thought that I could be of great help. There was another full-time fieldwork supervisor who had been in university training at a university in the United States for a year, so she knew something more than the others about casework. We also shared classroom teaching assignments.

Throughout much of your career you have enjoyed teaching, not only within the School of Social Work, but also with diverse groups in the larger community. Correct?

ABATE: Over the years I was asked to deliver classes to large groups of adults and young people. I remember a seminar for rural women; my assignment was to teach research in three sessions, six hours total. Some of these women had low levels of education, but all of them had influence in their communities. I kept the interest alive by making each one an active participant and using very simple language.

After agreeing on the definition of research, they were asked to think of what they could do in their communities, and to my surprise their examples gave evidence that they had grasped the concept creatively. They said some would go to the bus station to count how many left the village and how many came from other places to the village, noting age and sex. Others said they would go to the post office and study the correspondence between their village and the cities where the people migrated. If there were more outgoing letters, or the same amount of incoming letters, it might mean a good relationship still existed between those who left the village and those who remained. Others would go to the public water supply, the only faucet for the whole community, and ask those who came for water what they thought about the water quality and whether the amount of water was enough to meet the needs of those in the village. It was really very rewarding for me to be able to teach "research" at this level. When the course was over, these women stood up and applauded.

Another course was a seminar organized to prepare young people for summer programs in which they would work on projects in widely differing communities of Peru. I was asked to deliver six-hour classes on the subject of leadership to some 800 youths, mostly men, at the university level.

I also taught social problems and social institutions to students on the Women Police Force, but there I could not change the rigid discipline. I was escorted to the classroom by an attaché announcing my entry, so the students rose to attention. To my regret, I had to go back to lecturing because there was little feedback from the students. I could not participate in faculty meetings since I was a part-time professor and met with the students only two hours per week. I did this for two years, and then I gave up because I believed I couldn't do much to change such a rigid situation.

After three years as a member of the social work faculty in the classroom and field, was study abroad the next step in your career?

ABATE: Yes. New York City was a source of great excitement for me but one of sadness for my mother and grandma. I had applied to three American universities and was admitted to the master's program of the Columbia University School of Social Work, which granted me free tuition and allowances for personal expenses. I registered for the fall quarter of 1949. Most of my courses were in casework.

There were 13 foreign students at the time, and the school believed we needed special treatment, so instead of fieldwork placement, we were to attend weekly meetings with a faculty member. Weekly visits to social welfare institutions were organized so that we could learn about services in the New York area. In our meetings we had the opportunity to express our concerns, but the meetings served other purposes, helping us in the acculturation to new ways of living.

I was so proud to be a student in a school with such well-known faculty members: Lucille Austin, Gordon Hamilton, Virginia Bellsmith, and Marion Kenworthy. Also, the library was a luxury we could not afford in Lima. We took classes in a Carnegie mansion on Fifth Avenue, a building given to the university to house its school of social work for 50 years.

At the beginning, I felt it was impossible to read all the assigned materials. Each professor required three or four chapters per week, and I had four courses. Granted, I was a good reader, but not in a foreign language, and the English I had learned in Lima in secondary school did not include social work terminology.

In the winter quarter, I was placed in a family agency in Manhattan, not far from International House. My supervisor, Henry Freeman, had experience with one American student. Although he did not know much of my cultural background, he was receptive and understanding. All my clients were Puerto Ricans living around 100th Street and Fifth Avenue. The interviews were carried on in Spanish, but all of my reporting was done in English. My interviews were almost verbatim process recordings to help the supervisor follow what I was doing.

To accelerate my graduation, I requested a summer fieldwork placement in 1950 because my paid leave of absence from the Peruvian School of Social Work was only for one year. At the time, my mother didn't have economic support from my father, so my stipend went completely to my mother. Columbia made contacts to help me find funding for my second year, and the Children's Bureau from Health, Education and Welfare granted the fellowship I needed to complete the two-year program. Other organizations came forward to help. One was the Quota Club, and I obtained a loan from the Leo Rowe Foundation.

In my second year at Columbia, I was placed in an experimental fieldwork unit at Mount Sinai Hospital. The school provided a full-time supervisor and secretarial help; the hospital provided accommodations with spaces for individual work, as well as areas for group discussion. Cases were referred by psychiatrists, and a doctor assisted us in evaluating the patients. We students would be requested to present our findings to the psychiatric meetings. With the exception of an elderly Jewish woman, a survivor of the Holocaust, my clients were Puerto Ricans. The doctors acknowledged the importance of the rich cultural content of my findings in psychiatric diagnoses and treatments.

My second year in New York, I was invited to join the staff at the Dosoris House for juvenile delinquents on parole. I worked there for room and board and was on duty 16 hours per week. I was able to limit expenses and to gain new experiences with traumatized teenage girls who had lost interest in life. I got them involved in activities in a world they didn't seem to know. I organized visits to the zoo, museums, movies…

I would not like to pass over almost two years of professional training and life enrichment without mentioning how pleased I felt when taking case recording with Gordon Hamilton, who asked me to read my assignments to the class.

Then in my last quarter at the school, I worked on my thesis, a survey on the use of leisure time among young Puerto Rican males on the Lower East Side of Manhattan. Two American students and I shared responsibilities for drafting the questionnaire and selecting the sample. We carried out the interviews in Spanish, and we translated [the responses] into English. International House was a good environment for both studies and entertainment. I was exposed to many people from different parts of the world, as well as from the United States. We had weekly evening art and music performances by students. Among them was soprano Leontyne Price.

Through the Columbia University School of Social Work, I met graduates who wished to entertain foreign students, and I became a close friend of an extended family with grandparents and children in New Jersey. They reminded me of my own family.

When you returned to Peru, you assumed two successive positions in the public sector. What were your challenges there?

ABATE: Back in Peru, I resumed my full-time job as a fieldwork supervisor and as a classroom instructor, as well as a member of several committees. I was happy with my duties, but I realized that changes were urgently needed to update the professional training of social workers. Not much could be accomplished as long as the school was in the hands of an educator who did not understand the nature of the profession. Because of this, my time with the school was limited, but also had its rewards.

Some of the students were placed in a health center where the lines of responsibilities with the doctors and the nurses were very clearly understood and respected. When my fieldwork students left for vacation or for changes in their programs, I took over the cases because they could not be left unattended. While there were no social workers on the staff of this health center, social work was considered as important as the other professions.

Once a year, the school organized a trip. It could be to a vineyard south of Lima or historical places in the Andes—to Machu Picchu or to Cuzco. I was the official reporter.

One of the most important tasks I had during this period (1952) was to conduct a survey of the living conditions of newspaper, lottery, and magazine street vendors. Presiding over the Board for the Assistance to Newspaper, Magazine and Lottery Vendors, created by law, I developed questionnaires. The sample included some 900 vendors and their family members, totaling around 5,000 people. On the basis of the findings, I detailed a plan with specific functions and staff qualifications to meet the needs of these people.

I was then asked to become director of the board, which sounded like a very good opportunity to introduce innovative ways in social assistance. After discovering that I was not free to select the social workers or staff members to work under my direction, I resigned from this job, including my position at the school.

I accepted a job at the Board of Public Works in Callao, where I worked for four challenging and rewarding years as director of the Social Development Department. I was able to influence board policies and to help the staff—lawyers, engineers, architects—to realize that our target, our goal, was not simply to design public housing, but must also consider the people, most of whom were being forced to leave their old houses and move to make way for new highways and avenues.

While I was in charge of the Social Development Department (1952–1956), a number of programs were designed to help those relocated to the new housing units to organize themselves. They were buying their new homes in monthly payments over 20 years and were likely to be neighbors for a long time, since the shortage of houses and their limited budgets did not allow them to move elsewhere. By the time I left this position, a great number of residents' committees had been established, and they were performing very well. These groups received close advice until they could act on their own, with consultation always available. The groups contributed to developing community pride.

During this period our staff also increased; we had five full-time social workers, some part-time social workers, auxiliary personnel, volunteers, and fieldwork students. The latter were assigned to group work and community development practice, some preventive, some corrective, but all designed to help families enjoy a better standard of living. But the focus of our efforts was the grassroots leaders, who were helped not only to represent their community but also to act as interpreters of community needs.

Later, when I was no longer in charge of the Social Development Department, new board members were appointed. One of the first measures they discussed was how to reduce the budget. One way that was considered was to stop all social services. When I learned of this, I felt it was my moral obligation to intervene.

I alerted the grassroots leaders that these changes could not be made unilaterally by the board. When the time for an open general assembly came around, the mayor of the city, who was also the president of the board, spoke of the need to make changes. As if they had been summoned, the grassroots leaders advanced, crying out, "We want our social workers," and so on. They almost stripped the mayor of his power and he had to be retired for he had to leave the assembly. The Social Development Department and its programs went on, with the blessings of its best "clients," the people.

Soon you were to continue as an administrator, this time back at the School of Social Work.

ABATE: When I was asked by the Minister of Public Health to accept the position of director of the school, I was still working at the Board of Public Works. A third director with barely one year in office had been asked to resign; a medical doctor had been appointed to run the school. Realizing there was the danger that the school might be closed, I accepted the challenge. One of my conditions was that I needed a free hand to make the necessary changes. This was granted. So, in a few days I had to begin to reorganize all aspects of the school.

During the 11 years I was dean of the school (1956–1967), I never gave up teaching. Whether it was a regular course or short seminar, I always kept communicating, teaching, and sharing experiences.

Radical changes in administration were introduced. Religion, infirmary, anatomy, English, native languages, home economics—all were taken out of the curricula. This was not easy, since some of the faculty had been my own teachers. The number of secretaries and auxiliary personnel was increased. All of them were sent to government institutes to be trained for their specific work, free of charge.

A graduate librarian and two assistants were not sufficient, so we hired part-time helpers. We increased the library stock significantly through donations. The school was entitled to donations in kind, but not in cash; it would have taken a long bureaucratic process to use the money, and the risk was that the Minister of Public Health would decide to use it for other purposes. The institutions, national or international, that requested school participation in studies, census taking, surveys, and so on were asked to compensate us for our services by donating books. Fourteen-thousand volumes were added to the collection in this way.

Five full-time and several part-time social workers were put in charge of both fieldwork and social work classroom instruction. The school made arrangements with both public and private organizations to establish field placement units where our supervisors would spend two or three days per week with the students. Special seminars were conducted to bring student field instructors up to date.

You attached great importance to field instruction?

ABATE: Yes. A six-month block fieldwork placement was organized for students in their last semester, and for many years this practice proved successful. Students were sent outside Lima, sometimes as far as 1,000 kilometers away.

Our full-time supervisors were in charge of ensuring the terms of the school's agreements with the agencies. The first requirements were to secure good professional supervision on site and to approve the accommodations (room and board). The student placement sites were visited twice during the six-month period for evaluation and adjustments to the learning processes, if needed.

Most of the student field placements were in the private sector; the receiving organizations were oil and mining companies, sugar cane and vineyard haciendas, and fishery industries. The large corporations had a legal mandate to hire social workers, but if social workers were not available, the law could not be enforced. Since the industrial sector was paying the highest salaries and other attractive compensations, sometimes including accommodations, it was imperative that employers and social workers be brought together. In places where students could count on relatives for housing, field units often were organized under governmental agencies—health centers, hospitals, schools, social security offices, and so on. Within these private and public programs (many of them new partners of the school), the students had the opportunity not only to spend a semester working under the supervision of a professional social worker, but also to give those with whom they related a better understanding of social work. This was also a way to open up new job opportunities for graduates.

These block fieldwork placements became known nationally. I remember an invitation, for example, from the Catholic Bishop of a missionary order (Mercedarios). It was my turn to explore the local conditions. Getting to the location was not only time-consuming but also expensive and risky. The only way to get to the area was by air, and it was necessary to change planes on the way. Two of the four airports posed serious weather and geographical problems that sometimes required hours of waiting. In addition, since the area southeast of Lima bordering Bolivia and Brazil was crossed by many rivers, traveling by boat and canoe was also unavoidable. Once on site, the only means of transportation might be by bicycle or on foot.

This remote Catholic mission did have a radio station, and social workers might reach many people through these means, since radio was the only source of entertainment and information. There was a school for elementary education, a small church, and a few programs run by the missionaries. But it was clear that the inhabitants were nomadic, moving to hunt and fish, and all the efforts of the mission could only keep them in one place for a short time. Agriculture and raising small animals was out of the question. These people would remain a few months, if food was provided to them or when they were waiting for the yucca (cassava) harvest. So this request was not accepted. We could not expose our staff and students to the overall lack of infrastructure or of social workers in the area.

Aside from strengthening the school in the ways you describe, was it during your tenure as dean that the school became university-affiliated?

ABATE: While coping with all aspects of running the school of social work, it was clear to me that we needed higher levels of preparation. We needed a university atmosphere to make real progress. It took a long period of negotiations to achieve this goal. I had to work with the national congress, politicians, university professors, and other authorities to have a law passed approving the affiliation of the school with the National University of San Marcos, the oldest university in the country. Several faculties of the university expressed their desire to receive the school. After careful consideration, we thought that the school needed to be next to the sociology, anthropology, and psychology departments. Our viewpoint was accepted by the university. I obtained permission from the Lima City municipality to give the school space for its own building very close to the university campus.

We then pursued the idea that we needed centers for advanced courses in teaching, research, social policy, and so on. I requested advisors from the UN Latin American Development Branch (CEPAL), and a three-day meeting was held at the University of San Cristobal de Huamanga in the Andean region for the directors of the five schools of social work by then operating in Peru, all within university structures. This university had a strong reputation for its leftist orientation. (It was in this university that the Maoist movement called Sendero Luminoso, or Shining Path, was born, led by the dean of the faculty of social sciences, who, after several years of breaking the law was captured by the army and sentenced to life in prison, where he remains today.)

This meeting produced a document recommending the establishment of the Center for Advanced Studies in Social Work Education. Our school at San Marcos University accepted this challenge, and the other schools of social work were to cooperate. Our first task was to request assistance from the UN and from some Peruvian centers of similar nature already operating.

Back in Lima, the school was slowly growing in prestige. Government and private institutions requested its participation for special studies. The creation of an admissions department within the school was also a good step, as we were able to design criteria for selecting candidates. We arrived at a point where foreign universities (among them, Cornell University) and other organizations selected our school for full participation in all stages of social research.

In my last month at the school, I endured political retaliation from a group of university students. The senator who fought for the approval of the law to help the school become part of the university, for whom I felt great respect and gratitude, was not only a distinguished member of the national congress, but had also been the highest authority at San Marcos University three times. He had been a political enemy of the leftist movement within the university, and I, too, began experiencing some aggression from this group. Its practices were to "break someone," as I was informed by a person who knew the movement's tactics.

I imagine there is a great deal more to be told about this story.

ABATE: Sure, there were many other things. One that I would like to mention briefly is the reaction of the early graduates. When we were struggling to get the law for the school to become part of the university, they helped. They gave me support. But once the law was passed and we went into transition from being a unit of the Ministry of Public Health to a school under the university structure, the more radical wanted to be given a master's degree from the university without having to do any work (as a "reward" for their earlier support), which was quite impossible. Although I tried to be a mediator between them and the university, they believed that I was not doing all that I could for them. About that time I received an invitation from Columbia University to spend one year as a visiting scholar there, concentrating on social research and social policy. I decided that was a good way out.

So you went back to Columbia, this time as a visiting scholar.

ABATE: Yes. While at Columbia, I became extremely active in both national and international social work. I participated in the work of the International Committee of the Council on Social Work Education, preparing a paper on the problems of foreign students in schools of social work in the United States. I was appointed by the Colombian Council on Social Work Education as their representative to the XIVth Congress of the International Association of Schools of Social Work in Helsinki, and I was asked by the Latin American Association of Schools of Social Work to assist in the development of indigenous teaching material for use in Latin America, a project financed by UNICEF.

As an official representative of the Peruvian government, I attended the UN International Congress of Ministers Responsible for Social Welfare. Becoming visible at the headquarters to colleagues and friends, I was invited to accept a short mission of five weeks in Colombia as an adviser to determine the feasibility of initiating family planning programs in a rural area. I respected Julia Henderson and Marshall Woolf very much, and their encouragement made me accept the request.

The two agencies participating were the Pan American Health Organization (PAHO/WHO) and the UN Department of Social Welfare. Family planning was considered primarily a health concern, so the chief of the consulting group was a pediatrician (Chilean), and the others were a demographer (Argentinian), an expert statistician (from the United States), and myself.

My part of the mission became the study of attitudes, beliefs, and practices related to family planning in an area in the middle section of a large river, the Magdalena, which flows north, emptying into the Caribbean. With his keen interest in anthropology, the minister of health, Dr. Antonio Ordoñez Plaja, was very helpful. As if he were deciding on a touring route, he would say, "When you get to this island where two churches of different denominations operate, I want to know their position and influence in family planning."

I worked with personnel in the Malaria Department, all well-trained men who had been successful in working with the people of the region for several decades. Twenty-four hours a day I was under the care of the vice director of the department, who did not want me to be exposed to accidents, kidnapping, or, possibly, death from the rebel guerillas in the area. Whether by jeep, foot path, or small boat with a canvas cover, with my straw hat for protection against the tropical sun, I gathered a great amount of information. The experience was extremely rewarding, to the point that the mosquitoes, the flies, the heat, and climbing up the river banks became more tolerable.

The people were warm and came to greet the visitor. As an introduction to later conversations, I spoke with the people about their health. It was not altogether a surprise when a five-year-old boy not responding to folk medicine was brought to my attention. Among the treatments was a rusty door key hanging on the child's chest to open his congested bronchus. I commented to the parents and others that there were many other keys to clear the child's breathing.

Many people thought I was a health officer, perhaps a medical doctor. Others had the most funny ideas: "She is a crazy gringa looking for film location and casting." But mainly I learned from my questions that there were high birth rates in the area, but also high morbidity and mortality rates. Many children had been buried right next to their parents' houses. I also learned that the people in this remote area were ready for modern medicine, if made available, and for family planning.

Before I could leave the country, Dr. Ordoñez wanted a briefing. I provided it during a couple of hours while he was doing his walking exercise, but found it difficult to keep up with his pace. When I finished, he said I could not leave the country without submitting a written report. "Anything can happen to you on your way back to New York, and all your work would be lost!" Breaking UN rules, I typed all night before taking off the next day.

To my satisfaction, I learned later that new family programs had been started in rural areas of Colombia once malaria had been largely eradicated, and that the Malaria Department personnel (all male) had been retrained for this new responsibility.

During your period of administering the School of Social Work in Peru and after, you were engaged in other trips abroad to study and to teach. Could you tell us something about those experiences?

ABATE: When I was beginning my deanship, I was invited to participate in a UN seminar for directors of schools of social work. The seminar was held in Uruguay. At the time my experience as a dean had been very short, but those who attended the seminar acknowledged the important changes that I had been able to introduce in our school's curriculum. For another trip, to Brazil and Ecuador, I was invited by the UN as part of a Peruvian team to study government and private community development programs.

Taking advantage of a sabbatical, I accepted an invitation to study at the Institute of Social Policy at The Hague in the Netherlands. We had professors from Greece, Lebanon, Germany, India, all of whom were experts in their areas. The only negative aspect was the lack of integration between the social planners and policymakers and those in the areas of economics and engineering. We didn't have any contact with all three groups other than in sharing meals and recreation. That is why, in not an entirely joking way, I said to the engineers and economists, "You may be able to plan a utopia, a city beautifully organized from the point of view of roads and electric services, but where are the people who are to be served? And when you do add the people, there are going to be problems, and who is going to solve them?"

I understand that you have been engaged in a number of other international endeavors.

ABATE: It is hard to condense all the different activities I have performed, since some or most of them were concurrent. Perhaps my 10 years with United Nations responsibilities is a place to begin.

With the Pan American Health Organization I was a short-term consultant contracted to carry out an exploratory study to define responsibility of the health sector in social welfare matters. The study was performed in 1970 in four countries (Chile, Costa Rica, Jamaica, and Venezuela). While still with PAHO, I organized the First Advisory Committee on Health and Social Welfare convened in PAHO headquarters. This interdisciplinary group produced a document recommending PAHO's involvement in social welfare activities related to health objectives. A post of Regional Consultant on Social Welfare was created.

From 1971 to 1975, I worked full time as the PAHO/WHO Regional Adviser in Health and Social Welfare. During my tenure we served agencies in 11 countries, organizing six seminars and four workshops attended by 568 social workers. We assisted in the design of training courses for auxiliary personnel. Curricular content was developed to prepare social workers in public health at the master's level. Consultation was provided to ministries of health, institutes of social security, schools of public health and social work, institutes for family and child welfare, professional associations, and others.

In three countries, as the result of PAHO input, national departments of social welfare were established, providing the infrastructure to ensure integration of social services within the Ministries of Health. A roster of potential advisers was started. Several documents and working papers were produced and widely distributed, and a specialized library was established at headquarters. PAHO organized and financed a meeting in Costa Rica to study the feasibility of a regional center for training and research in social welfare and social policy. We revised and translated into Spanish a guidebook, *Social Work and Population, Family Planning and Sex Education.*

From 1977 to 1979, I was social affairs officer for the UN Center for Social Development and Humanitarian Affairs, Social Integration and Welfare Section, where we worked on the social aspects of family planning. In addition, I served as short-term adviser to the UN and UNICEF and in several capacities for the International and the Latin American Associations of Schools of Social Work, the Inter-American Commissions for Women, and Inter-American Council of Social Welfare. I was also president of the Peruvian Association of Social Workers, a member of the committee in charge of drafting the bylaws for the creation of the Colegio of Graduate Social Workers (an accreditation board), a member of International Planned Parenthood and of International Social Services, and Peruvian official delegate to the UN Assembly on Social Development.

I was asked to conduct a study of the use of indigenous teaching materials in schools of social work; the study was sponsored by UNICEF, the Latin American and the American Associations of Schools of Social Work, and the UN Social Welfare Office. I visited 33 schools in six countries (Argentina, Bolivia, Colombia, Chile, Ecuador, and Peru), and the final document was widely distributed.

Of course, my commitment to social work education prevailed for years, while my special interests shifted from social casework to social research, community development, and social policy. I continually shared experiences with representatives of other schools in Latin America...

Part of your career included addressing social concerns through the popular press, including a full-color magazine for which you assumed administrative responsibility.

ABATE: While I was in Peru, as well as when attending meetings in other countries—the United States, Costa Rica, Uruguay, Chile, Venezuela—I was interviewed by the press. Often my opinions were requested on social subjects that were of particular concern to Peru or my city, Lima.

Once I was asked to interview high-ranking officers, ministers, army generals, and university professors on highly sensitive subjects related to family planning, their thinking, their social behavior, means of birth control, and so on. It was felt that my post as the dean of the School of Social Work was a secure entree to these important people. The final report was published in a specialized magazine. This was a challenge that gave me great satisfaction—the fact that I had access to those hierarchies, to inquire into delicate matters.

My editorials have regularly appeared in publications such as Humanitas (published in Buenos Aires), where I reported on the regional and international seminars, conferences, and congresses I attended. I was named an itinerant correspondent for Humanitas.

As a member of the Peruvian Association of University Educators, I participated in forums addressed to teachers and professors on subjects related to social aspects of learning. Some of my interventions were published in the association magazine.

After I relocated to Guayaquil, Ecuador, I was asked to take charge of a weekly magazine, a full-color tabloid of 16 pages to be distributed on the Sunday edition of Expreso, a newspaper with wide national coverage. Granted, I had experience in writing and editing professional material, but this was quite different. In a few days I produced the first issue of Semana. I stayed in this job for 10 years.

After I had resigned my work with Semana, I became a freelance correspondent, working on book reviews and interviews. Sharing with writers, poets, critics, artists, musicians, and painters was very rewarding. I was able to help young poets obtain free airline tickets to Germany and France, where these young people, after completing their studies abroad, joined universities in departments of literature and became recognized in their area of specialization.

I also understand that you ventured into business enterprises and that you've served as coordinator of a cultural center promoting art and cultural activities. Tell us about those.

ABATE: As coordinator of a private cultural center for the promotion of arts and related activities, it is my duty to select the painters, most of them young and relatively unknown. This requires home visits to assess the works, and press bulletins to assure that each activity is well-attended. We have had a minimum of 80 people at an event, but we have sometimes had 400 at an opening. Some of the artists have been in great demand and have sold their works. We are now seeking sponsors to send promising artists abroad to continue their studies.

Once a year we invite an organization to make use of our center. A psychiatric hospital presented the works of patients receiving art therapy, and we have invited two organizations representing disabled people to present works of art. One newspaper dedicated a full-page color publication to the center, which would have cost several million sucres if we had paid for it. So far, 60 people have exhibited individually or collectively in our gallery in two and a half years. Twice a year, on civic holidays in Guayaquil, we invite masters of art to join the celebration. This Cultural Center is not a for-profit gallery and thus does not charge commissions.

Which honors or awards that you received do you particularly value?

ABATE: I do not deny that the prizes and rewards cheered me, but to me, all these activities were sharing happy moments.... I have never exhibited any of my credits. I have never hung a diploma on a wall. I never kept track of the number of rewards I received.

As a professional, I was recognized by the School of Social Work, by San Marcos University, by the Peruvian Association of Social Workers, by the City Hall in Callao, and by several international and national organizations and committees with which I have had the privilege to work.

Have you any thoughts for current social workers or for future members of the profession?

ABATE: Social work has made substantial improvements. Starting as a good will or charity endeavor, it has slowly entered formal ways of preparing its members to take on new challenges. The exchange of knowledge and experiences at international levels broadened the scope of the profession, and the integration of schools of social work into university structures has enhanced the levels of educational preparation.

But even with the progress made in social research, social planning, and social policy, in many countries the profession still has a low profile. Its interventions cannot yet be compared to those of other professions. But still, sociologists, psychologists, medical doctors, and lawyers consider social work as a good complement to their work, as an aid to fulfill their own goals.

Perhaps in the next century we can see social work taking its rightful role in modern society. The international social work community has a moral obligation to help in places where people have limited resources or need to be encouraged to adopt new professional approaches—practice approaches based on knowledge, discipline, and the enthusiasm of people being engaged as active participants in social change in tangible ways.

ANGELINA C. ALMANZOR

Angelina Almanzor obtained a teacher's certificate from the Philippine Normal College, a bachelor of science degree in education from the Far Eastern University, master's degrees in social work from the Philippine Women's University and Our Lady of the Lake College, and a doctorate in social welfare from Columbia University. Interspersed with her educational programs were several years of high school and university teaching, plus extensive volunteer work.

On completing her doctoral program in 1961, Dr. Almanzor became dean of the School of Social Work, Philippine Women's University, where she served until 1972. She was Asia Regional Representative on Social Work Education for the International Association of Schools of Social Work from 1972 to 1978. After that, she worked for a year with the United Nations Social Welfare Development Center for Asia and the Pacific, Manila. Then for five years she was regional adviser on training and education for social work and community development, United Nations Economic and Social Commission for Asia and the Pacific, Bangkok.

Dr. Almanzor also served as first vice president, Council of Welfare Agencies of the Philippines, 1962–1964; president, Schools of Social Work Association of the Philippines, 1969–1971; president, Asian Pacific Association for Social Work Education, 1972–1973; and vice president, International Association of Schools of Social Work, 1972–1978. She directed many national, regional, and international seminars and workshops and provided consultation and technical assistance on social work education, community development, and administrative management throughout Asia and the Pacific, for which she has received national and international awards and other recognition. The mother of a son and daughter, she has five grandchildren.

BILLUPS: *Could you share with us something of your early life experience or other influences that led you to enter into social work as a career pursuit?*

ALMANZOR: I was in college taking an education degree when I was asked to be a Girl Scout troop leader by the founder of Girl Scouting in the Philippines, Mrs. Josefa L. Escoda. We were to be among the first groups of Girl Scouts in the Philippines. That gave me the opportunity to work and play with children, and it was fun.

Then World War II broke out and everything stopped. About three years later, my husband, who was a lieutenant in the army, was killed. My two children never saw their father. For some time I didn't even think about working. I was completely paralyzed.

During the war, my family lost everything. We had to start from scratch. My family was in the printing business, and while my parents were rebuilding the business, I was thinking about what I should do with my life.

World War II was a defining and redefining period for many people in the Philippines. Was that true with you?

ALMANZOR: At the outbreak of World War II, I worked as a volunteer not only in scouting, but in the underground, taking food to the concentration camp internees, Americans, in Capas, Tarlac. I was particularly concerned about their children, who were housed at a college near Malacanan (home of our national President). I would go through Japanese checkpoints to get food and juice (or only juice if that was all we could afford) several days a week for the American children. It was a frightening experience but a challenging task that had to be done. With my background in Girl Scouting, I taught the children how to dance, play and work with their hands to occupy their time during the war. It led to my receiving a Diploma of Honor "in recognition of service for the cause of Filipino and Allied prisoners of war."

We collected clothes and medicines through the Federation of Women's Clubs and brought those to the concentration camp as well, but I continued to be particularly concerned about those kids.

Unfortunately, the founder of Girl Scouting and her husband were killed just before the end of the war. Their "crime" was that they were carrying, not only food, medicines, and clothing but also messages, so that families would know that the prisoners were alive. Through the inspiration of such people, how could I miss in my own career choices?

Please tell us about your early career development.

ALMANZOR: In 1950, the sister of the founder of scouting came to visit me. Knowing that scouting was my extracurricular activity while I was in college, my mother had told her that I might want to do it again. The sister had continued the founder's interest and asked me if I might want to go back to scouting. I replied that I did not know if I wanted to.

I did think about it. Once again as a volunteer I started training Girl Scout leaders, went to camps, and led troop activities. I got wholly involved in scouting. I forgot all about my problems.

In the meantime, my mother cared for my small children. This situation is not unusual in the Philippines. The extended family is very supportive. My children lost their father, but my parents, brothers, and sisters helped us, so there was really no problem about either a father or mother figure.

Then I met a priest from Catholic Charities, Father Mitchell. My major in college had been physical education, character education, and health. He suggested that I teach at La Consolacion College, a private school for girls. I began teaching at the high school level and later taught beginning teachers too. I did not know it at the time, but I was getting drawn increasingly into activities that I would later learn were known as social group work.

After I had been teaching for a while, Father Mitchell encouraged me to go to the United States to study social work. That was in the late 1950s. As my children were still small, I discussed it with my parents, and they said that I could go if I wished. But there was a delay.

I had graduated with honors from college a few years earlier, and my father had promised me that he was going to send me to the United States for further study. He asked what social work was. I said, "I have actually been doing a form of social work already—training leaders, organizing, playing and working with young girls, except that I need to learn more about scientific approaches to ensure success in what I was doing."

In the meantime, the first school of social work had opened in the Philippines. Mrs. Josefa Jara Martinez (mother of Mrs. Amelita Martinez Ramos, former first lady of the Philippines) was the founder of the Philippine School of Social Work (PSSW). She knew about me because of my volunteer work with the Community Chest, the United Fund, Catholic Charities, and the United Nations Children's Fund. As a young woman, I was doing both fundraising and committee organizing.

Mrs. Martinez offered about 20 of us from different social welfare fields a year of training in social work. I won a scholarship. Within one year, most of the members of the initial group of students had completed the master's degree in social administration. The program included not only group work (my principal interest), but casework, communication arts, administration, and other social work courses.

Josefa Martinez was the only professionally trained social worker in the country at the time. Later, she was joined by another, a graduate of the Catholic University of America. Most of our teachers were either medical doctors or psychologists.

There was a close bond among graduates of the first class. We went to work after graduation in 1951 in key places like the National Development Board, Red Cross, Social Welfare Department, Girl Scouts, and new schools of social work in the Philippines. While completing my master's degree, I was recruited to teach at another new school of social work at the University of Santo Tomas. I taught social group work there for some time.

In scouting the important thing I had gained was the motivation, the dedication, and the desire to do something for the girls. I think that was what pushed me into social work.

What more can you tell us about your educational preparation for the two professions, first teaching and then social work?

ALMANZOR: My first credential was a teaching certificate in elementary education from the Philippine Normal College in 1939. Then I earned a bachelor's degree in education in 1941 at the Far Eastern University in Manila in preparation for teaching high school students. Then I took special courses like history and humanities. That helped prepare me for teaching in high school and for other aspects of my career later on.

I hardly thought about social work at the time, even though much of what I had been doing was social group work. Then Father Mitchell again said that maybe it was time for me to go abroad. He helped me to obtain a scholarship to the Worden School of Social Service at Our Lady of the Lake College in San Antonio, Texas. It was a beautiful place, a good school. I am glad he steered me there even though the MSW degree that I earned in 1957 was more or less a repeat of my program in social administration at the Philippine School of Social Work. For my student fieldwork I was assigned to Ripley House (a social settlement house) in Houston, where I became director of programs; I did my thesis on Ripley House community development projects.

One of the Catholic sisters, who later was to become a classmate of mine at Columbia University, suggested that I go on for a doctoral program in social work. That summer I obtained a position as director of program activities at a girls' summer camp in Wisconsin, and I earned enough to pay my first semester tuition at Columbia, where I had been admitted. I had a brother who was already studying at Columbia. Fortunately, once confirmed that I was qualified for doctoral study, Columbia gave me a full scholarship that included board and lodging at International House near the campus.

Dr. Herman Stein, Dr. Alfred Kahn, and Dean Kenneth Johnson encouraged me. They helped me obtain additional scholarships. After finishing all the academic course requirements in one year, I worked on my dissertation and finished the entire program for my doctor of social welfare degree in 1961.

The library was an unbelievable and unlimited source of academic and intellectual resources. My professors, like Dr. Stein, Dr. Kahn, and Professor Clara Kaiser, to mention a few, were perhaps the best and the most brilliant professors I ever had. Alfred Kahn (and later Herman Stein) was my dissertation adviser, and Professor Clara Kaiser, who was teaching social group work, was a terrific teacher. Discussions were intellectually stimulating and full of substantial work experience. Those few years gave me an excellent preparation to cope with the demands of the new and growing profession of social work in my country and the Asian region. What I learned has been a lifetime source of knowledge, values, and skills that I treasure.

My parents were very helpful and I was able to complete my educational programs.

After your academic pursuits and accomplishments, I should not be surprised that you continued on in an academic setting soon after returning to the Philippines.

ALMANZOR: When I returned home I was walking down the airplane ramp, and there to greet me was a friend, a teacher from the PSSW. She told me that the president of the Philippine Women's University (PWU) would like to talk with me. The director of the school had died while attending a conference. They were looking for a successor and asked that I visit the school. I thanked her, but said that I wanted to settle down first and find out what it was that I wanted to do.

A few months later, a PSSW representative called, so I went to the school, and I was offered the position of director. I said I first wanted to do an evaluative study— how the school began, what it had done, and so forth—so that if I accepted the position I would know what I was getting into. After conducting the study, I gave the results and recommendations to the president of the Philippine Women's University. She said that I should be challenged because I had found that the school had not developed as fast as it might, considering the staffing and other resources available. Finally, I decided to accept the position of director, equivalent to a deanship, as I was directly responsible to the president of the PWU.

This was the same school of social work (the first in the country) at which I had been one of the first graduates, so I had a strong emotional feeling for it. Plus my former mentor, Mrs. Martinez, was an outstanding social worker and a gem of a person. Between her and the founder of Girl Scouting, Mrs. Escoda, I had learned much about how to put into practice sound methods of organizing learning experiences and how to teach in formal and informal settings.

During my tenure at PSSW, we increased the course offerings in the undergraduate and graduate programs, as well as the number of students taking the courses. The creation of PSSW was in line with the philosophical mission of the PWU, which is to gear education to maximum service to the nation. The university as a whole has been committed to train women (and later men) for their roles in home and family life, community participation, and vocational and professional careers.

PWU President Benitez helped to open the PSSW in 1950. She initiated moves to open doors of higher education in social work to volunteer social workers, community leaders, and professionals from other disciplines. Over the years, many civic organizations that played significant roles in building the nation were founded at PWU, among them the Civic Assembly of Women (CAWP), the Home Economics Association of the Philippines, the Philippine Rural Reconstruction Movement (PRRM), and the Family Life Workshop.

The PSSW saw the multifaceted challenges and problems of the Philippines as a developing nation and the critical roles of trained social workers concerned for the rights of people in meeting the basic needs of life in the family and the larger human environment. The exchanges between university learning and community service requirements helped PSSW to realize its significant role as a catalyst for change, an active partner in the country's development.

I represented the university at various national committees and civic organizations concerned with social welfare, such as the UN Commission on the Status of Women, United Nations Appeal for Children, UNICEF, the Council of Social Welfare, and so on. As a social worker and educator, I worked with groups concerned with orphaned and abused children, old age and foster homes, the Damas de Filipines Settlement House, the Civic Assembly of Women, the Girl Scouts, the YWCA, the Council for the Handicapped, and others.

Were there particular problems in taking on all of these responsibilities?

ALMANZOR: Yes; even as my responsibilities at the PSSW were very demanding, most of our instructors taught on a part-time basis. They also worked with the Department of Social Work or Child Welfare, engaged in research at universities, practicing casework, or working in staff positions in some governmental department or private agency. It was not possible to employ full-time teachers then. I was for a while the only full-time staff member at the school.

Most of the teachers did not have the time to commit solely to social work education. The challenge was how to bring this group of part-time faculty instructors together so that they could become the kind of social work role models that we would like our students to follow.

Toward this end, I chaired a committee organized to plan and prepare the teachers' training programs. Through this program, the part-time instructors began to spend more time in the school and have more contact with students. However, during much of the day, there were still no teachers available to talk to students. Only the director and the part-time (later, full-time) assistant director were accessible. Fortunately, later we were able to get full-timers.

One way to grapple with the problem of getting the faculty to become more involved in the program of the school presented itself when I met with the director of the Foster Parents Plan. He said that he had 150 foster children and did not know what might be provided for them during the summer. He asked if we could organize something for them. So for about three years I got the faculty and other people to organize and offer a two-week summer camp outside Manila for the children, for whom we got sponsors. By operating this summer camp, we were able to help foster families and their children get a reprieve in the summer months and, at the same time, raise some income to pay faculty salaries and increase resources for the school.

The PSSW also managed to set up community development work and activities for organizations that paid the school for running the programs. In this way, PSSW was able to provide for our library and other school needs. PSSW was also able to help individual faculty members supplement their small salaries by applying for research grants. In this way, we were able to provide additional income for faculty. That's very important for the retention of good faculty members.

I imagine that there were other challenges and rewards that you experienced while at PSSW.

ALMANZOR: After the war, we had no books. I used to write to Katherine Kendall at the Council on Social Work Education (CSWE) in the United States, and later at the International Association of Schools of Social Work (IASSW). I would order books through her. Our first books were written by Americans. The published material was almost all social casework, but we often could not work on a case-by-case basis in the Philippines. The needs were so extensive that we had to work with groups that gave us direct exposure to community problems. As a group worker, I had to relate social casework to other methods. We introduced community work into the curriculum, and we moved on to social development—a most difficult concept, but one that almost everybody talks about as an important approach for social workers to adopt, especially in dealing with macro-focused problems and solutions.

In the Philippines, poverty is all around us—as seen in our street children, abandoned and sexually abused kids, and homeless families. These are among the most complicated, widespread problems. How do we handle them? Where we had worked before with orphans of the war, children abandoned because their parents had died, not long afterwards we found that we had to work increasingly with problems concerning drug use, child abuse, single parenthood, and so on. How was social work going to address these concerns?

When we were developing and modifying our course content at PSSW, we had to allocate time for teaching about the problems and services that were already present in the Philippines and also find ways in which we could adapt these services to the emerging problems. We used to invite agency staff people to tell us what they were doing and what social workers could and should do in the future. That's how we developed much of our curriculum—straight from the field. The schools of social work and major governmental departments and many of the private services were mostly in Manila then, and that made it easier.

I understand that it was not long after you were at PSSW that you became internationally involved.

ALMANZOR: During my first year as director of the PSSW, 1961–1962, we embarked on a special project for the development of indigenous teaching materials. Eventually we designed a Philippine social work curriculum for both the bachelor's and the MSSW degrees. The school sponsored seminars, workshops, and interagency service training courses to record knowledge and information obtained from the field and to incorporate these in the planned curriculum.

The other schools improvised their own curricular content until the passage of RA 4373, which required civil service board examination for social workers. That law brought the schools together to come out with a basic curriculum content for both the bachelor's and master's degree programs.

During this period we tried to get in touch with other schools of social work abroad to exchange experiences and share teaching materials. The most important contact was with the Council of Social Work Education (CSWE) in the United States; shortly thereafter the PSSW became a member of the International Association of Schools of Social Work (IASSW). Dr. Katherine Kendall, by then the secretary-general of IASSW, has made a difference not only in the Philippines but all over Asia. I have looked up to her as the "angel" who has guided me in my career in social work. The close association with IASSW, through her, brought social workers from the Philippines closer to colleagues abroad.

IASSW facilitated the organization of the Schools of Social Work Association in the Philippines (SSWAP), and I was serving as its president when in 1968 I was elected vice president of IASSW at the Helsinki Congress of Schools of Social Work. At that Congress the Philippines was invited to host the XVth Congress of the International Association of Schools of Social Work held in 1970.

The opportunity given to the Philippines to plan, organize, and host the 1970 Congress was the greatest challenge to me and to the newly formed SSWAP. About 3,000 delegates, roughly 1,500 from abroad, attended the Congress. The Congress emphasized the increasing ties between social work and community development, interdisciplinary and interprofessional education, team efforts to anticipate and cope with current and emerging social problems, and education of social workers to help people work toward the attainment of both social and economic goals.

As chair of the Congress held in Manila, I had the most exciting opportunity to meet and talk to the outstanding leaders of international social work: Dr. Herman Stein, then president of IASSW; Dame Eileen Younghusband; Robin Huws Jones; and, of course, Katherine Kendall, who supported the Congress Organizing Committee.

The Congress was held in the midst of typhoon season, but the program went on despite howling winds and a raging storm. To the credit of the Organizing Committee, all the major speakers arrived safely and, overall, the Congress was a success. The following year, Dr. Kendall asked me to work for IASSW as the Asia Regional Representative on Social Work Education for a family planning project. I accepted.

The new responsibility required that I go to the various schools of social work in Asia and in the Pacific, organizing curricula and developing seminars, workshops, and meetings that dealt with family planning or problems of overpopulation, within the context of the cultures of the various societies. I was a bit concerned about how family planning would be accepted in the region, especially in the Philippines, a Catholic country. That is why we started defining family planning in my country within the context of family welfare. There was no abortion or birth control talk; we talked about what the Catholic Church approved. For societies and schools that were not Catholic and were in favor of birth control, we were able to teach family planning directly in socially acceptable terms.

In the meantime, the UN Economic Social Commission for Asia and the Pacific (ESCAP) had heard about the work I was doing. After the first year of the program, they sent a long telex offering me a job as field adviser. The UN was going to pay me four or five times what IASSW was giving me.

I told Katherine that because of the IASSW opportunity, and the chance to work with people like her, I was not going to accept the ESCAP offer. She realized what

I was giving up, and I think she appreciated that. In fact, I continued with the IASSW work for five years. I then told Katherine that I really should now give the opportunity to somebody else. I recommended Evelyn Pangalangan from the University of the Philippines, who took over for about two or three more years.

In the meantime, the UN had established in the Philippines a Social Welfare and Development Center headed by a man from Iran. Because we used to meet at conferences and because he knew about my IASSW work, he asked me to join the staff. I accepted and became a project director and field representative of the UN's Social Welfare and Development Center for the Asia-Pacific region (SWADCAP).

After one year of successful work with the Center, ESCAP asked me again if I was willing to work in Bangkok. This time I agreed. I worked at ESCAP for a few years (1979–1984) as regional adviser on training and education for social work and community development.

Having been a representative and consultant for three organizational bodies in the Asia-Pacific region of the world, is there more that you wish to tell us about those experiences?

ALMANZOR: First, as IASSW Regional Representative and then as Regional Representative of the UN ESCAP, I worked mostly with educators and persons in the area of social welfare who were connected with governments and nongovernmental organizations (NGOs). They were staff members of the national departments of social welfare, as well as the deans, educators, and lecturers of both government-supported and private schools of social work in Asia and the Pacific. As far as the Pacific part of the region was concerned, there were hardly any schools of social work except, I think, in Hawaii and Guam. So there was very little contact with schools of social work in countries other than in Southeast Asia.

Different countries had various attitudes and policies that applied to the question of family planning. In India, we had no problem. They accepted the idea of abortion and birth control. It was the same thing in Sri Lanka. In Indonesia, they were a little bit unsure about the idea, and in Thailand it was accepted as long as we called it family welfare. The greatest difficulty was in the Philippines, the only primarily Catholic country in Asia, where there was great resistance to abortion and family planning. I spent more of my time consulting and working with representatives and schools of the other countries. The major focus of my approach was to point out the problems of feeding and maintaining big families.

The social welfare courses that were modified during my time with IASSW to include family planning content throughout the region are still there today. The content is included in various courses having to do with social development, family welfare, and child welfare, and it deals with developing policies, programs, and practice approaches and services for taking care of the planned family, how to control the number of children for those who cannot afford to care for them, and so forth.

A most important part of the IASSW experience for me was the relationships that I developed with the faculty members of the schools of social work. I developed very good friendships, longtime friends.

Working at the United Nations was a different matter. As a regional representative, I had to deal with national government officials of departments responsible for social development and social welfare. In that context, I might never get to work with people at the grassroots levels until I asked whether I could talk to welfare workers, including the people at schools of social work, staff and volunteers of voluntary organizations, and members of people's organizations.

Did you encounter unique difficulties or challenges?

ALMANZOR: The most difficult part of the job was working in places where living facilities and transport were very limited. I did not want to stay in first-class hotels because I did not think it was proper: I was supposed to be helping poor people. So most of the time I stayed on the top floor of public housing projects. Because of this, I was able to relate to the people more readily. This made for a very broadening but trying and tiring experience. I worked with people at different levels, but sometimes even if they wanted to work with me, they were held back by all kinds of bureaucratic constraints.

The most dissatisfying part of my job was finding out that my work was being duplicated by other people in other units in the large United Nations system. Unfortunately, there was too little coordination going on at the UN at that time.

There was another issue. In the UN system, you had to be requested by a government before making a consultation visit to a particular country. Fortunately, there were many requests for my services, and it was satisfying to help so many agencies. While with IASSW, I believed I was able to come to grips with the real problems—family planning, family welfare, and social work education. But with the United Nations, the activities to be monitored were so broad that I sometimes felt that my efforts were being stretched too thin. Trying to do whatever I could, I did not always know if what I was doing was adequate or was being followed through. After turning in my reports, that was often the end of it. Because of layers of bureaucracy in governments and organizations, it was not easy to see the implementation of my recommendations. That was the main difference between the two positions. IASSW work was not so heavily layered with hierarchies and could be followed up on relatively easily. In the UN, unless countries requested follow-ups, I could do no more.

Let's turn now to your service as an officer, board and committee member, consultant, and volunteer for various organizations.

ALMANZOR: I was an officer of the Association of Schools of Social Work, both nationally and regionally. As president of the Philippine and the Asian Regional Associations, I organized workshops and seminars. In addition, I served as vice president of the IASSW from 1968 to 1976.

I've been a member of the board of a number of organizations. One of my more recent involvements is with the Tahanan Outreach Project and Services (TOPS) in the Philippines for boys found in the streets. Tahanan in Tagalog means home. I have served as a member of its board since my stint with the United Nations was completed in 1980. I thought that was fine for a while. However, as TOPS has only a limited number of staff members, I now volunteer as a front-line social worker as well.

I was part of the organizing group of Tuloy Don Bosco Center, setting up procedures and standards for helping boys from the streets. A very innovative part of the work was setting up an outdoor open space (a reception area) for boys to come and go to as they pleased; it's called "The Patio." It's a place where they can come before they are prepared to enter the Center.

The boys usually come to us dirty, some a little woozy because of drugs. Initially, they are given food and allowed to take a bath and sleep there. The new boys stay at The Patio until the staff or the volunteers feel that they are ready to be with the rest of the group. (We do not simply bring boys in from the streets. Sometimes they come on their own. But at first, the boys tend to steal or break rules and do all sorts of things that are not acceptable. I guess that can be expected because they have lived with no control.) The Center has been given special permission by the Department of Education to offer a vocational educational program designed to help the boys to learn skills to become self-sufficient as soon as possible. But when the boys are accepted into the Center they first are taught their ABCs. When they are a bit older, they go into vocational training courses for tailoring, auto mechanics, air conditioning repair, television and radio repair, and even art. The Center has received funds to build a four-story building.

Much of the credit goes to Father Evangelista, the director of Tuloy Don Bosco. He is a management expert, a fantastic fundraiser, and an excellent media person with a doctorate in development from a university in the United States. His staff members are either priests or seminarians, and there are social workers as well.

I am now voluntarily tutoring a little boy, a street child named J. R. It is a very challenging task that I have not done before.

At our meetings I bring him books, notebooks, a pencil sharpener, candies, and cookies. After some meetings, he has become more responsive and friendly. One day he said, "I hope you bring me something to drink." So the next meeting, I brought him his snack and watched him drink his milk. He asked me why it was tasteless. I said because the milk is pasteurized and has no sugar added; therefore, it is not sweet. Imagine! This was the first time he had tasted real milk!

One day I said, "If you continue to learn until you can read, you can ask me for anything you want, as long as it is something that you need and I can afford." I asked him whether he believed it, and he said, "Yes." After a few minutes he asked if I would give him a basketball. He said he really wants it badly. He said it so seriously. I said, "O.K., I'll give you that."

I'm only concentrating on one child for now. If I can help save this child, then I was thinking that it would be okay. But he asked, "Why don't you also teach my friend?" I said, "Why?" "He doesn't know anything." I said, "Well, let's see how you learn first, and when you are doing okay, we will help him." I guess that this thought gave him a little self-esteem, feeling he could help this other boy someday instead of only receiving help himself all of the time.

Don't you think that this is social work too? Or is it more like mothering? Since the Don Bosco outreach program is staffed mostly by priests and seminarians, the boys have few mother or sister figures in their lives. I have thought that this issue of having a "complete family" should be dealt with vis-à-vis the boys at the Center. Eventually, this is what I hope to promote, starting with this one boy.

Turning to your professional publications and presentations, which issues have you addressed as being of paramount importance for the profession?

ALMANZOR: I have always advocated, as in the title of one paper I presented, that "Schools of Social Work Could Be a Deliberate Force for Change." Many of my other papers have focused on community organization and development and the organization and management of volunteers at the community levels. In my doctoral dissertation, I studied the Young Women's Christian Association, the YWCAs of the eastern United States. When I came back to my country, I found that what I had learned about the work of the YWCA was really valuable in my work with the local YWCA and with various other groups and organizations in my home country, and in my work with the IASSW and UN as well. This is something that I later wanted to tell my students—that when going abroad to study you must choose the kind of subject matter that can be useful in your home country. We must learn what they are doing "over there" but must be able to apply and adapt it to our own country, society, and world region.

So, when I came back from study in the United States, the most important task I had was to promote and develop community work, for the American versions of community organization could not be carried out within our cultural context without serious modifications. However, a problem in the developing countries has often been that we cannot seem to put down in writing, in good form, enough of the real-life recording of case, group, or community situations that we would like to use in our teaching. Also, there's little money or incentive for widespread production of literature. Here in the Philippines it is so expensive to publish teaching materials.

A role for retired faculty, it seems to me, is to volunteer to assist younger faculty members in any way they can to help meet the challenge I have outlined. They could make a contribution to whatever the younger faculty members are researching and teaching in today's increasingly complex and dangerous world. We have so many serious problems with drugs, child abuse, homelessness, poverty, and so on. The need for improved research on how to deal with such community and society-wide issues on both the macro and micro levels should be an ongoing concern.

One example of what I am referring to may illustrate this. Do you know who helped to set the combined model of community organization and community development syllabi for the PSSW? It was Mrs. Josefa Martinez, the founder of the school. She had just come back from a trip to South America when she asked me what she could do to help the school. At that time she was in her seventies. She was very sharp and mentally alert. So we teamed up and worked on the syllabi of the community organization–community development educational program, and all related course content and teaching materials.

In a presentation on "Poverty, Social Welfare and the University," the Eileen Younghusband Memorial Lecture at the 25th IASSW Conference in Lima in 1990, you drew upon the Philippine experience to argue for a "new view" of social welfare and social work. Do you recall?

ALMANZOR: I cited a social malady in my country that is affecting the lives of many and how I believe it serves as an example of the need for a new view. I will begin with a quote from my presentation: "Landless sugar farmers (sacadas) have been oppressed throughout this and the last century by the Spanish, Americans, Japanese, and the various political regimes since the Philippines became independent. Their lives have been controlled by the landlords (hacenderos). Social workers have tended to work directly with the sacadas, trying to liberate them from deprivation and injustice by helping them to change their thinking and attitudes toward their life situation. Unfortunately, the hacenderos, having inherited their land and with it the oppressive tactics, were difficult to reach and so they continued in the ways of their forefathers. Hopefully, a younger and more visionary generation of social workers may be able to be agents of change on both sides—sacadas and hacenderos—for the betterment of the social situation and the lives of all concerned."

A few social workers in the rural areas have worked directly with the farmers and their families, using their expertise in casework, changing attitudes, improving methods of work in the home and on the farm, helping the children to go to school, helping the mothers procure daily sustenance. While the very basic needs of the farmers' families may be met, the poverty situation—a hand-to-mouth existence—is never resolved. Clearly, the missing element is the direct intervention to open the eyes and pockets of landlords. The new view, when it is put into operational form, is to work with both farmers and landowners to change their attitudes so that a more equitable distribution of yield of profits from the farms may be attained.

This new government that won the most recent national election because of its pro-poor program has succeeded in influencing the Philippine Congress to create the Comprehensive Agrarian Reform Program (CARP) to address the problems of the sacadas and of the hacenderos.

Following from this new law, on July 7, 1999, President Joseph Estrada launched a program "to liberate 10 million Filipinos from poverty." The Department of Social Welfare and Development, headed by no less than the vice president of the Philippines, is expected to influence Congress to allot more funds for the millions of poor Filipinos nationwide. Vice President Arroyo also has the clout to deal with powerful landowners. She can talk with influential rich people, as she comes from the same group.

Never before has social welfare received this attention from the government and the public. What I had advocated nearly 10 years ago as the "new view" of social welfare may finally be coming to full realization.

You are still taking on teaching and speaking assignments. I understand that you are to address the Hundredth Anniversary Celebration at your alma mater, the School of Social Work at Columbia University.

ALMANZOR: Yes, I am to speak on what Columbia University graduates might do in the next millennium. I will focus on an important concern of social workers—human rights. So often the violations of human rights come about as a result of the highly competitive pursuit of economic goals within the free market economy now being so widely touted as the way for societies to progress.

Drawing on my experience in the Philippines, I will note that while policies may be enacted and clarified as to the social and human aspects of development in society, the competition for national budget allocations is a fierce and serious concern. There is an ongoing struggle to obtain the resources needed to effect a three-way approach to human rights involving three P's: provision, protection, and participation. Social rights of provision include the right of people, such as the farmers in the fields, to receive adequate compensation for work done and for basic medical care. Still using the farm laborers and their families as the example, they also have the right to protection from all forms of exploitation or abuse by landowners. Finally, they have the right to participation, to be heard on all of their problems in the farm fields and in the community.

I will speak about the few brave social workers who are working in Mindanao, where the Muslims and other minority non-Christian groups are just beginning to be schooled in their human rights, an emotionally charged issue with different groups owning the land and working the land. Some social workers have lost their lives in the crossfire.

More of these sorts of problems between wealthy owners of businesses of all kinds and their workers will likely arise in the new millennium, and not only in the so-called developing countries. Social workers will need to be educated in the new concerns, the newly articulated human rights, and the new sorts of practice approaches if they are to help people to obtain and maintain their rights within highly competitive market-driven environments.

I will also note that by the year 2000, a majority of the world's people will be living in urban areas. As the physical environment changes, so will the lives of people, as is being experienced by a great number of people living today in Philippine cities. How will social workers cope with these inevitable changes that bring about so many social problems? Social workers are most often pressed into service at the remedial end of the continuum only after problems become full-blown. There is almost no adequate professional attention to preventive programs. Community development per se, which includes the participation of the people themselves working collectively on problems they identify as or before they emerge, must become the inevitable entry point in helping newly urbanized people. I have seen the beginning of this community approach in Manila, but I wonder how well-prepared the profession will be to help nurture and extend it, not only in Manila, but in the many new cities in our country.

Were there any challenges that you faced in your career that you would have liked to have handled differently?

ALMANZOR: There was a time when I thought that I would not stay in social work. When I came back to the Philippines, even with my additional graduate degrees, I was not adequately paid. However, my family has been very good to me and to my children. They said to just go ahead and do what I wanted, and they would take care of the rest. That helped. That's how I was able to go full-time into social work. I should quickly add that I have received a lot of satisfaction from my social work endeavors, even if they did not always pay well.

For your many contributions to social welfare and civic services, you have been the recipient of several honors and awards. Could you share with us something about those recognitions?

ALMANZOR: For my work during the war, I was awarded a diploma of honor for valuable services rendered to Filipino–Allied soldiers of World War II.

For my work at the Philippine Women's University, I was awarded the University's Highest Achievement Faculty Award. The Girl Scouts also presented me with an achievement award. In 1998 the Philippine Association of Social Workers recognized my national and international performance, honoring me with their Social Work Achiever Award for my 'social work education, social welfare, and social development endeavors, which elevated the status of social work as a discipline and profession." There is also the Recognition Award from the National Citizens' Movement for Free Elections and Honest Government (NAMFREL). The award was for my work with a group of volunteers who were given the task of monitoring election procedures from the voting in the precincts through the counting of the ballots. Our major objective was to prevent cheating in the electoral process.

Do you have any closing thoughts?

I have received a lot of satisfaction from my social work endeavors. I really love to work with people, reach out to the young people and get involved in community work. I pray that I may have a little more time, strength, and resources to go on to serve those in dire need. Truly, social work never ends. There is always something to do if one wants to go on helping people.

SENO CORNELY

Born in 1929, Seno Cornely spent his early years in a small Brazilian farming community. From ages 10 to 17, he was educated in a Jesuit seminary. He completed his undergraduate work and, in 1975, received a doctorate in social work from the Catholic University, Porto Alegre. He earned a master's degree in city and regional planning from the Federal University and pursued postdoctoral studies in Germany.

Dr. Cornely's earliest professional practice was in industrial social work and community development in work with fishermen and their families on the southern Brazilian seashore. He also worked as a private-sector consultant and as technical director of social investigations and social planning projects in Rio de Janeiro and elsewhere.

In the public sector, Dr. Cornely served as director and coordinator of large public assistance and city planning offices while teaching part-time at Catholic University, Porto Alegre. He was also a visiting professor at many Brazilian and foreign universities, beginning in 1962. As one of those most active in reconceptualizing Latin American social work, he has written extensively; during the military dictatorship of Brazil (1964–1984), much of his writing had to be published outside the country.

Dr. Cornely has served as president and executive secretary of the Brazilian Union of Social Workers, president of the Latin American Association of Schools of Social Work, and vice president of both the International Association of Schools of Social Work and the International Council of Social Welfare. He has been recognized for his work. He is married and has four children and eight grandchildren.

BILLUPS: *Please share with us something of your family context and overall impressions of your boyhood.*

CORNELY: I was born in São João do Deserto, a very small village in the rural district of Lomba Grande, approximately 50 kilometers from Porto Alegre, the capital of the southern state of Rio Grande do Sul in Brazil. There, farmers of German ancestry ran small farms. My father was a mason and owned a small farm. My mother was a homemaker who also farmed a bit for our food. Of course we all helped our mother in her tasks. My father came home only on weekends.

I was the oldest of 13 children: nine boys and four girls. Although we were poor, my father built our house and we were self-sufficient. At age seven, I started to go to the community elementary school.

What were the influences that steered you toward social work?

CORNELY: When I was 10, I met a Jesuit priest, Father Urbano Thiesen, who told me he thought I could become a Jesuit. He told me about life in the seminary, where I would have opportunities to study, to learn new subjects. That was the most important factor in my decision to abandon São João do Deserto.

Father Thiesen got me a scholarship, and I went to the Kappesberg Seminary. It was an impressive building in the mountains, about 150 kilometers from my home, with 220 young students and a lot of wise Jesuit teachers. I was anxious to learn better Portuguese, English, Latin and Greek, and higher mathematics. I really don't remember having serious teenage crises during my seven years there. The whole psychological and physical environment was very healthy. We had two months of vacation yearly, and I used it to visit home.

But after seven years my spiritual counselor, Father Herzog, told me, "Cornely, you are a good guy, very intelligent and creative. We all like you. But you really don't have a vocation to be a priest, so I suggest you try some course in a university. You can become an effective Christian leader, but not a priest." It did not sound too dramatic, but it was definitive.

Those seven years were basic to my education, both for the moral values and humanistic studies. Jesuits were—and still are—excellent teachers, and I used all the occasions they afforded me to learn.

Once out of the seminary, I tried a lot of occupations: mason, farmer, factory worker (producing bricks, sugar cane rum, manioc flour), store clerk, private teacher, agent in an air company, but always for short periods and without any financial success.

During my compulsory military service, I took all of the possible courses and training, such as in Morse code and weapons. In four months, I was promoted to soldier first class, and in eight months I was a sergeant.

At night I went to a preparatory course for admission to the university. I decided to try engineering, as I knew a lot of mathematics. I did not pass the admission examination because I had a heavy hand and I was not trained in drawing. I had to try again the next year. Then a friend of mine said, "Well, Seno, why should you lose an entire year? There is something new here at the Catholic University. It's called social work. I don't know exactly what it means, but in the curriculum there are subjects like psychology, sociology, and social research. Maybe it could interest you for this year."

So this led to your discovering social work?

CORNELY: Yes. After passing the admission examination for the new school of social work in the Pontific Catholic University in Porto Alegre, I was interviewed by the director, an engineer, Mário G. Reis. He emphasized some points in my favor: my gender (more than 90 percent of the candidates were women); my background as a seminarist with Christian ideals; my curiosity about discovering new worlds; and my ambition to surpass limits and to fly higher. So he selected me.

As a student, maybe because I was one of the few males, I was elected executive secretary of our Students' Center, where I had permanent contacts with students of other university faculties. We had hot debates with the teachers and our directors, and sometimes with the rector. Besides our intellectual battling, we participated in many negotiations. We also often had long and boring discussions on ideology. I identified myself as a progressive Christian committed to social justice.

The director of the school of social work guided my studies. I remember he lent me a new book by an Egyptian social worker, Mohammed Shalaby. This book, translated only into German, was about community organization among *fellahinor,* the mix of fishermen and small farmers living along the banks of the Nile. At age 20, this book revealed to me a new world, one in which a social worker decided to live with the people, sharing their daily lives, discussing with them issues and ways for collective solutions. I remember vividly that, using a microscope, the author and the villagers examined the water they drank from the "holy" Nile. They discovered the pollution, germs, viruses, and other dirty substances in the river water. Then they decided, during many meetings with the leaders and in community assemblies, to purify the water. They also organized themselves to build a small health center and to develop, with Shalaby's advice, their other local potentialities to empower themselves.

In my fantasy, I was there with the *fellahin,* motivating them toward a better quality of life. And I brought them to my country, to our peasants or to our *favelas* or slums, to share their experiences. I went to the school director's office and told him preemptively, "Well, I feel strongly that I've met myself. This is what I want: to be a social worker."

What were some of your first professional activities and responsibilities?

CORNELY: As I was finishing my sixth semester (at the time, the requirement was eight), the Social Service of Industry (SESI) came looking for young social workers and exceptional students to start a new kind of social services for fishermen. SESI was a big private national organization sponsored by the National Confederation of Industry, with an annual budget of more than $700 million.

I enrolled in the program and presented a proposal for organizing the eight fishing settlements on the southern Brazilian seashore. The proposal was based on organizing the people's efforts through initiatives like cooperatives, local education, and self-help and self-reliance—emphasizing the people's power to solve their own problems. My unknown Egyptian colleague, Mohammed Shalaby, was my inspiration. In addition, I had discovered reports on the fishermen's cooperatives in Saskatchewan, Canada.

My proposal was approved by SESI's board, chaired by the former director of the Faculty of Social Work, the engineer Mário G. Reis.

About this time, other big events took place in your life. Correct?

CORNELY: In 1953, at age 24, I married Therezinha, a social work colleague. We're still married. We have four children, one girl and three boys, and eight grandchildren. My wife has made a career as a social worker within the state government, where she worked in mental health, then with children, and later in public assistance, where she was director, coordinator of planning, and general director. She completed her master's degree, but, unlike me, she never liked to teach. She is now retired.

After I graduated, while working with SESI, I was elected executive secretary of the Brazilian Association of Social Workers in the state of Rio Grande do Sul. There we promoted courses, social programs, and research studies, as well as social activities. Let me tell you how this came about.

In 1957 SESI sent me to the Pan-American Congress on Social Work in Puerto Rico. There I got to know some outstanding people whom I already knew through the literature (Katherine A. Kendall, Herman Stein, and Caroline Ware). I was also highly interested in one of the discussions at the Congress, which was about unionizing social workers.

Before returning, I discovered a special $10 airfare from Puerto Rico to New York to attract migrant worker immigrants from the island. I got myself on the cheap flight and spent two weeks in New York. Besides the fascination of the Big Apple, I got in touch with labor unions, in order to observe their organization, their programs, and learn how they got the participation of workers. I also contacted some street social workers.

Back in Porto Alegre, I joined a group of social workers connected with the Labor Party who were already discussing the advantages of a professional association. Under Brazilian law, in order to organize a union, any category of workers needs to organize first a professional association, which must function for a minimum of six months. We created our association and, after six months, we got permission from the Ministry of Labor to start our union.

For the election, two groups presented their program proposals. I headed one, and the other was led by a university professor. Some respectable colleagues fought against me because they thought I was too young, did not have enough political experience, was not closely enough linked to the political left, and so on. However, we campaigned with an issue-oriented agenda and won by only two votes.

My opponent was very elegant. She congratulated me and offered her support. As we were a new, small, and weak union, I thought we should not feed internal divisions, and I invited her to be my adviser. She accepted. So we started to heal the wounds of the campaign. (By the way, we are still good friends—and respect our differences.)

The election was in November 1958, and I became president on January 1, 1959, for a two-year term. Our first important cause was defending in court a colleague, a university professor who had been dismissed in error. The union won the case, and she was reinstated into her job. It was the second important opposition leader we had won over.

After winning in court, we implemented several projects:

- We organized Rio Grande Week of Studies on Social Work, with hundreds of participants and good coverage by the media, which brought the state governor and other authorities to the opening and closing sessions. We did three of these weeks, producing 92 papers that were later published.
- We participated in the design of governmental social programs and social action projects signed by all the political candidates before the election. Those elected created a state Secretary of Labor and Housing, and a municipal Secretary of Health and Social Work, and our union served on the working groups that outlined their responsibilities and those of their commissioners.
- We gained important political leverage as the union got a permanent seat in the working groups, planning state and municipal social policies on housing, health, education, social insurance, social leisure, labor, and public assistance.
- We conducted studies funded by the government on issues such as prostitution, criminality, domestic violence, rural-area-to-city immigration, and drug addiction.
- We engaged in studies and proposals for social services for private organizations and big companies, as well as cooperatives and other unions.

All of this brought social work permanently before the media. It helped us to gain prestige and better leverage for our proposals. In addition, it produced higher status and salaries. As a matter of fact, during the term of Governor Leonel Brizola of the Labor party, our salary doubled from level 7 to 14, the top of the civil service scale. When my term of office was over, it was really not hard to elect my candidate as my successor.

Because of my suggestion, SESI created a Sector of Fishermen's Assistance, and I was appointed as chief. I did this work for six years, and I trained three other social workers and a great number of collaborators. There were 25,000 fishermen and their families in four cooperatives that we helped to initiate and advise. We also developed more than 40 professional courses for fishermen, from enhancing their domestic economy to improving their health, housing, sanitation, and other services.

In one fishing settlement, the Faculty of Medicine's laboratory examined samples of human excrement and discovered that 100 percent of the people had at least one kind of internal parasite (and many had several). So we had to fight against disease. In an agreement with the Health Department of the state government, we implemented a big campaign, to persuade families to boil or filter their water, use wooden clogs for walking in unsanitary areas, and build simple sanitary tanks.

People usually attended the experts' speeches and appreciated the posters and educational films, but that was all. The community leaders told us that they were convinced of the importance of preventing infestation by parasites, but the services were too expensive. If SESI or the government could finance them in small installments, well . . . maybe. So SESI asked me for an economic study. Buying the recommended clogs, water filters, and septic tanks in large quantities directly from the industrial plants at cost, we would pay less than 50 percent of the retail price in local shops. These articles could be sold by the fishermen's cooperatives or in small shops in the fishermen's colonies.

SESI agreed to lend $500,000 in U.S. dollars for a demonstration project; the loan was to be repaid without interest within 12 months. The fishermen's organizations designed an installment financing system (wooden clogs and filters to be paid in five monthly installments and septic tanks in 10, always without interest). The cooperatives and colonies signed agreements directly with SESI and paid their debts directly to the SESI treasury. The loan was paid back in full and on time. We professionals did not involve ourselves in the business.

In the first year we advertised in the press and talked with municipal health commissioners about how the program could work. The municipalities of Rio Grande, Pelotas, Porto Alegre, and São Lourenco do Sul decided to take responsibility for the program, while the fishermen's cooperatives of Torres and Tramandaí negotiated directly with the industries. The small colony of Itapuá got support from the state Department of Health, while in São Jose do Norte some companies decided to sell the products directly to the fishermen.

Through a survey, we then tried to justify the financing of modern tools for fishing (nylon nets highly resistant to salt water, larger boats for fishing by the cooperatives, powerful engines to move these boats, and so on). The board of SESI, arguing that its objective was not social service, suggested we try to sell the idea to a development bank. The BADESUL (Southern Development Bank) was interested. The fishermen's organizations received financing for five years at very attractive interest rates.

After our report was approved by SESI's board and published by the state Parliament, we sent it to the Brazilian president, who used it to support negotiations with the Food and Agriculture Organization (FAO). I participated in the FAO mission for two years under Mr. John Fritjof's chairmanship. I learned a lot while working with this Norwegian expert and his colleagues. Eventually, the mission proposed two big national programs to President Kubischek: a national program of assistance to the seashore fishermen, to be led by the government and inspired by SESI's experience; and a national campaign to increase consumption of fish, as Brazilians generally ate little of this nutritious and inexpensive food. The president created the National Fishing Authority, using part of the FAO mission's suggestions.

We had designed a social security project for fishermen, including pensions and protections for their families. Like many other projects, this one was "sleeping" in the Congress, so we got the support of a deputy for this and for more medical and dental assistance for the communities. The projects were approved in less than one year.

In what other areas did you work early in your career?

CORNELY: I traveled often to Argentina and Uruguay, not far from my home in southern Brazil. On one occasion I met with Father Lebret of the Latin American

Center of Economy and Humanism in Montevideo. In 1956, he had invited me to participate as a junior professional in a survey of the needs and potential of the Paraná-Uruguay Rivers Basin (a region of five southern states of Brazil with about 70 million inhabitants).

I had read about the Tennessee Valley Authority in the United States, and I noted a parallel between the two regions. Father Lebret personally supervised the whole study and the team of more than 70 professionals; I was the only social worker. The team agreed in our weekly meetings on the immense potential of the region if social, political, and economic changes were introduced in an integrated fashion. These changes would include land reform, correction of the huge social differences, equality of opportunities for all social groups, and socialization of the results of these collective efforts. Three governors supported our proposals and implemented a good part—not all—of our recommendations. Even now, 40 years later, it is easy to see some of the recommendations in the state's policies.

This activity was particularly valuable for two main reasons: It was something big, encompassing almost 50 percent of the Brazilian population, and it was the first time I interacted professionally with the left wing of the Catholic Church.

In your busy life, was this also about the time that you formally continued your education?

CORNELY: Yes. I was always a voracious reader. By the time I was 24, I read German, Portuguese, and some English, but many publications were accessible only in French or Spanish. So I decided to study French (just enough to be able to read it) and Spanish in a course in the university.

My wife and I also enrolled in a one-year postgraduate course at night, "The Sociopolitical Situation of Latin America," organized by the Department of Geography and Political Sciences of our Federal University in Porto Alegre. The teachers, most of them very competent, gave us a list of 58 books. My wife and I decided to read all of them, and we divided the task. Therezinha, more busy than I, read 23, and I read 35. We wrote short summaries and discussed them. We both discovered a new and fantastic world of rich lands and subsoils, forests and well-distributed water, natural resources, and climates inhabited by miserable and deprived people surrounded by corruption and the omnipresence of international capital. Later I enrolled in a three-month seminar on social work supervision organized by seven professors from Brazil, Argentina, Chile, and Uruguay. Our meetings were on weekends in Porto Alegre, Montevideo, Buenos Aires, or Santiago, so that we had some direct opportunity to observe different realities. In spite of some superficiality and lack of unity, the seminar opened up the technical literature on supervision to me.

My interest in broader matters (I would never have been an efficient caseworker) led me to read more about planning. In Chile during the supervision seminar, I visited the offices of CEPAL, the United Nations Economic Office for Latin America, where I bought many documents on the continent's social situation and on planning.

All of this motivated me to apply for a new postgraduate program on city and regional planning in the Federal University in Porto Alegre. I was the only social worker among 15 students from different backgrounds. I wrote my thesis on partic-ipatory planning and graduated in 1963.

I continued my studies and received a doctorate in social work from the Catholic University in Porto Alegre in 1975. My final research was an investigation of people's participation in the local planning process of five municipalities in three southern states of Brazil, entitled "Popular Participation: A Crucial Factor for the Success of Local Comprehensive Plans." Visiting Professor Judson Marshall de Cew from the University of California was my adviser for the study.

A scholarship from the social worker Mary Catherine Jennings, social work attaché to the American embassy in Brazil, led to opportunities to study and observe social work planning and administration in universities and public organizations in the United States—in Pennsylvania and Wisconsin as well as Washington.

Among your many endeavors, you also have worked both in group practice and as an independent consultant.

CORNELY: A friend and I founded a small social research firm. We organized a bank of human resource experts and advertised our services to government and private agencies. Although it was not a financial success, we designed more than 30 propos-als for social investigations. Seven of them were funded and implemented.

In 1968 in Rio de Janeiro, I participated in a new enterprise, the ISSI (Institute of Integrated Social Services), which included a physician, nurse, another social work-er, and myself. We trained volunteers and others in health and social services for aux-iliary personnel and volunteers in such matters as nutrition, domestic sciences, vac-cination programs, self-help and community projects, leadership, and group work. We made some money and had a lot of fun, but, in 1970, I was transferred to Porto Alegre and the others took on new duties, so we closed the firm.

These were my two attempts at being an entrepreneur, but I did continue to work in the private sector as a consultant. The Deutsches Volksverein, an association of small farmers of German ancestry, asked me to design a development plan. After hear-ings with leaders, I proposed land reform that was approved by the board. The asso-ciation bought large areas of land, paying for them through its credit cooperatives. Then the land was divided into family-sized plots and sold to farmers, with 10-year financing. The Deutsches Volksverein populated seven municipalities with a total of more than 100,000 inhabitants.

In addition, the governor of Acre in the Amazon rainforest approved a proposal I developed to move thousands of families there from the south of Brazil. However, the board of the Deutsches Volksverein association recommended against the project after their commission found climatic and other problems.

When I first went to Rio, I was superintendent of Community Action, a private organization intended to lead projects in five big *favelas* with participation by local leaders. The projects were supported by private firms and banks, most of them multi-national. I had conflicts with their orientation to community development, and after six months I left the organization.

Years later, I was a technical consultant to SESI regarding cooperation with other international partners. This lasted 30 months. I consider it valuable that the UN acknowledged SESI's projects against drug addiction in industries as a model.

I have used many negotiation techniques, especially to attenuate the impact of big public investments, such as electrical plants and petroleum processing facilities, on large groups of people. It was possible to advise people through their organizations so that they could negotiate collectively and help preserve their interests. One example was the Regional Commission of the Victims of Barrages (CRAB), people whose land would be inundated by large new artificial lakes. CRAB is now acting in the whole southern area of Brazil, as well as in Paraguay and some areas of Argentina.

As I chaired this activity and worked with a team of five social workers, one social engineer, one economist, and one journalist, I later proposed that negotiation become part of the curriculum. It became a special unit within the political science curriculum of our Catholic University in Porto Alegre.

Tell me about your work in the public sector.

CORNELY: I had a lot of prejudices against public service. I saw too much bureaucracy and too few results. But as I had a good experience with the fishermen's organization, the president of CODEL (Commission for Development of the Seashore), a new state government agency, wanted to interview me. He had an interprofessional team of 35, but not one social worker. He told me that I would be free to investigate and to draft proposals, and that he, as a politician, would fight for the proposals. I decided to try this experiment for two years.

We assessed the region of 25 municipalities and about 1 million inhabitants, including its problems and potential. My training in the Movement of Economy and Humanism was useful as I coordinated the sociodemographic surveys. We designed a regional development plan, most of which was eventually implemented. My first experience in public service was not frustrating, but to the contrary, was quite rewarding, because more than 75 percent of the projects in the social area were implemented.

After my two years with CODEL and a change of government, the new state Commissioner of Labor and Housing invited me to be his technical adviser in social work and, simultaneously, to lead the Division of Public Assistance. After 18 months, he changed my function to director of social planning. There I chaired a team of 45 people from 13 different professions.

We devised a State Plan of Community Development with eight programs and many projects. We were able to attract grants from the Brazilian government and from USAID. Professor Louis Miniclier, director of an international community development institute, was sent by USAID to examine our plan, and his positive recommendation was vital. This was leverage to advertise the plan—the first state-level plan of community development, in the Organization of American States (OAS) and the UN. The plan had short-, middle- and long-term goals, and we accomplished most of them. The long-term goals were interrupted by changes of government and, in our case, with the military dictatorship of 1964–1984.

I left for Rio de Janeiro, and after some years became social work supervisor in the national Ministry of Social Security. Later I was commissioned as technical adviser on social affairs at the Federal Bureau for Housing and City Planning (SERFIIAU). Next, I was commissioned as coordinator of the Federal Bureau for the Southern Region (the states of Paraná, Santa Catarina and Rio Grande do Sul, with approximately 26 million inhabitants). I had a leading role in designing, financing, and implementing more than 100 local development plans and 31 microregional plans, plus 12 schools for city hall employees, a regional training center, and three large investigations—one for each state—on city infrastructures, as well as two metropolitan area plans. We did a good job in increasing the efficiency of three states and almost 800 municipal administrations.

My last public job was as senior social worker at the Metropolitan Planning Foundation of Porto Alegre, a position I held for nine years. There I was chief adviser to the superintendent, as well as coordinator of the Social Infrastructure Planning Office. I chaired the interdisciplinary team that elaborated on and implemented the Plano Participação, with projects to encourage social participation in 28 municipalities. At least 150 social workers are working for these municipalities.

What was next?

CORNELY: In May 1983, during a routine visit, my dermatologist detected a skin cancer lesion. He suggested operating immediately. It was a simple surgery followed by 10 applications of radium therapy. I was healed. But Brazilian law obliges compulsory retirement of all civil servants affected by tuberculosis, AIDS, cancer, cardiopathy, leprosy, or dementia. But I continue to do what I really like—teaching part time, doing volunteer work, consulting, writing, traveling, and working internationally.

You have mentioned your love of teaching in the university. What about that part of your life?

CORNELY: I had some experiences as a teacher while still a university student. I was a private instructor preparing candidates for the university entrance examinations in mathematics, Portuguese, German, and Latin. At the time, I was also a teacher in night school.

I was also selected to be a professor for 120 hours of higher mathematics—trigonometry—to prepare captains and majors of our air bases for their entrance examinations for advanced studies in the Aeronautic Engineering Institute. To pass was sine que non or absolutely necessary for important commands, such as colonels and brigadiers. I was proud that all 120 air military officers in my four courses did pass.

At age 33, I joined the social work faculty at the Catholic University in Porto Alegre as an assistant professor of community development for 10 hours weekly. I was never a full-time professor, because I prefer a mix of academic and field work. It has helped me to feed my university teaching with practical activities and examples.

I discovered that some students did not know a real community, especially in the rural areas, nor had they seen professional social workers in action. So we scheduled weekend visits to rural communities with the help of students from those areas. We would stay two to three days, living with families, sometimes helping in their work (or disturbing it), but getting to know real people in the hinterland (people of German, Italian, or Portuguese ancestry).

As a result of these visits, I observed how students became more interested in the classes. Theory had come alive. The students participated more actively in classroom discussions, building more bridges between theory and practice when they compared the community examples from books, usually from the United States, Great Britain, Israel, or Germany, with the examples they had observed.

With time, we broadened the community visitation projects, constituting teams of students from various backgrounds—not only social work but also agronomy, medicine, veterinary medicine, nursing, nutrition, domestic sciences, sociology, psychology—often accompanied by their professors. For these expanded groups, we needed careful preparation, including written materials as guidelines for surveys, basic techniques for conducting interviews, and the use of different kinds of approaches.

We promoted on-campus seminars on these themes. Our social work faculty, as well as some others, materially supported the projects (as did the university) with didactic materials, buses for transportation, food, and sometimes lodging when it was impossible to accommodate the whole group of students.

The Lages Project became the largest and most elaborate of your community visitation efforts. Is that so?

CORNELY: Yes, Lages is a city of 200,000 in the south of the state of Santa Catarina (300 kilometers north of Porto Alegre). Its young mayor, architect Dirceu Carneiro, was leading a big people's participatory endeavor. It included two large housing projects built by the people; community fishing pools; community reforestation throughout the whole surrounding rural area; popular education using the Paulo Freire method of conscientization; cooperatives for job creation; a community health system; popular culture through theater, poetry, and other folklore rising from the people; and a lot of other activities.

At this time, I was teaching city planning three hours a week in the faculty of architecture at the Lutheran University in Canõas. I had spoken of the Lages experience during a class, and some students showed interest in visiting, as did my social work students at the Catholic University in Porto Alegre. Elso Helm, our dean at the time, encouraged me to contact other academic areas. One Friday in September 1978, a total of 27 teachers and 412 students from 17 faculties at three universities (the Federal, the Catholic, and the Lutheran) left Porto Alegre for Lages in a convoy of buses and airplanes piloted by an Air Force major and captain, two of my students.

We were received at City Hall by the mayor and the municipal administration, as well as many community groups, and stayed in hotels, colleges, and barracks. It was a well-organized operation, orchestrated by the municipality. The professors, students, and people of Lages learned a lot from each other. Subsequently, our university rector opened more possibilities for future projects by our faculty. The mayor of Lages became a congressman and later a senator. He has supported some of our other projects in the social area, such as scholarships for poor university students.

Almost simultaneously with these initiatives, I understand that a new prospect for social work education at your university was being raised.

CORNELY: In 1976, Professor Helm, dean of the faculty of social work at the Catholic University in Porto Alegre, called a meeting to ask, "What about a postgraduate department?" At the time, only two universities in Brazil, the Catholic Universities of São Paulo and Rio de Janeiro, had postgraduate social work courses of study.

The Ministry of Education was very stringent in authorizing new courses, but the southern states of Brazil needed a more scientific social work approach to study our peculiar problems. The same was true in neighboring Uruguay and Argentina, which had no postgraduate social work offerings. We had three faculty members with doctorates in social work and six with master's degrees, plus others studying for these credentials, so we designed the program that was accepted by university authorities and then, experimentally, by the Ministry of Education.

In September 1977, Professor Helm pronounced the inaugural lecture for 15 selected students from Brazil and Argentina. I served as professor for social planning, and in more than 20 years in this capacity, I've had very exciting experiences with master's students from various countries of the continent. Many of them are now teachers or directors of schools of social work.

The success of the experience encouraged us to carefully prepare for a doctoral program. We attracted faculty from Brazilian and foreign universities, some of them as visiting professors. The university also signed an agreement with the Gesamthoschschule Universität Kassel, guaranteeing the participation of six German professors in our department.

In the second semester of 1998, we enrolled the first 12 students in our social work doctoral program from throughout Brazil and other Latin American countries. Ours is the fourth Brazilian doctoral program in social work (the others being in São Paulo, Rio de Janeiro, and Recife). I was accepted as professor of social policies and am guiding two students in their theses.

What about your faculty experiences elsewhere?

CORNELY: While I was living in Rio de Janeiro in 1968, I accepted an invitation from the Catholic University there to create and lead a course, "Synthesis of Social Work." As all of the students came from the Brazilian elite, I concluded that the most important deficiency to be addressed was their lack of knowledge about the misery of so many people and the sociopolitical causes of that misery. I invited the students to move some classroom sessions to *favelas*, which was easy to arrange as I was at the time the superintendent of community action.

The effects were impressive. Students started to read critical analyses on crucial issues affecting Brazilian society. They questioned their families' lifestyles, contrasting them with those of the *favelados* or slum dwellers. All of the students concluded that this was the most important subject matter of their whole course of study, that it should be offered during the 10 semesters of the program, that the university should be more radical, and so on. However, despite good evaluations and acceptance by the dean and most of the professors, the course could not be repeated in 1969 because the fascist wing within the military dictatorship became predominant in Brazil.

Nevertheless, the student centers designed unofficial courses on the Brazilian social reality, not only at the Catholic University but also at the federal universities. I was the professor in charge, and 765 students enrolled. It was a hidden, underground activity. I also lectured for three years on community development in the university's faculty of social work. There, too, we had programmed practice in *favelas*, including a project on "brown ecology" that still exists.

Meanwhile, your professional involvement led you increasingly to other parts of Brazil and beyond.

CORNELY: Yes. In 1977, in the worst period of the dictatorship, the Federal Council on Social Work decided to hold a national congress of social workers in Recife. I was an invited speaker, having had my first important book on planning just published.

I decided to challenge my colleagues to critically examine the concentration of national wealth and the exclusion of the majority of our people, the landless peasants and homeless *favelados*. I pointed out the illiteracy of 37 percent of the population, the 32 percent of our people living under the poverty line, the general lack of opportunities, and the rising negative social indicators (unemployment, criminality, prostitution, disease, and child mortality). I suggested we discuss our roles as political animals and as professionals.

I was afraid of two possible unknowns: the reaction of the audience and the action of the security police, who were always present.

As to the first concern, the audience was highly enthusiastic because I was the only one who took a political approach. As to the second, it was benevolent because I had twice mentioned General Geisel, who was dictator at the time, and his proclaimed purpose of "a gradual and progressive distension" of economic opportunity. The chief of police told me that he agreed with me because he received a meager salary insufficient for his family.

The Recife Congress made me known all over the country. I received many invitations to lecture on social policy and related matters. I accepted most of them.

As I was at the time president of the Latin American Association of Schools of Social Work, the opportunity to spread my message increased. In some cases, I was invited to speak on multiple occasions—in Argentina to eight schools; in Colombia to five; in Mexico to four; and to three schools each in Ecuador, Venezuela, and Peru. I also became a visiting professor at the University of Puerto Rico and the Gesamthochschule Universtät Kassel.

I understand that you were very involved in the Latin American reconceptualization process as well.

CORNELY: In 1962, at the Eleventh International Conference on Social Welfare in Rio de Janeiro, I presented a paper on community development in Rio Grande do Sul. I affirmed that we should try new approaches to social work in situations of generalized misery and marginalization, and that we should produce indigenous social work literature independent from that produced in the so-called First World. Many colleagues approached me to chat about these ideas. One of these was an Uruguayan Methodist minister, Herman Kruse, also a social work teacher at the Universidad de la Republica in Montevideo, Uruguay.

Herman Kruse and I discussed organizing a regional meeting with Brazilian, Uruguayan, and Argentinian colleagues. We engaged the Union of Social Workers, the Regional Council on Social Work, the Faculty of Social Work, and the Student's Center of the Catholic University, Porto Alegre, and gained the support of the new state Secretary of Labor and Housing and then of Argentinian colleagues. The result was the Regional Seminar on Social Work Facing Social Changes within Latin America in May 1965 at the Federal University in Porto Alegre. Students from Argentina, Brazil, Chile, and Uruguay, including a large delegation brought by Professor Kruse, and 415 social workers attended. This seminar generally is considered to be the first public activity of the reconceptualization process of Latin American social work.

I was elected chair of the seminar. We invited five official papers and welcomed "free themes," papers linked to new approaches of social work in Latin America. We selected 58 papers. Seminar proceedings were published and distributed in Portuguese and Spanish.

By the time we returned to Puerto Alegre in 1972 for the sixth seminar, there were 2,200 colleagues from all the countries of Latin America and the Caribbean.

We have since created an informal network of all former seminar presidents, as well as a journal of reconceptualized social work. We thought that we needed a formal organization through which faculty and students could connect between seminars. As a result, our ideas have spread all over Latin America and the Caribbean.

I understand that you were engaged extensively with other international organizations as well.

CORNELY: In July 1977, the Latin American Association of Schools of Social Work (ALAETS) called for its general assembly in the Dominican Republic, where I represented the Brazilian Association of Schools of Social Work (ABESS). South American colleagues and I decided that I should run for the presidency of ALAETS.

My opponent was a young and charming professor from the hosting school of social work. I won by two votes. Following my experience with the Porto Alegre social workers' union, I immediately invited my opponent to advise me, and she accepted. Then I consulted the former presidents of reconceptualization seminars, and they all accepted ALAETS leadership. We also used the services of CELATS (the Latin American Center on Social Work)—the academic branch of ALAETS—under my chairmanship. Subsequently, the ALAETS board designed three reconceptualization seminars in the series: the eighth in Guayaquil, Ecuador, in 1978; the ninth in Caracas, Venezuela, in 1979; and the tenth in São Paulo, Brazil, in 1980.

As president of ALAETS, I chaired these seminars. These public forums drew thousands of participants. Reconceptualization ideas and academic outcomes were adapted to the common needs of those present. The outstanding theme during this period was forging links to public policies. This was a reaction to the first period of seminars when ALAETS was invaded by a radical Marxist influence, the Althousserian structuralism that rejected social workers who performed civil services and believed the state was necessarily a repressive apparatus. We had fought hard to conquer social work space within civil services, where more than 50 percent of our colleagues worked. So we always had discussions with the surviving Althousserians, the Trotskyites, the anarchists, and other Marxist groups. (It's important to add that the association has continued leading the reconceptualization seminars. The nineteenth was held in Santiago, Chile, in 1999.)

What more do you care to share about the ALAETS/CELATS portion of your career?

CORNELY: We worked on various fronts during my period in office:
- We supported a Latin American Congress of Students in La Paz, Bolivia, in 1979.
- We encouraged meetings of unions of social workers at a continental level to facilitate the Latin American Federation of Social Workers as a regional branch of the International Federation of Social Workers (IFSW).
- We edited *Acción Crítica*, the journal of reconceptualized social work, our information bulletin, and a number of progressive books.
- We conducted social investigations, all published, and we supported many research studies (both technically and financially) in most of the countries of Latin America.
- We worked with universities in designing in-service courses, including five correspondence courses for social workers far from academic centers. (More than 4,000 colleagues from all Latin American countries participated.)
- We established the Latin American Master's Program in Social Work through an agreement between ALAETS/CELATS and the National Autonomous University of Honduras.

To support all of these activities financially, ALAETS negotiated an agreement with the Konrad Adenauer Stiftung valued at DM 650,000 (approximately U.S. $350,000) yearly, which continued until 1985. I traveled three times to Germany to negotiate the agreement.

Do you care to add anything more about the political situations in Latin America, their effects, and the profession's response during your service?

CORNELY: ALAETS was very politically active during the period, not only internally but in schools of social work or among teachers with political problems with the dictatorships in Brazil, Argentina, Uruguay, Chile, Bolivia, and Paraguay. We denounced internationally ideological terrorism against colleagues and protested energetically against prosecution of crimes of opinion. We were deeply linked to human rights organizations in many countries of Latin America, Europe, and North America. So we've been able to effectively protect a great number of colleagues, getting them political asylum. (I have more than 50 letters of gratitude from colleagues for whom ALAETS was very helpful.)

I imagine that surviving the military dictatorship was a special chore and challenge.

CORNELY: I was under some espionage control and vigilance by security police in Brazil because of my liberal ideas, and in 1967 I faced a military tribunal in Porto Alegre and was accused of political subversion. Before being sentenced, I resigned my civil service job, so the tribunal closed the case.

I then accepted the job with the private community development organization in Rio de Janeiro. Because the Information Service in the first years of our dictatorship was precarious, I decided to try for a new identity card. This new card, officially delivered by the state of Rio de Janeiro, declared me a clean citizen not suspected of political subversion, and, with this document, I received a new passport from the federal government.

In Rio, many colleagues and organizations offered me good professional opportunities, including the Catholic University faculty of social work. So I survived the dictatorship.

Many colleagues did not have the same opportunity. Many were jailed and others were condemned to death.

You went on to assume the vice presidency of IASSW. Could you tell us something about that?

CORNELY: During the IASSW conference in Vienna chaired by Robin Huws Jones, I met Professor Heinrich Schiller, rector of the School of Social Work of Nuremberg. We decided to run for election, he as president and I as vice president. We were elected for the 1980–1984 term.

We actively recruited Latin American schools for affiliation with IASSW, signing agreements with the Brazilian Association of Schools of Social Work to represent its 65 affiliated schools. In addition, we were able to obtain important IASSW partners for a large Seminar on Social Work in the Latin American Unity. A total of 2,217 participants from all countries of the continent convened in Porto Alegre. I chaired the session, and IASSW President Schiller was our guest of honor. The seminar had as its political leitmotif to support Argentinian sovereignty over the Malvinas Islands in its conflict with Great Britain.

We faced enormous conflicts during the seminar. The only question on which we got unanimity was solidarity with Argentina.

Another highlight of my term of office was attending the combined international meetings of the sister organizations—IASSW, IFSW and ICSW—held in

Montreal in 1984. Beforehand, the Canadian schools and social work organizations designed a program of visits and speeches by Third World social workers. I was selected, as were colleagues from 13 other countries. It was an intelligent way to facilitate our participation in international meetings.

As part of my trip to North America, I was invited to a five-day international seminar of social work educators sponsored for the IASSW by Katherine Kendall, at the Hunter College in New York. The seminar was chaired by Professor Charles Guzzetta. This was my first contact with teachers from Iron Curtain countries. We mostly discussed the trends and challenges of social work education in times of globalization. It was good preparation for Montreal.

With your IASSW term of office about to conclude, you were soon to be elected to the vice presidency of another international body.

CORNELY: For the meetings in Montreal, some Latin American colleagues and national branches of ICSW (Jamaica, Belize, Brazil) had nominated me for Latin American regional vice president of ICSW. I was elected for the 1984–1988 term, and the new ICSW president, Norbert Préfontaine of Canada, promised me his support to improve ICSW within my region.

Back in Brazil, I immediately prepared a questionnaire for a comprehensive plan of regional ICSW development. I sent this document to all national ICSW committees within the region.

The picture was anything but optimistic. Most of the committees were not functioning or were in a state of financial emergency. Only five (Argentina, Belize, Brazil, Chile, and Jamaica) had paid their annual contributions to international headquarters. Some national committees had explicit relationships with the military governments, and in at least one case the annual fees were paid by the Ministry of Foreign Affairs of the military in power.

I decided to try to change this landscape. First, I sent the questionnaire not only to national committees but also to a great number of colleagues, friends, and organizations, including many progressive-oriented colleagues. Of the 220 questionnaires mailed, more than 130 came back, some of them with very helpful suggestions and offering more permanent cooperation.

In Porto Alegre, I invited colleagues and institutional representatives to form a steering committee to elaborate a plan for the region. Some 66 professionals volunteered and formed this committee. We prepared the plan with five programs: social investigations, training, publications, seminars and workshops, and political action. Then we sent it to funding agencies within Latin America. With the vital support of President Préfontaine, we were able to interest the Canadian International Development Agency (CIDA). I immediately traveled to Ottawa. Supported by Norbert Préfontaine, Pierre Dionne, and other Canadian ICSW officers, we got support of CIDA for the whole training component, the most expensive part of the plan, with 200,000 Canadian dollars (about U.S. $150,000). It represented an important signal for smaller Latin American agencies, as well as some in Spain, to support other components of the plan.

During my period of office and the next two periods, Jorge G. Krug, my friend and successor, and I helped to inaugurate new committees in Mexico, Guatemala, Honduras, Costa Rica, Colombia, Venezuela, Ecuador, Bolivia, Puerto Rico, and the Dominican Republic and subcommittees in Paraguay, Panama, El Salvador, and Cuba. There are small groups, not committees or subcommittees, in Haiti and some countries in the Caribbean region. This changed the political weight of the Latin American region with more votes in the ICSW.

Programs under ICSW auspices included a 1986 Latin American and Caribbean Seminar on Family and Community held in Porto Alegre, where more than 1,200 experts from 17 countries convened, along with Mr. Préfontaine, the vice presidents from the European and Asian regions, and the president of the IFSW. In 1987, again in Porto Alegre, we convened from the Seminar on Legislation and Social Welfare. In 1988, in Mar del Plata, Argentina, more than 900 experts from the social welfare community met to discuss "Children in Work."

I led our region's delegations to ICSW conferences in Tokyo (1986) and Berlin (1988). In Tokyo, I was a plenary speaker addressing the outcomes of our Latin America and Caribbean Seminar on Family and Community.

Following my term, I continued with ICSW endeavors. In 1989, Mr. Krug asked me to chair the Regional Seminar on Social Work and Social Policy in Mexico, as well as another one on social ecology in Porto Alegre, in preparation for the UN Summit on the Environment in Rio in 1992.

Then our Latin American ICSW vice president decided to hold a Caribbean workshop on social ecology in Cuba, also in 1992, and asked me to chair it. We held a very productive regional project with participants from all over the Caribbean, as well as some experts from Central America, Mexico, and Brazil. The results were presented by the Cuban delegation at the UN summit.

You have been involved with still another international organization, one concerned with children.

CORNELY: I started to work with the International Bureau for Children's Rights in 1996, when at its Paris meeting I was elected vice president for the Latin America and Caribbean region. We planned the 1998 International Tribunal on Child Prostitution, including sexual tourism, in Fortaleza, Brazil. In this moral tribunal, five judges from five countries held a trial on the matter, which drew extensive coverage by the media. Later we evaluated the tribunal and its considerable influence over Brazilian judiciary authorities and decided to repeat it in Colombo, Sri Lanka, early in 1999.

I continue to serve on the board of the bureau. Our next objective is to address the protection of child victims of violence, particularly in times of war.

Social planning from an interdisciplinary frame of reference is another of your major interests. Is there more to say about that?

CORNELY: As I worked in public and private organizations, we thought that we needed an interprofessional organization to defend our interests as planners. In 1974 in Porto Alegre, we created the Brazilian Institute of Planning. Our president was a very busy architect, and I was elected (four times) first vice president, which meant that many of the tasks were mine.

To increase visibility, we organized two Brazilian Congresses on Planning, as well as one Southern Cone Seminar on Comprehensive Planning, all with hundreds of participants and all held in Porto Alegre. I chaired these congresses, and the institute became the voice of Brazilian planners, nationally and internationally. At peak times, about 3,000 Brazilian planners were associated with it.

SIAP has nominated me to chair six Latin American courses in metropolitan planning and a seminar on administration and managing the metropolitan areas.

Our institute produced a journal in which I published my first articles on participatory planning. Many of these articles were translated into Spanish and published by *Revista InterAmericana de Planificación*, the journal of SIAP.

In 1980, the International Society of City and Regional Planners (ISOCARP) invited me to present a paper on planner training in Latin America during the International Congress of City and Regional Planners in Tunis, Tunisia. There I was elected a bureau member. I've been reelected in the World Congresses of 1982, 1984, and 1988. I've continued to work with them, and I've sent prominent young city planners from Latin America to their congresses and training workshops.

Could you tell us more about your publications?

CORNELY: As a student, I worked for years as a freelance journalist for newspapers.

My first professional publication was the survey of the south Brazilian fishermen's situation published by the state Congress of Rio Grande do Sul. As I made speeches or presented papers in seminars and conferences on social affairs—on community development, social planning, participatory planning, social policy, and social ecology—these usually were published in proceedings or in books or journals. Many of these materials are still used in faculties of social work within Latin America.

In association with an architect, I've written a book on public housing, published in 1962 by the Federal Saving Bank. Another survey on the fishermen's situation in the state of Santa Catarina was published by the presidency of the republic. Another, on the social situation and perspectives of the coal mining workers, was published by SESI.

My doctoral thesis went through three printings by Cortez Editorial in Portuguese and two by ECRO in Spanish. My *Handbook for Designing Social Projects* was reprinted 18 times in Spanish and five in Portuguese. My plenary speech on "Family and Community," presented at the 23rd ICSW conference in Tokyo, was printed not only in the proceedings but also by the Anglican Church of Australia.

During the military dictatorship in Brazil, most of my writings were issued in Argentina, Peru, Colombia, and Mexico, for obvious reasons.

In the last five years, I've investigated the social impacts of MERCOSUR (the Southern Cone Common Market), producing 22 documents in Spanish and some in Portuguese.

On reflection, are there particular issues that come to mind with respect to your international endeavors and leadership experiences?

CORNELY: I've always had significant support, both from individuals and organizations all over the world. I will not mention anyone because I'm afraid I'll forget some important people, but I cannot omit the name of Dr. Katherine Kendall. From the early years of my presidency of ALAETS, she has always supported and challenged me, despite some differences we've had.

On the other hand, I've had to fight some obstacles. One has been the enormous time away from home for travel. (My wife, a social worker, has understood the situation, but my children probably felt my absence.) Another obstacle has been the lack of support of my government in international meetings. Third, overcoming differences in cultural contexts has sometimes been a challenge in parts of Asia and Africa. Finally, there has been my own impatience. I like to see and to touch the results of my work, but on the world scene things tend to move slowly.

Could you share with us something about your awards and honors?

CORNELY: In 1955 I received a medal during the First Brazilian Congress of Professional Fishermen for extraordinary social services delivered to fishermen and their families. In 1970, while I was chair of a federal agency that financed the Plan for Local Development of Novo Hamburgo (the county where I was born), the City Hall organized a big solemnity where I was given a decoration with the title of "outstanding citizen." In 1972, the Federal Rondon Program, which promotes integration of the Indian communities while respecting their native culture, presented me a diploma of "great benefactor." In 1979, during my term as president of ALAETS, a medal with this same title of "great benefactor" was presented to me by the Colombian National Council for Education in Social Work after successful negotiations with the Minister of Education to increase university-affiliated social work education in Colombia. In 1984, at the World Congress of ISOCARP in Braga, Portugal, my project on participatory planning (grassroots participation in planning) won first prize. In 1987, the Superior Council of the Pontific Catholic University gave me its Brother Alphonsus Medal. In 1997, the Brazilian Association of Education and Investigation on Social Work, commemorating its 50th anniversary, presented me with the diploma for "outstanding educator in social work."

What are your most recent professional interests, as well as your perspectives on the future of social work?

CORNELY: In 1998, the Catholic University offered a special postgraduate course on domestic violence and social policy for an interdisciplinary group of 30 professionals. I coordinated 45 hours of this offering, including a survey of public and community resources to assist the victims of violence. The resources were totally insufficient for the size of the problem. I have encouraged a group of my former students to create the Institute for Studies and Action on Domestic Violence. The needs of the victims will become an increasingly large issue for social workers in our male-dominated society.

Other emergent issues are social ecology and ecosocial work. I've offered short courses (30 hours) on each of these topics, the first a postgraduate course at the Catholic University faculty of medicine, and the second at the Jesuit-chaired University of the Sinos Valley.

Outside the university, through an engineering firm where I'm senior consultant, my work is with the people to be displaced (about 950 families) for construction of a new subway line in the São Paulo Metropolitan Region. The families are to be reimbursed for 125 percent of the market value of their properties and resettled in areas with at least the same infrastructure and external advantages. I've proposed managing this process through a collective negotiation; it's vital that the people organize themselves.

ARMAITY S. DESAI

Born in 1934, Armaity S. Desai earned a bachelor of arts degree with honors in sociology and anthropology from Bombay University in 1955. This was followed by a diploma in social service administration from the Tata Institute of Social Sciences in 1957 and master's and doctoral degrees in social work from the University of Chicago in 1959 and 1969. Before she completed her master's degree, and interspersed between her work toward the two graduate degrees, Dr. Desai served as a lecturer in the College of Social Work affiliated with the University of Mumbai (Bombay; 1957–1958 and 1961–1965). In addition, for almost two years immediately after completing her master's program, she worked with the Chicago Child Care Society and for one year at the Tata Institute of Social Sciences.

Before completing her doctorate, Dr. Desai was involved in teaching and supervising social workers at Loyola University and the University of Chicago. Upon her return to India, she became vice principal and then principal of the College of Social Work in Bombay from 1969 to 1982. She served 13 years as director of the Tata Institute of Social Sciences. Subsequently, she was called to serve a four-year term as chairperson of the University Grants Commission (UGC) from 1995 to 1999.

Dr. Desai has held many special assignments as a consultant, trustee, and adviser on various professional and governmental bodies within India and elsewhere, including South Africa. Her offices have included president of the Association of Indian Universities, vice president of the International Association of Schools of Social Work, and president of the Asian Regional Association for Social Work Education. She has written widely and has served for a number of years as editor of the *Indian Journal of Social Work*. She is the recipient of a variety of scholarships and awards. Since retiring from UGC responsibilities, Dr. Desai now lives in Mumbai.

BILLUPS: *Please share with us something about your childhood or adolescent years, as well as any experiences of those years that may have prompted you to consider social work as a career.*

DESAI: Well, in my case, my entry into social work was greatly inspired by my family. Both of my parents were in social work. My father, Sapur F. Desai, was the secretary of an organization called the Parsi Punchayat Funds and Properties, which is more than 300 years old. This is a very large welfare organization of the Parsi community, who are Zoroastrians by religion. They came to India 1,300 years ago from Persia to preserve their religion, which was under threat. This group of fewer than 100,000 has contributed to its adopted country far out of proportion to its numbers. My father was the joint secretary of this large trust and directed its activities. The trust provided for the disadvantaged members of the community from womb to tomb. He oversaw a wide spectrum of social services. My father tried to modernize and professionalize the programs and methods of service delivery. I was interested in what he was doing.

My father was the first to start vocational guidance through his organization. He wanted to help young people to choose their careers with the help of two trained vocational education specialists who had studied in the United States and who had come back to India. Later on, the Government of India took this on, and now they do it as part of the normal government machinery.

Naturally, my father was keen that I should take a placement test, but I wasn't too happy about it. I said, "I know what I want. I want to be a social worker." He said, "Never mind, wait to decide until you take the test." So, I did. And it was very interesting that my results were the highest for teaching. Number two was agriculture. I said, "What a silly test. I don't believe in any of this. I don't want to be a schoolteacher." I didn't think of teaching beyond that stage. I stuck to social work and was admitted to a postgraduate school of social work after my bachelor's degree. Yet I am in education and have been in education all of these years.

My mother, Tehmina S. Desai, was a schoolteacher and the principal of a girls' school. When she left full-time teaching, she went into social work as a volunteer. During World War II she developed a day care program for the organization that my father worked for, serving Parsi children who were malnourished and faced other problems in an area where many low-income families were living. She started a day care center for preschool children, when comparable ones hardly existed; later this program became a model for others. Then she went into many other activities, including an organization called the Maharashtra State Women's Council, where she was convener of the Child Welfare Committee. Among other activities, the council also established a child guidance clinic. She did a tremendous amount of other volunteer work in the council in several committees and in the Women Graduates Union. So, from the beginning, I had this kind of family influence given the nature of involvement of both my parents.

Then, to add to all of this, my father's youngest sister, Aloo, was one of the earliest social work graduates from the Tata Institute of Social Sciences, which I attended years later. It was the first institution in this part of the world, in the whole of Asia, to begin training for social work. An American missionary from Chicago, Clifford Manshardt, had set up a settlement house in Bombay, which led to the establishment of this institution. I would ask my aunt what she did as a medical social worker. She was the first one to be appointed to such a position in India in a large city public hospital supported by the State Government. I was very fond of my aunt, and this also furthered my interest in social work.

And what about the influences of your early schooling?

DESAI: I went to a Christian Protestant missionary school where they helped me develop a natural empathy toward others. In fact, the school motto was "Others." I remember, as a small girl in second grade, that I was asked to write an essay about "My Dolls" and I wrote something about my dolls being in an orphanage and how I would look after them. I would give all of them chicken soup, which seemed to me like an expensive thing to do at the time! All of this encouraged my interest in the profession. I couldn't wait to go into social work training.

In those days, as you know, in the United States most schools of social work did not have a bachelor's degree program in social work, and the program in India also started with a two-year diploma after the first degree, based on the American model. One had to wait until after graduation at the bachelor's level to enter social work education at the master's level for professional practice preparation. I hoped that I could be admitted directly after completing high school, as I was in a hurry to enter preparation for social work. I approached one of the faculty members whom I knew, emphasizing to him, "I'm quite mature. I'm ready for this." However, it was not possible since qualifications for entering the program were well-defined. Hence, I took sociology as my major for the undergraduate degree, because I thought that would be a good background for social work. I was very fortunate because in this Jesuit college, St. Xavier's, they were very keen on students being involved in social service activity. We had a Social Service League, and that gave me ample opportunity to do things. I put my heart and soul into working in the slums of Bombay. We not only volunteered there on a regular basis, but we also spent 10 days of our vacations living with the people, making physical improvements and offering recreation programs for children. We built a platform with a line of faucets for them to wash; otherwise, they had to wash standing in muddy slush. We had other campaigns as well. We learned many things, one of which was how difficult it was for anyone to remain clean under such conditions.

We also spent one summer in a village doing some work with a women's group, and we did some construction there, as well. We tried to build a school, but it was not a very good effort because we made mud bricks, covered with sticks and straw, and put them to dry, and in the night the cows ate the straw and smashed all of our bricks! But we learned a lot about social issues, culture, and building relationships with people. These were my very good first lessons in social work, which later on came in handy.

I understand that you graduated with a bachelor of arts with honors from Bombay University before going on to study at the Tata Institute of Social Sciences. What else would you like to share about your undergraduate experiences?

DESAI: Well, I took sociology and anthropology as a combined major and political science as my minor. I did those courses as a kind of foundation that I thought would be very useful for social work. I enjoyed sociology and anthropology a great deal more than I enjoyed political science, and I did a lot of reading on my own.

Sociology had some very fine courses, but I found them a bit boring because of the method of teaching. Sometimes in class I would break the boredom when I would ask a question that would make the professor digress from his lecture notes. Then the discussion became more interesting. This professor also took us out of class into the field. He said, "Let's go and see the 'tribals'"—after all, we were in anthropology—and we went off campus and studied the tribal group living very close to Bombay.

A stark incident during the visit to the tribal village is engraved on my mind. We stayed with some nuns for the night, sleeping on their verandah as they had no other accommodations; the male students stayed with the priests. We had just lain down on our bedrolls when we heard some rather fearsome sounds coming from the dark outside, as though a person were being strangled. There was no electricity in that village, and we could not see anything. We all felt distressed. I was too uncomfortable to be able to sleep. I announced that I was going out to investigate and picked up a lantern. Two other girls also volunteered. We went out and followed the sound.

We soon came to a small building that was a row of rooms with tile roofing and which served as a dispensary-cum-cottage hospital for the nuns. There were some adult men and women sleeping outside—relatives of the patients inside, they said.

I could distinctly hear the sounds coming from one of the rooms. I asked the people what was happening. They explained that the patient had received a "ghost." Of course, I did not believe them, so I went to the room and opened the door. I saw a tribal boy of about 16, lying on the floor next to a dim lamp in the corner. His hair was tousled and his eyes were red. He was shouting, in delirium, apparently, or out of fear. I sat next to him while one of the other girls went to awaken the nuns.

I will never forget the sight that greeted us when I opened that door, not knowing what I would find. Maybe in our youth, we did not know fear (we were just 19 or 20), and maybe our desire to act was stronger than the fear of the unknown.

So we certainly learned a lot from firsthand field experiences. All in all, I think that the college did a lot of good for me. And now, when I look back, I'm glad that I had a liberal arts education first.

Would you please tell us something about your entry into your social work education through your experiences at the Tata Institute of Social Sciences?

DESAI: I entered the Tata Institute at the time when it had shifted from its city location to a new suburban campus. The campus was surrounded then by orchards and green fields, a lovely location. It was an adventure in those days because there were no proper buses. The city service had not yet been extended. Sharing a room with two students from Myanmar, I stayed on campus because both bus and train connections were poor, and so it was not possible to commute every day. Today, this area is indistinguishable from the city; but in those days, at night, you could hear the jackals calling. I thoroughly enjoyed my social life in addition to the studies. It was a lovely life-given opportunity with good faculty, and I was doing what I really wanted to do. The idea of being placed in student field practice was a very appealing part of my course of study.

I was placed part-time in a Remand Home to work with children who were awaiting their appearances in the Children's Court, and I worked with the probation officers. The other half-day was spent in the community, a housing project for the employees of the Bombay Port Trust, where I worked with children in groups. I had Girl Guide experience in my school years (I captained a Girl Guide group for five years) and so I knew how to conduct group programs. It was a group work field practice placement, basically, and in those days the idea that you should combine group work with casework in the same agency was more unusual than it is today.

The Tata Institute has always offered a specialized curriculum in the second year. I decided to enroll in community development. I was clear on what I wanted, based on my experience of working in slums and in the village. I was very community-oriented but, unfortunately, the specialization was closed down for that year. I was advised by one of the teachers to specialize in Family and Child Welfare. So I met with Mrs. Manu Desai (no relation to me) and she agreed to place me for a half-day in the community and a half-day in a place where I could do casework. I agreed. I was placed in a day care program for children from disadvantaged homes, which, unbeknownst to the institute, my parents had helped set up. Afternoons, I went out for community work, where I started a project for potters residing in a Dharavi, a large slum.

At the end of my first year of graduate study, a French Catholic nun who had been instrumental in starting another school of social work in Bombay contacted me and said, "We should be very happy if you join us as a teacher at the end of your graduation." They knew of me because one of their nuns had accompanied us, as students, to the slums and the village where I worked as an undergraduate student from the Social Service League of my college. One of the visiting teachers of this new school of social work had also suggested me. I met the new director of the school who was an American nun, and I agreed to consider it. "But, in the meantime," she said, "we would like you to start a community project that will become a fieldwork center for student field placement." So I started community work in this particular slum community as my second-year field placement, and three first-year students were placed under my supervision. They didn't know I was a student for a long while. We were doing fine and had no problem working in this traditional, highly cohesive, and very interesting community. However, the cat was out of the bag when I sent one of them to the public hospital in connection with the referral of a patient in the community. She met my classmate in the hospital, from whom she came to know my status.

Fortunately, it did not affect my role and relationships as a supervisor, because they felt they were getting an adequate learning experience. Thus, I did casework, group work, and community work, and also supervised students. It was an interesting mix.

That was also the year we had a Technical Cooperation Mission in India. The United States Agency for International Development (USAID) in collaboration with the Council on Social Work Education (from the United States) and the Government of India, had supported a group of social work educators to come to India. One of them was Professor Manning, a black American from California who worked with the Urban League serving African Americans in the United States. He was a community organization expert and really helpful to me. My department of Family and Child Welfare didn't have any faculty with a background in community specialization, so his help was important to the Institute and to me.

My Tata Institute years laid the foundation for all that I did later, for I really never liked following only one practice method. In fact, my placement in the slum provided me the opportunity to develop an integrated approach, using all the methods. Coincidentally, the leader of the U.S. team that brought Professor Manning and several experts to other schools of social work was Dean Wright, a former dean of the University of Chicago, where I subsequently went for my master's and doctorate.

What happened after your graduation from the Tata Institute?

DESAI: As you know, I had already been promised a job in the school of social work. I started working for a very meager salary, but the work was enjoyable in a new and struggling institution that was just starting. I joined in their second year of operation. It was the tenth school of social work to be established in India. Most of the students were older. Quite a few students were married women who came to class and fieldwork after fulfilling their household responsibilities in the morning. The classes were held in the late afternoon or evening. Though they were older, we got along rather well. The only time I had a clue to their thinking that I was younger than they were was when we went to a rural area to which we wanted our students to be exposed. Returning on the train, because my shoulder-length hair was flying, I tied my hair in two pigtails. When we were nearing Bombay, my students requested that I remove the pigtails because it made me look young. They said that their parents had been rather surprised and apprehensive to see me escorting the whole group when they came to the station to see their daughters off to the camp. In spite of problems such as bedbugs biting one of the girls, the trip went well. I enjoyed being a teacher. Because I came from a family of teachers, it came very naturally.

Something more was going on in your life at about the same time.

DESAI: During that year, I was corresponding with the University of Chicago and Columbia University about enrolling for the master's degree. My heart originally was set on studying at Columbia, but I didn't want to put all of my eggs in one basket so I applied to both Columbia and Chicago. I would have to depend on some fellowship funding. I couldn't have gone on my own. I needed at least my tuition to be covered, but a private trust in India, the Meherbai D. Tata Trust, was willing to finance my travel and living expenses, with some other smaller trusts giving me loans. Chicago gave me a tuition scholarship, which I accepted. Later, I received a scholarship offer from Columbia, but I remained loyal to Chicago.

Could you tell us a bit about your experience in Chicago?

DESAI: It was an interesting experience because in those days they allowed foreign students with a background in social work to begin in the summer months by taking a "bridge course," offered to the doctoral students as an introduction for direct entry in the second year of the master's degree. It was mainly casework, and some other subjects like social policy and social welfare in the United States. The highlight of this summer program was to be taught by a sensitive teacher, Charlotte Towle. She taught a course in casework. Later, in the second year, I took two other courses offered by her related to fieldwork supervision and teaching. Both courses were excellent and later inspired me to develop suitable courses in India.

In the master's program, I was placed with the Jewish Family and Community Services as part of my fieldwork. It was one of the top agencies for casework. This was the first year that the school had introduced community organization, and a new person had just joined the faculty for that purpose. But there were only two students, myself and an Australian woman student. No American students joined the specialization at that point.

The professor placed me in the famous Urban Renewal Project of Hyde Park–Kenwood, which was going through great change. It was an interesting experience working with the neighborhood block organizations with all of the problems they were facing with black and white integration and fear of displacement by the expansion requirements of the University. So that's what I did, along with my casework in the Jewish Family and Community Services agency.

The coursework during my master's program was heavily oriented toward casework, but I also took a course in community organization. As I mentioned earlier, I also took one of Charlotte Towle's courses on teaching and field instruction since I had already worked in the educational system in India. I thought these two courses would be very valuable for me when I returned to the College of Social Work.

My doctoral research at the University of Chicago looked at social work education for foreign students—the context and the materials of social work education in the United States with its cultural parameters and its degree of applicability and transferability for practice in other countries. I was especially interested in developing countries and non-Western cultures. How should social work practice, and, therefore, social work education be restructured for foreign students? What should an institution in the United States, which receives students from other lands, understand about the students? It was a study based on a questionnaire I sent to all the schools of social work in the United States in 1967, which I followed by interviewing a smaller sample. The 166 enrolled students were asked to complete the detailed questionnaire, and 25 were interviewed Dr. Donald Brieland was my research guide. This study was very interesting. It uncovered many misconceptions on the part of the schools of social work about the requirements of foreign students and their learning needs, especially with respect to fieldwork. It made me sensitive to how in my own situation—coming back to India after having studied in the United States—I would need to work with my students in a culturally sensitive way. I thought that was very important.

I completed the master's degree in one year, and decided to gain some full-time experience as a fieldworker. I knew that I could be going back to teach and I thought that such a field practice base would help me in my teaching. I also wanted to work in a field in which I could learn to practice in an area that did not yet exist in India. One such area was adoption and foster care. Hence, I found employment in the Chicago Child Care Society, located within walking distance of the university. My familiarity with adoption legislation proved very useful when I returned to India. I learned a great deal about the process of adoption, foster care, and working with unmarried mothers.

I also had other memorable experiences in Chicago. While studying for my doctorate, I took a part-time job at the University of Chicago (Billings) Hospitals where I supervised some social workers. I thoroughly enjoyed it, but medical social work was never my cup of tea; so I looked around for something in social work education. I took a job at Loyola University supervising students in a school social work field placement. In addition, I taught a casework course for one year. One student said they enjoyed the course because I was always bringing out the cultural elements, even in the American situation. That was never a part of the course content, as they were more heavily weighted toward the individual psyche. I think I heightened my own sensitivity a great deal in understanding how people behave because of their culture and the larger societal context.

The fieldwork placement also was a challenge. I started a field placement in a school that received a large number of Cuban refugee families. The 1960s had seen a large exodus. We learned a great deal about the impact of displacement to another cultural environment, affecting each member differentially—the husband, the wife, and the children. The children were the quickest to absorb the language (English) and, as interpreters, seemed to gain a superior position over their parents. The mothers were the least exposed to the language, sequestered as they were in their homes. Hence, we started English language classes. Its spin-off effect was that some of the mothers found friendship and support from the group in handling the trauma of displacement and also in sharing ways of dealing with their children.

I liked supervising the social workers in the hospital. During that period I had the good fortune of seeing and hearing Anna Freud. She was marvelous. I can still see her on that stage, simply dressed and wearing her tennis shoes. There were these intellectually serious-looking psychiatrists of the University of Chicago Hospitals, all well-dressed, who spoke and analyzed a case in highly sophisticated medical language. Then Anna Freud got to the microphone and gave a simple explanation of the whole thing. I wondered whether some intellectual egos were deflated.

There were several times that other doctoral students commiserated about the stresses in our program, but I enjoyed all I was doing while working on my dissertation studies and my research work. Helen Perlman and Bernice Simon ran stimulating classes, and I feel fortunate to have been their student. I was happy doing what I was doing even though it took me a little while (about four years) to complete the entire doctoral program, including the initial nine months to complete the doctoral comprehensives. I worked consistently part-time after my comprehensives—first at the University of Chicago Hospitals and then Loyola University in the downtown campus of the School of Social Work. I greatly enjoyed the interaction with the faculty members at the school. I was instrumental in suggesting the use of Bloom's Taxonomy of Educational Objectives to develop objectives in field instruction and a more detailed sequential framework for fieldwork for each semester. I worked on this much further on my return to India with my colleagues at the College of Social Work. The classroom teacher has the advantage of a course outline and units for teaching. The field instructor is left to consider his or her own idea of what is to be taught. We spent considerable time evolving an outline for field instruction for each semester, sequentially from the first semester through the last.

Following your studies at the University of Chicago, you returned to India?

DESAI: I came back to India after my studies and my work in the United States even though legally, at that time, I would have been allowed to teach approximately 18 more months on a visa allowing work experience. However, my college of social work was pressing me to return.

The first time I came back to India after earning the master's degree, I worked in child adoption on a systematic basis in one of the family agencies. I worked at setting up a network of existing institutions that had children in their care who could be adopted. It was very tough in those days because adoption of unrelated children was an alien idea. The challenge was tremendous as even some children's institutions were reluctant to release the child for adoption. Of course, today, the picture has changed significantly. Foster care was also just being promoted by the Government of India, but, at the time, they wanted somebody with some experience to get the program under way. I accepted the challenge, though I could do only some preliminary planning as I left for the United States for the doctoral program.

On my return to employment, first at the college affiliated with the University of Bombay (now known as Mumbai) and, later, at the Tata Institute, I expected that the students learn more than one or two methods of practice, both in the classroom and student fieldwork placement. It is a holistic practice that I have been trying to promote. I thought that was a very useful way of approaching social work practice, so I developed an integrated social work practice syllabus. I enjoyed teaching it. I used the students' field practice experiences to promote classroom learning. In the College of Social Work, we even had a seminar course, in the last semester of the master's degree, designed for students to form groups with identified faculty members and make presentations based on a specific area of field intervention, using integrated practice.

There was a Family Service Center that was a part of the College of Social Work and that served as a practical learning laboratory for our students, but it was not doing well. So I used my fieldwork experience with the Jewish Family and Community Services and helped to develop adoption, foster care, and a proper family social casework program. We also had an income-generation activity for the women because many women who came to the agency for assistance were heads of single-parent families, or their husbands were not in a position to work for one reason or another. In India, we do not have public aid programs as in the West, so we had to find other means of generating income support for women. We started a tailoring class for the women that would take orders from a pharmaceutical company that required muslin mouth protectors/veils and aprons, easy things for the women to sew and that did not require many backward and forward linkages in procuring raw materials or arranging sales. We tried to develop other methods of income generation as well.

You became involved in a succession of administrative responsibilities once you returned to India from doctoral studies. Could you please fill us in on some of those roles and duties, starting with the college affiliated with the University of Mumbai?

DESAI: Subsequently, on my return to India from doctoral studies, I really was much more involved in administrative work because I became the vice principal of that college and, later, the principal. Those were very interesting years in Bombay because not only did we restructure our master's curriculum, but the college also became affiliated with the University of Bombay in 1969. That's when I tried to begin to shift the curriculum from what was highly oriented toward casework and group work toward a social development framework. A workshop presented by the Social Development Division in Bangkok (ESCAP) was particularly useful in consolidating my thinking.

We only had a few teachers, but we had a system. We always met regularly, once a week. And we would do all of our administrative and academic work together as a group in staff meetings on a regular basis. Later on, we grew into a larger group of 16 to 18, but we continued to meet to do all the planning, policy development, content of curriculum, and fieldwork.

We also developed a bachelor's degree program in social work because we saw the need to open the door to social work at an earlier stage of student career choice. Eventually, it became quite a good model of what a bachelor's degree should be in a developing country. In fact, the first year had a number of components that were program- and not process-related so that the students could function in specific activities as paraprofessional workers. The university awarded a certificate at the end of the first year for those who did not wish to continue but who wanted to work at that level, though few did. The paraprofessional training program didn't survive fully, but parts of it continued in a different form.

Another problem was how the bachelor's and the master's degrees might meld together. This was quite a problem because we were admitting students directly from other majors as well as from our own bachelor's of social work program. We did not want a bachelor's student to have a repetitive program. So we developed a new approach by which bachelor's students in social work would go directly to the second-year MSW methods courses, combined with a new requirement for completing certain courses in their second year, such as an advanced practice methods course. That course turned out to be most interesting and enjoyable—for the students and for me—as we examined various practice-related issues and as students made presentations on self-selected topics that they prepared through library research. Students could opt between clinical practice (casework and group work) or social policy and development (taught by another teacher).

We would also give social work bachelor's graduates more freedom to decide their MSW-level field placement than was allowed baccalaureate graduates from other disciplines. For example, we developed an interslums youth program that later became an important youth agency. We developed youth groups in the Bombay slums. The students had to work with whatever structure there was in the slums and with whichever nongovernmental organization (NGO) worked there, identifying the youth and developing a group for development work in urban slums. (By that time, these students, with three years of undergraduate social work preparation and the first year of their master's degree program completed, were expected to be reasonably independent practitioners.)

This strategy of working with youth was also part of the thinking we did about community organization. We thought that working in one slum could not have the desired impact. Unless we helped to federate the slums to bring pressure for change on the power structure of the city, there was no way that desired change could be achieved. So we wanted to develop the youth groups as part of that attempt to bring these slum neighborhoods together into some kind of a power bloc. It didn't quite work out that way because this effort was not sustained. We thought that our students often had to make their own way as relatively autonomous practitioners. These experiences in a restructured social work education program, we hoped, would eventually help to restructure social work practice in India as well. The work we undertook was challenging. Parallel to this effort, we put in place a paraprofessional training program of nine months, and several youths from these groups and slum communities joined it.

The college also developed an activist orientation. We worked on the issue of slum and pavement dwellers' right to housing close to their places of work. We took up for pavement dwellers, who, at one stage, were unceremoniously removed and sent back to their own states. Subsequently, the college worked on other issues such as the rights of construction workers, women, and street children.

You then went to the Tata Institute?

DESAI: Yes, my work in India with the College of Social Work spanned 25 years after my graduation with the diploma in social service administration from the Tata Institute in 1957. I joined the College in June 1957 and left for the Tata Institute, my alma mater in November 1982. The former director at the Tata Institute had retired. They were looking for a person to head the organization, but I didn't even pay any attention to the vacancy because the Tata Institute of Social Sciences had begun to emphasize social science research, and I was sure that they would look for a good social scientist. There are plenty of them in India, and I was enjoying my job at the College of Social Work affiliated with Bombay University.

Then I learned that my name was being mentioned by everybody except me. It was a little embarrassing. I was called to meet a couple of the trustees of the Tata Institute at Bombay House. They called me back and asked me if I would join their faculty and head the institute. It was too traumatic for me. I first said "No." It would be a major separation from an institution I had helped to nurture for 25 years.

Finally, after much discussion with my own faculty at the college, I took the plunge. One reason was that I had about 12 years left of my professional life before retirement. Sixty is considered retirement age in India, and I thought, "Well, what else would I like to do in these last years?" I lived with my parents, who were very old. I knew I wouldn't want to take on something that would take me somewhere they couldn't go. My parents still had their home, but at the same time they could be more with me at the institute campus as it was in the same city and, therefore, they could carry on some of their activities and maintain their contacts.

I was pleasantly surprised that over the 12 ½ years that I was there, we did quite a few things, including changing the social work curriculum and enriching the field-work program. We significantly modified the PhD program as well. For one thing, we decided to introduce the concept of writing a monograph instead of three papers in a selected area. The monograph was based on experience in the field for those who had been practitioners, and those who had inadequate field experience produced a monograph on an action they were required to carry out. The monograph explored implications of theory for practice. This was possible to do in all the professional programs we offered, including social work, personnel management, industrial relations, and hospital or health administration. However, even some social and behavioral science students, such as those in criminology and psychology, demanded to do likewise. The problem was how to provide a guide for this specific module with the relevant field practice.

We also developed a lot of new programs. One of our faculty who had a social work background had been developing hospital administration as an area of interest. He had developed a certificate program (and later a diploma) for the local hospitals. We developed it into a master's degree program and redesigned it so a doctor could take the course from a minimum of two years to a maximum of five years. If he or she successfully completed a certain number of modules, he or she could earn a certificate, and with further modules a diploma and then a degree. Also, at the Tata Institute we developed the tradition of successful field action projects, as in the College of Social Work. These were projects in areas where we thought we needed to demonstrate what social work could do. When I left the institute, we had 16 projects in different fields. I had undertaken similar projects when I was at the College of Social Work.

Could you give an example?

DESAI: Besides the family agency I mentioned earlier and the community project in a slum occupied by potters at the College of Social Work, I was very much involved with the problem of primary education, where there was a tremendous stagnation and waste. Children dropped out of school very early. Illiteracy was increasing, not only in Bombay but throughout the country. There is a high percentage of students who drop out in India, besides those who never enroll. I began in private schools. Later, I decided to invest in schools that children of the disadvantaged population attended—the schools of the Municipal Corporation of Greater Bombay. I met the education officer at the time and told him I wanted our social work students to practice with disadvantaged children in her schools. We worked with the child, family, school, community and the administration of the Department of Education of the Municipal Corporation. We revolutionized the first-year school environment. We threw out all of the tables and chairs, so that there was enough room to move around. We began with games for the children, and teachers developed new, more flexible teaching materials. We introduced play-way, informal methods of teaching.

The school's textbooks were not relevant to the children's societal and cultural context and what was in their immediate environment. For example, we avoided using pictures of a flower in their textbook that didn't grow in a city like Bombay and, therefore, made little sense to the children. There were other things in the environment that were much more meaningful and, therefore, could be more readily learned. With the help of the students placed for fieldwork and the school social workers, we began to modify the curriculum and the teaching approaches involving the teachers who had many ideas, along with modifying the physical environment of the classroom. In the process, we tried to make school an enjoyable experience through various new activities. We also provided evening study centers in the schools, since children did not have available spaces within their crowded, noisy homes.

We also went into the slum community, where we tried to get the families of children who had dropped out involved in helping these children return to school. We also worked with groups that were regarded as delinquents by the school and the community. We formed them into very useful and productive youth groups that helped us in our work with the younger children. This helped to lift the self-esteem of these older children who had dropped out, and the community came to see them as useful members. Many years later, some of these children became leaders in their own communities, and some of them are paraprofessional workers in social work agencies.

I understand that you helped to introduce other innovative projects while serving as Director of the Tata Institute of Social Sciences.

DESAI: The teachers were highly innovative and my role was to stimulate them and support them, to create a climate for their initiative. We had projects for street children. We've had programs for battered women. We placed full-time social workers and students in the Bombay police commissioner's office, where they worked with police taking complaints regarding domestic violence against women. Another project operated in the local police station, the magistrate's courts, and the jail to secure poor people's human rights and obtain justice in the labyrinth of the legal system. There were many other such programs—about 16 or 18 by the time I left the Tata Institute.

Another area that we thought was our responsibility was intervention in disasters, both man-made and natural ones. For example, the Institute was involved in Kurukshetra, where there was a refugee camp.

From then on the Institute always acted in times of crisis: when communal riots broke out in Bombay in 1984 and in 1992–93, and after the Union Carbide plant gas leak at its plant in Bhopal in 1986. After the gas leak, between the end of December and end of February, we did a survey of 24,000 households in Bhopal through Tata Institute-coordinated work with nine schools of social work. We identified the level of loss, who was affected and who required compensation. Unfortunately, although we produced piles of data, mounds of it, we never saw it again. We think that the government, the chemical industry, and the insurers got into a legal hassle. They used our findings in the beginning for entitlements such as ration cards and when they tried to settle initial financial compensation, but, later on, the expected compensation benefits to the disaster victims disappeared. So the next time we did something like that, we did our homework and reported our findings entirely on our own terms. We have learned from that experience a good lesson on how to work in a highly politicized arena.

Another example was an earthquake that occurred in two districts of Latur and Osmanabad in our state (Maharashtra). Our students were raring to volunteer, so we rescheduled our examinations and cut short the vacation. We asked everybody who wanted to go, so many students, so many teachers, even library staff and one watchman who said, "I'm coming too." We surveyed the villages that were demolished, identifying the people who had died and those who were injured, the losses of dwelling units and other property. Students from local colleges and some area schools of social work also participated. These data were then collated and processed, and we didn't let it out of our hands this time. The World Bank and the government of Maharashtra later used it to aid the victims. We placed one social worker at the disposal of the data collector to aid him in his tasks.

We also assisted the well-known industrial house of the Tata group of companies and its Trust (which also founded the Tata Institute) in adopting two villages to help in their reconstruction. We were invited by the government, at the insistence of the World Bank, to ensure that the community was involved in its own rehabilitation. To achieve this objective, the project trained government staff and community members.

These practice-oriented projects not only provided valuable learning for our students but also kept our teachers actively involved in practice in one way or another—supervising students, managing the programs, coordinating the overall practice strategies and methodologies used, and documenting what they were doing. The faculty members not only demonstrated to the community how social work could and should be done but also helped to further the learning and research of the students. In all our educational programs, we were innovative in teaching courses, guiding research of students, participating in community projects that I just mentioned, and intervening in crises. Also, I think that a background in social work was useful in administration. I had learned to understand people, why they do what they do, to understand group forces and conflict resolution in ways that can be applied to the administration of educational programs.

While you were the Director of the Tata Institute, the widely recognized doctoral program was inaugurated, or was it just that it was greatly modified?

DESAI: Our doctoral program is old; it started in 1966. However, in the 1980s, we decided that certain modifications would be useful for social work faculty and students, or even for personnel management and industrial relations students, to understand the relationship of theory to practice. Earlier I referred to the idea of an action-based monograph. Our curriculum required that the PhD scholar produce nine papers in three broad areas. The student went to the library, read, and prepared papers. There was an oral examination on the topics of the nine papers. Only after that hurdle was crossed was the student cleared to go on to the thesis. We made some modifications, but retained the basic educational model. What we did was to provide the option of a field practice component, which I mentioned earlier. Experienced practitioners would have to look at their practice in relation to the readings they would do and conceptualize it. Those who had little field experience would carry out a project and relate it to theoretical concepts. These were equivalent to one area of three papers, and a monograph was produced. Some excellent ones have been published, and this is one way of developing indigenous field-based teaching materials.

In addition to your academic responsibilities, there have been special assignments by way of commissions, committees, and consultancies in professional organizations in your country. Could you recount some of your work along these lines?

DESAI: I was a member of the Commission on Self-employed Women and Women in the Informal Sector. This was a commission appointed by the late Rajiv Gandhi when he was India's Prime Minister. Ninety percent of women in this country are outside the formally organized sector, working in innumerable types of activities dealing with producing and selling consumer goods, and largely in agricultural-related occupations. Women play a major role in looking after animals and such things as animal feeding, crop or forestry transplantation, and many other activities in the agricultural sector.

Women are engaged in very hard work in India, both domestic work and production-related activity that may be home-based or outside. Domestic labor is complicated by the fact that piped running water often is not available and women sometimes have to go long distances to bring water. Fuel is not easily available; they often have to go long distances to find fuel wood, which is becoming scarcer, as is fodder for the animals. So the women work very hard in this country. A majority of them are self-employed, and many of them are heads of households.

I enjoyed thoroughly the work that I did while on this commission. It was different in the sense that, unlike most commissions, it was not based on a pattern of sitting in public hearings someplace. We went to where the women worked. For instance, if the women were cleaning shellfish as part of an industry that did not want to consider their work as part of an organized business sector, but in actuality was an industry for freezing and exporting shrimp, then we went there. We studied women in the coir sector as well as in the areas of production of matches and the processing of cashew nuts. We had long discussions with the women about their work, the issues and the problems they faced, including the health hazards. To facilitate change, we had the additional job of sensitizing the government administration to what we found to be the problems the women faced.

For example, government officials were mostly men who were totally unaware that there were so many women who either were the sole or the major providers in their families and that, to maintain themselves and their children, the women had to work in what was often a little-regulated informal economic sector. In one Indian state, I asked the head of the district administration how many women he would estimate were single-parent household heads. He was quite astonished by my question. He said, "Every woman has either a father, a husband, a brother, or a son. Somebody's there, so how could she be alone?" This is the traditional belief in India. He thought I was very Western in my concept of the family for posing this question. But when we went into the field to meet with this group of women in the fishing community, and he asked them how many of them were either sole earners or major providers for their families, about 60 percent of the women raised their hands. "Now I see what you mean," He said. Old cultural values and views such as his were often in conflict with major social changes that were taking place.

In another situation, we were in Kashmir where there was rice transplantation work going on, men working in the fields on one side of the road and the women on the other side. The women were bending as they engaged in the traditional style of transplanting (stoop labor, as it is sometimes called), but some of the men brought folding stools and were seated comfortably. One even had a transistor radio to entertain himself while he was doing the work, so I asked, "How come you are sitting, and they are stooping, doing it the old way?" He said, "They like it that way." There was no sensitivity that women might need the same kind of conveniences as the men doing the same work.

We also visited a nomadic group of sheep herders. In the summer, they go up to the hills, and in the winter they go to pasture in the valley. They had put up their tents, so we started talking to the women. We discovered that in the state of Kashmir, there is a law by which every such tribe has a teacher that moves with the group and teaches the children. In discussion, we found that their medical needs are the least attended to as they were always on the move and had little access to services. In discussion with one of the ministers in the state, I asked, "Why don't we do something similar for health as well, with a paramedical person sent with each group who will give health information, help with the delivery of babies, and assist with so many other problems of people when they do not have access to regular medical care while on the move?"

Once I was ordered by Supreme Court Chief Justice Bhagwati to look into the issue of mistreatment of women-under-trial prisoners in relation to a public interest litigation that was before him. My colleagues and I completed the interviews and study in 10 to 15 days. We put the information together and gave it to the Supreme Court. It was way back in the 1980s, but this judge still remembers the report, and he always talks about it when he sees me. I believe he is the first judge to commence public interest litigation in India by turning a postcard complaint, on an issue pertaining to children, into a petition.

As the director of the Tata Institute, I was also becoming more involved in Indian higher education. I used to attend the regular vice chancellor conferences held every year in India. Also, I took my turn as the president of the Association of Indian Universities, when we presented a memorandum to the Finance Minister on the problem of financial crunch faced by the universities. We were able to get a 100 percent tax deduction for donations to universities. I was also a member of the Council of the Commonwealth Universities. Because of these positions, I had interacted with the University Grants Commission (UGC) long before I was appointed as its chairperson, which was a great asset for me.

In addition, I had a lot of other things to do with the UGC even before I became its chairperson. One of the first things I did for the UGC was the Review of Social Work Education in India. The UGC has always had subject panels to look at the status of each major subject area taught in the universities and make recommendations for its development. The review recommended norms for the schools of social work. Later, when I became the vice president of the Association of Indian Universities, I was able to take up these norms at one of the meetings of vice chancellors. Most of them expressed a lack of awareness about social work education and were glad to receive the information.

Please share with us some of your other activities, particularly in the international arena.

DESAI: In addition to my involvement with the Association of Schools of Social Work in India, of which I had served as president, I helped to establish the Asian Regional Association for Social Work Education (ARASWE) for which the initial push was given by Angelina Almanzor of the Philippines when she worked with the IASSW on an Asian project. The first committee laid the foundations for the activities of the organization such as seminars, biennial conferences, and publications. Later, it became known as the Asian and Pacific Association for Social Work Education since it included the schools in Australia and the Pacific. I was the first president of the association and was involved for almost five years. I was also a member of the board and also vice president, for a period of time, of the international body, the IASSW.

I did some work in Bangkok with the Social Development Division of the UN, and in Manila, where they set up the Social Welfare and Development Center for Asia and the Pacific (SWADCAP) for training. I was involved periodically as consultant/adviser, but not on a regular basis.

I might mention that the Secretary General, Commonwealth Secretariat, London, had come to Bombay, and asked to see me. He called me and said, "We are setting up a small group to assist human resource development in post-apartheid South Africa." (This was when South Africa was still under apartheid rule.) "We would like to set up a group to look at the Human Resource Development Program in South Africa." While I agreed to join the group, I was a little confused as to what we would do. However, it turned out to be an interesting exercise.

At first, the committee appeared to be focused only on turning out accountants, computer specialists, and doctors. I argued that development does not take place with focus only on the top layer. It's the people at the grassroots in the community that you start with and people at the lower level of skills. That is the bulk of people outside the economy for whom human resource development is required. They were frustrated and were angry with me because they were all from Western and developed countries, Australia, Canada, and the United Kingdom, and they didn't understand when I said, "They need paraprofessional health workers before they need doctors. Doctors alone cannot handle the need." They had to look at it from that point of view, but they were not prepared to take a holistic view of development. This discussion took place on the first day before tea. At teatime I talked to a professor from South Africa and an ANC member. They both agreed with me. I said, "Are you going to accept something like this? I'm not going to sign a report with such a limited focus." So we had a frontal attack and finally succeeded in changing their concept of what the committee's work was to be. The meetings took place several times before the report was finalized.

When I was chairperson of UGC, the Commonwealth Secretariat invited me to go to South Africa, after Nelson Mandela came into power, because the Higher Education Commission for South Africa was set up to look at their whole academic scene and to recommend changing whatever was needed. I visited there several times. Finally they came out with draft legislation. It's not particularly what I think it should have been, but they have made a sincere attempt to look at their educational system. It was a very good working group, with various task force groups obtaining the material needed. I enjoyed participating and in assisting this process.

Back to the Tata Institute, I understand that you retired from the Institute and then came to the University Grants Commission. Could you please tell us something about this transition and your present responsibility?

DESAI: Never in my wildest dreams would I have thought of becoming the UGC chairperson, so I was very shocked when I got a phone call from the Department of Education, Ministry of Human Resource Development, requesting that I take the post, and I finally agreed. (By then my parents were no longer alive and, therefore, I was free to move.) My greatest regret was that my parents were not there when this happened, because both of them had put such great emphasis on education.

Could you elaborate on the structure and responsibility of the Commission (UGC)?

DESAI: There are 10 members of the Commission, eight of whom generally are academicians and the other two ex officio—the Secretary of Education and the Secretary of Finance (Revenue) of the Government of India. The Commission meets every four to five weeks.

The Commission is the standard-setting and funding body for the development of higher education in India. However, its decisions are not always binding on the universities and colleges. Our work is to set the pace, put forward ideas, start experiments, encourage and demonstrate new work.

We also are responsible for regulating our universities. Regulations relate, for example, to the number of years for a degree course, number of days in an academic year, and qualifications for teachers.

I understand you have more than 70 professional papers and articles and have also served for 12 years as editor of the Indian Journal of Social Work.

DESAI: During the last few years, I handed over the responsibilities of the journal to the managing editor. I tried to redesign the journal's appearance and the quality of its articles. We actually accepted very few of the papers that were submitted. They were subjected to peer review. We had an editorial board, an internal board representing practically all of the major social work areas. Articles had to have some practical orientation. We were the only Indian journal in the social science field to be published regularly from 1940 to the present.

I have had such a busy life that finding time for writing was very difficult, but important. I made sure that I wrote articles on whatever I presented. I tried to make sure that I wrote at least two articles a year, even though I haven't had much time to write books. I have had time for two books, one written with Angelina Almanzor, which was a report of the first Asian meeting of social work educators.

The second was the *Review of Social Work Education in India: Retrospect and Prospects.* I also did a massive research project on social work education in India spanning a number of years. It was an effort to look at social work education from several points of view. I looked at students and their families and their motivations and commitments. Similarly, I studied teachers in social work, and what and how they taught. I looked at the curriculum and student perceptions of it. Then I looked at the future careers of the students, what kind of jobs they were seeking, and the kind of salaries. I was looking at many things; too many, actually. I drew on the experience of 34 schools of social work, the total number at that time, and some nine or 10 bachelor's degree programs. I sampled 1,176 students and 70 teachers and a lot of curriculum and administrative material. It took me a long time using my weekends and vacations, but finally I produced three volumes. It was financed by the Government of India, Ministry of Social Welfare (now known as Social Justice and Empowerment). They were breathing down my neck to submit the research for several years, and somehow I finished it. The data by then were old, but in a way they were very important because they provided baseline information on social work education in India. Nothing like it existed. The data were from the mid-1970s, and social work education was still very young in India then.

You've received a number of scholarships and awards. Would you please share with us something about those?

DESAI: Well, I had a few scholarships that helped me to go to the United States and also maintain myself in the United States, like the Lady Meherbai D. Tata Scholarship, the Fulbright Travel Grant, the Altrusa and PEO Scholarships, and scholarships from the University of Chicago.

The honor that I value a lot is the Katherine A. Kendall Distinguished Service Award in 1992, the first time the award was given, because Katherine has played such a very important role in my professional development internationally. Her enthusiasm, her incisive mind, and her capacity to see things clearly, to articulate them, and to find an innovative approach have made her my role model.

Now that you have only recently retired from UCG, do you have any concluding thoughts for today's professional social work colleagues or for social work students soon to be entering the profession?

DESAI: Within each of our countries, we have the polarization between the rich and the poor, and their ratio depends on whether they live in a so-called "developed" or developing country. The issues that arise in each of these situations are different.

Social work education will have to respond to the needs of these graduates to be able to function with flexibility in a changing social structure, to learn to live with ambiguity, and to be able to evolve the required strategies in the fast-changing scenario anticipated in the 21st century. In a developing country like India, the major issue will be how to narrow the gap between those enjoying the fruits of development of the 21st century and beyond, and those who have been denied those fruits. They include the families of small and marginal farmers, those working for wage labor and the informal self-employed sector, migrant labor, and those displaced by development such as dams, bridges, roads, ports, and industries causing large-scale dislocation and relocation. Then there are those who have traditionally been outside the pale of society (in India these are specific caste groups and tribes) and the minorities. While women belong to all of these categories and are oppressed by their circumstances, they also face the problems unique to them when living in a patriarchal society. Then there are children and youth in difficult situations in which the girl child is the most vulnerable—child laborers, street children, child sex workers, out-of-school children, and many others who cannot be enumerated here.

Motivation to work with such groups and a long-term commitment are key issues for the profession that must be addressed. Fortunately, the democratic framework of the Constitution of India guarantees equality of opportunity regardless of gender, religion, or caste. However, with these enabling provisions, what is required now is to make our fundamental rights a reality in the structure of a society whose past goes back 5,000 years and whose centuries of tradition are deeply rooted in the psyche of the individual and the community—those who have power and those who are powerless. This will be the challenge for social workers. However, as I see the involvement of some of the present generation of social workers undertaking difficult and innovative tasks in challenging situations outside the customary social agency framework, I believe that it can happen. Ultimately, "we shall overcome" as young people join from other disciplines to form multidisciplinary groups to bring about change.

ℰℰ✺ℰℰ

SATTAREH FARMAN-FARMAIAN

Born in the 1920s in Iran, Sattareh Farman-Farmaian grew
up as the daughter of a Qajar prince. She studied at the
University of Southern California, earned her bachelor's
degree in sociology and a master's degree in social work, and then
studied family and child law at the University of Chicago from
1944 to 1954. She also worked for Travelers' Aid and the
International Institute.

After leaving the United States, Ms. Farman-Farmaian worked as
a social welfare expert for the Middle East at the UN Bureau of
Social Affairs in Baghdad from 1954 to 1958. She founded the
Teheran School of Social Work after returning to Iran in 1958, and
served as director until 1979. At the same time, she founded and
served as executive director of both the Family Planning Association
of Iran and the Community Welfare Centers of Iran. After a narrow
escape from execution by a firing squad, she left the country at the
height of the Islamic Revolution to return to the United States and
began working for the Los Angeles County Department of Social
Services, Children's Services from 1980 to 1992, continuing a career-
long effort to advance women's rights worldwide.

Ms. Farman-Farmaian has served on the board of the International
Planned Parenthood Federation, the International Association of
Schools of Social Work, and other international bodies. She has written many articles and several books, including her autobiography,
Daughter of Persia, which has been translated into several languages
and was on the bestseller list in Germany. *Daughter of Persia* is used in
courses on social work, women's studies, and Middle Eastern history.
Ms. Farman-Farmaian has received honors and awards for her efforts
and continues to lecture around the world.

BILLUPS: *Please share with us something about your family in Iran,
and your father's influence in particular.*

FARMAN-FARMAIAN: My father was the grandson of Abbas Mirza, the Crown Prince of Fath Ali Shah Qajar. The Qajar tribe is of Turkic origin, brought to Iran by Tamerlane in the 14th century and settled along the Gorgan River north of Iran. Agha Mohammad Khan united Iran and proclaimed himself shah in 1796, the first of a long line of Qajar shahs who ruled Iran from 1795 to 1925.

My father, Prince Farman Farma, was born in 1857 and died in 1939. He is considered one of the most influential Qajar princes. From his early youth he showed a keen interest in the political and social development of the country. As a participant in the turbulent affairs of his country, my father sometimes was at the helm as a governor, commander of the Army, minister, and prime minister. At other times he was incarcerated or exiled. Always, he was generous, caring, and just. He worked for the people and brought about better education, health facilities, and roads.

One of the major preoccupations of his life was the full and proper education of his 36 children. Most of us completed university education.

I came into the world at the time of the Qajars' downfall in the British-engineered coup d'état that brought Reza Khan to power. He was later crowned Reza Shah Pahlavi. During his reign, my father and two of his elder sons were imprisoned for several months. Later my father was released, but was forced to spend the remainder of his days under house arrest, under the watchful eyes of the Pahlavi shah's secret police. My eldest brother was killed in prison.

My father was over 60 when I was born, and old when I knew him, but in the world in which I moved and lived, he ruled supreme. Though a political moderate and a firm supporter of the democratic Iranian constitution, my father was a man born to power and privilege. I accepted his rule, as did everyone, with fear and reverence and distant adoration. I would have done anything to please him.

My father married eight wives, but when I was growing up only four lived in our compound. Each had her own home; collectively they were called *andarun*, the inner quarter or harem where the women and children lived. Everything else, including the central garden and the other buildings surrounding it, was the *biruni*. This was the outer or public quarter where my father lived and was the realm of men. The greater world beyond was also the men's realm. On Friday, the Muslim holiday, our mothers and we trotted up the white gravel road to the big house to pay a formal call on my father.

My father had decided that we, his younger children, must have something more solid to depend on than politics after he was no longer there to watch over us. He was adamant that we learn to be self-reliant. Every day except Friday we were busy from dawn until dusk with school homework, math tutors, Persian poetry tutors, and other pedagogical what-have-yous. My father tended each one of us like a gardener fostering orchids. "Nothing is more important," he would admonish us, "than your education. Times are changing, and what counts nowadays is not who your father was, but what you make of your own lives."

One week I recited for him a poem by the great 13th century Persian poet Sa'adi, which he had assigned me:

Human beings are like parts of the body,
created from the same essence.
When one part is hurt and in pain,
The others cannot remain in peace and be quiet.
If the misery of others leaves you indifferent
and with no feelings of sorrow,
You cannot be called a human being.

I loved Sa'adi, and I especially loved this poem, which always made me think of the petitioners in the park or the crippled old soldiers and nearly blind pensioners, who sat all day under the trees and who always had a hug and a few pieces of candy for us children who came along.

"Very good," said Shazdeh (everyone called him by this name, which meant "king" or "prince") approvingly. "Do you know the meaning of that poem Satti has just recited?" he continued, addressing us children. "It means that a country is a nation made of individuals. Every one of these individuals is important. Without seeing to people's welfare, a nation cannot become great. That is why it is your duty to work for the progress and well-being of others, so that our country can become a great nation again."

Even though my father died when I was in high school, his teachings have remained with me all my life.

Is it correct to say that, while a schoolgirl, you tested yourself for what was eventually to be a social work career by engaging in more and more volunteer work?

FARMAN-FARMAIAN: Yes, after I completed primary school, my father wanted me to go to "American school." He became very fond of the American doctors who were running the hospital, and he found out that they had a school, which was run by Presbyterian missionaries. I was lucky. I was the first of his children to attend this school.

These missionaries had hospitals and clinics, including one in the south of Teheran, and they said I could go with them as a volunteer and see what they were doing. I was maybe 14 or 15 when I followed the missionaries, Mrs. McDowell, and Mrs. Blair around. They knew what they were doing, and I just imitated them.

The people in the south of Teheran, because of the dirt and malnutrition, had a lot of diseases, and there were many street kids. The missionaries would give me a swab to rub on the heads of the children who were affected by scalp ringworm or would ask me to teach them the alphabet. I enjoyed that very much. For a long time I did not tell my family I was going there, because it was far away from home.

When the school year ended, I would continue as a volunteer, because I had become good friends with these missionaries and I knew that the children needed help. By the time my mother knew what I was up to she did not mind; she herself was always helping others.

When and how did you decide to gain a social work education?

FARMAN-FARMAIAN: As I was doing this volunteer work, I was in touch with a lot of destitute people. I would see children and babies, many of them naked, playing in the dirty running water of the street. People were getting their water from these open canals. At one point people were drinking the water; at another point people were washing their clothes in it; and at another point a donkey was being washed. The children were especially affected by disease, and I was appalled.

By that time my father had died, and I asked Mrs. McDowell, "Where should I get further education?" Iranian women had no place to go after high school. So Mrs. McDowell said she would write to the college that she came from. Some time later she came and told me that I had been accepted at the college in her hometown, Heidelberg College in Tiffin, Ohio.

However, World War II had broken out. The Allies occupied Iran. The war had moved to North Africa, and there was no way for me to leave until 1944. Finally, I could not wait any longer. The American consulate told me that people had been going to America by way of the East, and that I could go in that direction. My mother was very upset with this plan, but my eldest brother persuaded my mother to let me go. Iranian women were not, and still are not, considered equal to men. My mother wanted me to be a wife and mother.

It took four months for me to get to the United States. I had to go by land and sea, through India, sailing from Bombay and crossing the Pacific. Finally, I arrived in Los Angeles.

A missionary friend of my father, Samuel S. Jordan, was in Los Angeles and took me under his wing. He had been head of Alborz College in Teheran. He recognized that I did not know what I wanted to do and that I could use some help. He took me to the University of Southern California. I hardly knew enough English to sit in a classroom. I had no credentials, only an acceptance letter from the college in Ohio, but nothing more to show. At my interview the admissions officer asked questions, and Dr. Jordan answered. "She has had American history?" "Oh, of course, and she got an A." I did not know what American history courses were at all, but whatever he was asked, Dr. Jordan said that I had gotten an A.

I was admitted as a freshman, and I started school. When asked what I wanted to study, I did not know, but I said, "We have a lot of poor people in Iran. I want to learn to do something with them." The adviser said, "All right, sociology."

The four-month trip from Iran to the United States must have been quite an ordeal.

FARMAN-FARMAIAN: Oh yes, but the good thing was that wherever I had to stay, I found friends and relatives. There are advantages to being from a large family and knowing a lot of people.

At one point, on the Northwestern Railroad, the train was sabotaged by followers of Gandhi, and they put all of us on the street. I did not know where I was. This man came to me and said, "Were you on the train that came from Iran?" I said, "Yes," and when he found out my name, he asked me, "Are you the daughter of Prince Farman Farma?" I said, "Yes!" He fell at my feet and went on, "I am a merchant. I was going to the south of Iran years ago, and bandits got hold of all my merchandise and they were going to kill me. Your father, who was the governor of South Persia, saved my life and got the bandits to return my merchandise to me. I have not forgotten that, and I want to take you to my wife and my family. Stay here until the next train comes."

You mentioned that initially you had difficulty learning English while a freshman in college, but that you completed your undergraduate degree nonetheless. Please tell us more.

FARMAN-FARMAIAN: Knowing little English, I was lucky in that I reached the United States in the summer. My dormitory in university housing was where a lot of teachers who had come to summer school stayed. These teachers were older than the regular students and were a big help. They said, "Write down what you hear the professor say in class." With some of the professors' accents, that was a very difficult thing for me to do. I would come back to my room and read what I thought they had said. The teachers would say, "No, this word is this, and you have to write it this way." That was free tutoring every night throughout the whole summer.

As soon as the summer courses were over and I had learned more English, I moved to a student cooperative house with six or seven students from other countries. It was there that I learned to cook, to do dishes, and to garden. All of us were in need of money, and we took jobs on campus. I would go to classes, come home and do my housekeeping chores, and go to work. I was working all the time, either at the library or the art store, making 60 cents an hour, but this, too, was part of my education.

I had never attended a class with men sitting next to me. At first, it was very disturbing. But eventually I got used to them being around.

In addition to my major courses, I took a lot of English classes and some writing classes too. It took hours and hours for me to read what my American student friends were reading in half the time.

Could you tell us about your graduate education?

FARMAN-FARMAIAN: I enjoyed graduate school, because I went to the school of social work, and I was able to study for the first time what was happening in social services in America. I wanted to see Americans with problems and learn what to do about poverty, what to do about sickness, what to do about all sorts of problems that I was to be encountering professionally in Iran on my return. When I went to social work graduate school they immediately sent me two days a week to fieldwork, and I saw what was really going on. I found out when poor people were ill they were sent to the county hospital free of charge. The county government was giving out aid to children who were orphaned and aid to elderly people.

I felt that I must return to my home country and try to do something similar. I had all of the information and research reports from my classes stored in orange crates, especially materials that I thought would be helpful in improving the condition of women, children, poor people, and sick people. My whole idea was, "What I am learning here is going to help me in Iran."

Nevertheless, I had a lot of problems in the classroom. For example, I had difficulty with the teacher who was teaching social casework. The professor's most important concept was self-determination: "If the client doesn't want it, don't give it to them." But I was thinking, "What about all the children and mothers I saw in the street drinking from the open sewer water that was so dirty? They are not going to have self-determination, because generations have been drinking from it." This one-by-one individual practice concept and approach to social work—how was I going to apply that in my country?

This matter of being a self-determining citizen is easier for people in the relatively open and free American society. In the Persian language, which is 3,000 years old, there was no word for "citizen." Historically, Persia has been a country largely of "subjects" and "slaves."

One-on-one social work, especially psychiatric social work, would not be appropriate. Many of the people in my country were physically ill. Religious people in Iran believe that if you have pain it is the will of God; it is written on your forehead; it is your destiny. So there were many cultural and religious beliefs and traditions that I had to work through to be able to think about how to apply in Iran what I had learned in the United States.

You touched briefly on your study at the University of Chicago. Was that immediately after your work toward your master's degree?

FARMAN-FARMAIAN: Yes, I thought that I would go to the University of Chicago for one semester to immerse myself in American social legislation. I did not go there to get another degree, but I knew that I needed more knowledge. Also, I knew that I would have to train others on my return to Iran, and I would need to learn more to help me to teach. My one-semester plan extended into a year in the School of Education, learning the philosophy of education and its major concepts while earning a teaching credential.

I came to the United States in 1944 and left in 1954. I took a lot of different jobs. I wanted to see how the programs worked in what was then called "public assistance." My first full-time job was with the International Institute, dealing with problems encountered by Chinese, Japanese, and Mexican immigrants, as well as many from European countries. Then, because of my interest in rural and urban migration, I went to work for the Travelers' Aid Society, working with people, especially youth, traveling from one part of the country to another. They were often stranded or encountered difficulties because they lacked financial resources or had run away from home.

While these experiences had relevance to problems in my home country, the kind of experience that I really wanted most to take back with me was social work that had to do with the application of laws in public agencies—for example, in work with juvenile delinquents. We had so many young street children in Iran who would steal a piece of bread or an apple or something else just to survive the hunger. I wanted to learn how to work with these youth in rehabilitation programs. I did a lot of study of the juvenile court system on my own.

Then I had an offer from the United Nations Bureau of Social Affairs to work as what they called in those days a Social Welfare Expert. They hired me in that capacity for the government of Iraq and various other countries in the Middle East. My headquarters was in Baghdad from 1954 until my return to Iran in 1958.

The job called for promoting social development. I was back in touch again with people from my own part of the world. This helped to prepare me for my return to Iran.

Then you went back to your home country.

FARMAN-FARMAIAN: Yes, I had the good fortune to play a major role when social work had its beginnings in Iran in 1958 with the creation of the Teheran School of Social Work. The word *madadkar* (meaning "one who helps") was coined for social workers, thus establishing a new cadre of professionals.

Iran was a feudal society with a very low standard of living. More than 70 percent of its estimated 20 million people lived in rural areas and isolated villages. The illiteracy rate was more than 85 percent, 95 percent among women. People struggled to survive.

A few years before, the Iranian government initiated an economic development program and land reform to transform the country into a prosperous industrialized nation. Unfortunately, one of the unexpected consequences was that a large number of illiterate, unskilled peasants migrated to the cities in search of a better life. The city of Teheran suffered the most from the social problems stemming from unplanned urbanization. These problems were aggravated by the country's birthrate, one of the highest in the world. Desperate parents sent their children out into the streets to beg or abandoned them on the doorsteps of mosques.

The tasks facing social workers were virtually unlimited. They had to deal with urgent problems and plan for long-term social development. Social workers were optimistic that they could improve people's lives. They also believed that any such improvements could only be possible with the help and participation of the people themselves. However, popular participation implied a struggle for greater self-empowerment, which was difficult in this authoritarian society.

What were some of the social work activities that were initiated?

FARMAN-FARMAIAN: Social work emerged most vividly during a massive flood that devastated the slums of Teheran, leaving the poor residents homeless. Social workers put up large tents and took care of abandoned children. They recruited volunteers to help with food, clothing, and other urgent needs of homeless families.

With the arrival of winter, a local landowner, impressed with the efforts of the social workers, donated his house for the care and shelter of children. Social workers named this house the Community Welfare Center. At the center, permanent day care for the children of working mothers was established. A local midwife was recruited to instruct mothers in child care, hygiene, nutrition, and family planning. The International Planned Parenthood Federation (IPPF) assigned to this project a gynecologist with special training in reproductive physiology, and a full-time family planning clinic was established. This resulted in the creation of the Family Planning Association of Iran. Meanwhile, the Community Welfare Center was expanded to include literacy classes for women, job training, and youth activities.

Shortly after the formation of the Community Welfare Center, activists in neighboring areas donated land, building materials, and services to create similar centers in their communities. Social workers mobilized people of all social classes to take responsibility for helping poor people improve their quality of life. During the 20-year history of the Teheran School of Social Work, many community welfare centers were established all over the country, with the help of citizens, government, and the international community.

What happened with the social work education that you instigated in your home country?

FARMAN-FARMAIAN: Iran, like most developing countries, had initiated economic development programs during the second half of the century. However, economic growth in itself does not improve the social well-being of the community and does not benefit all sectors of the population. Affluence and poverty march side by side. Although Iranian social workers believed in economic growth, we believed that such growth in itself was insufficient to address the needs of poor and oppressed people.

An essential part of social work education is the selection of qualified students who are committed to practice social work among poor people and in slums and rural areas. Since jobs are scarce in most developing countries, candidates must not be attracted merely by the monetary inducements. They must have compassion for the people they will help and be committed to the work. Furthermore, schools must select candidates from minority groups. For example, in Iran, 10 million people speak Azari instead of the official language, Persian. These linguistic and religious minorities are in great need of social services.

The curriculum of social work education in countries like Iran must be adapted to the needs and problems of the people social workers are serving. This meant that we needed to find and train most of our social work educators from within our own borders. In addition to practice methodologies, we needed to teach classes in the history, culture, philosophy, and ethics of the people, as well as the various beliefs and lifestyles of minorities. Subjects such as nutrition, child care, hygiene, first aid, family planning, and family finance also became necessary for practicing social workers.

We learned from our experience that field practice is a major source of knowledge and must be greatly emphasized in the education of social workers. At the Teheran

School of Social Work (TSS), we organized summer block placements in provinces and rural areas in addition to the regular three days a week of field practice during the academic year. Small groups of students, guided by full-time field instructors, were sent to remote communities for 10 weeks, studying and researching the social needs of the people, always with an eye to achieving social reform and social development. This program was helpful in motivating the people to raise themselves out of poverty. It also helped the social workers create jobs for themselves. Many of them returned to these areas after graduation.

Students must also be taught that social development is not a quick process or an easy way to achieve a better quality of life. Personal effectiveness and deep relationships with people are only possible through working and growing together.

Conflicts occurred frequently between young idealists who wanted immediate progress and traditional people who resisted change and were suspicious of social workers. Fortunately, the school was able to pave the way for peaceful solutions.

We learned that schools such as ours in Iran should be instrumental in finding resources, both local and international, to provide material and technical assistance to social development projects. For example, TSS was able to procure mobile units for maternity and children's health from UNICEF. These units accompanied social workers to remote areas, providing services in child care, family planning, environmental sanitation, and other urgent family needs.

Recognizing that social workers play a vital role during national emergencies, TSS initiated and supported programs for earthquake and flood victims and dispatched students, graduates, field instructors, and supervisors to serve in such disasters.

Social work being a new profession in Iran, TSS took the initiative in creating jobs in both the public and private sectors. Pilot projects were initiated in various agencies and industries to demonstrate the role of social workers. As a result, graduates were employed in many industries, schools, prisons, health facilities, and other social agencies working with families and children.

We discovered that schools of social work in Iran should play a role in promoting social legislation that addressed the special needs of women and children. As we all know, women have long been neglected in developing countries. We needed to make an absolute commitment to improve the status of women.

I also believed that we had to include among the basic needs not only of food, clothing, shelter, education, and health services, but also population control and concern for the environment. Moreover, social workers' studies and research projects had to be made available to governments to instigate social reform. TSS was instrumental in passing the Family Protection Law in the late 1960s.

In summary, the role of the schools of social work in developing countries such as Iran seem to me to be: (1) selecting and educating committed, professional social workers; (2) creating pilot projects and demonstrating possible solutions to social needs, as suggested by social research; (3) initiating social legislation that promotes legal rights and responsibilities for women and children; (4) helping in disaster areas during emergencies; and (5) creating jobs for social workers in all sectors of society where they are needed.

Could you tell us more about the Family Planning Project that you have initiated?

FARMAN-FARMAIAN: Iran had one of the highest birth rates. Families of 11, with one breadwinner, were not uncommon.

We decided to recruit a volunteer midwife as a first step toward helping these families. Family planning, contraception, and prevention of a population explosion were very new to us. We knew we needed to do something, but we were not sure what.

We were told to contact an organization in the United States called Pathfinders. This group immediately sent a woman who told us that unwanted pregnancies could be prevented using a method they supported—a very primitive method when I think of it now. Women would be given a sponge dipped in a saline solution to insert within themselves before they had sexual relations with their husbands.

There was a 100-bed maternity hospital in the area. One-third of the beds in this hospital were occupied by women who had committed self-induced abortion using a turkey feather. All of the women had come to the hospital with tremendous infections and fever; some died.

The director at the hospital heard about our program and was very excited. He offered to help, but told us that because of traditional beliefs, our program would be resented. We literally needed to go underground, so he gave us the basement. We recruited and organized this program with people who believed in it. These volunteers cut the sponges, dipped them into the saline solution, and gave the sponges to the midwife, who distributed them to the families.

Fortunately, after a few months, the IPPF learned about our project and sent one of their employees to bring pills. (Oral contraceptives had just been introduced in the West.) They also assigned to our program a gynecologist who was trained in reproductive physiology. This individual provided us with much needed information and was paid for by the IPPF.

What about the Community Centers that you helped to establish?

FARMAN-FARMAIAN: After the massive floods, the community saw the benefits of our work and wanted us to remain. The children, the volunteers, and student social workers had moved into the donated house and had put up a sign that said "Community Welfare Center."

One of the rooms in this house was given to the gynecologist, with a sign on the door that read "Family Planning Clinic." This was the beginnings of the Family Planning Association of Iran.

After several months of working in family planning with mothers and providing a day care program for children, we noticed that many teenagers had no school to go to or program to attend. We extended the house and created a recreational area for these teenagers. We encouraged both the boys and girls to come and attend literacy classes. We also taught classes in personal hygiene. We did a great deal of teaching about nutrition as well, for both the teenagers and the mothers that came to the center.

Many activists approached us requesting that we set up similar programs within their communities and neighborhoods. We knew, however, that the only way for such programs to be successful was to have the participation of the people within the communities. But any participation by people meant self-empowerment, and this is only possible in a free society. Our society was authoritarian. We were afraid that the government would close down the community center, because it provided a place for group meetings and a forum for people to talk.

We decided that the best thing to do was to have the people participate only in matters relating to their social problems, not in anything political. By limiting the areas in which people participated, we thought we could protect our workers from the government and its agents.

We social workers always talk about those people who are excluded from social reform or social development. For instance, in the developing countries we exclude poor people, or we exclude women. But, in a country that has an authoritarian government, everyone is excluded but the government itself. We wanted both men and women to come to our center to work and learn how they could lift themselves out of poverty.

In the 20-year history of the Teheran School of Social Work, some 250 such community welfare centers were created throughout the country. The services provided within each center were tailored to meet the needs of the community it served. Whenever a community group approached TSS with a request to create a community center, we immediately sent a team from the school to the community. This team collected data such as age and gender of the population, the number of school-age children in school, literacy rates, pregnancy rates and income.

In some centers, we provided as many as 12 different services. We might have literacy classes; a day care center; a family planning clinic; vocational training for children who dropped out of primary school; and classes in carpentry, blacksmithing, drama, painting, and poetry for teenagers. Girls and women were given classes in typing and office work, sewing, weaving, knitting, and embroidery. These were meaningful skills that could be potential sources of additional income. Many husbands were unskilled laborers who did not have steady jobs. And with the help of these community center classes, family planning, and contraception, women could learn meaningful skills that would help them to get a job.

A woman who owned a sewing machine business became interested in our work at a center. The women she taught to sew eventually signed contracts to buy their own sewing machines with the money they earned from the sales of the products they made. We eventually created a shop for these women at the community center where they could sell the items they produced. They kept all of the proceeds from their sales. People had for some time believed that the government lied and was corrupt. We, on the other hand, demonstrated that we were trustworthy. Many people could not believe that we did not take anything from them.

What else do you want to share with us about the graduates of your social work program and their work?

FARMAN-FARMAIAN: They were in industries because the industries had a lot of laborers who would not show up for work. So we developed a social service department in all the government factories, and then in the private industries that were developing during the 1960s and 1970s. I would have the factory hire one of our graduates to be responsible for that department, and then I would place two or three students under him for their student field practice, and the industry would pay the school to supervise our students.

The students in each factory were responsible for facilitating the health and welfare of the laborers and their families. If a laborer did not show up for work, they would visit his home. They might learn that his wife was pregnant, was not feeling well, and had to be taken to the doctor. So the social worker would make arrangements for someone to take care of the wife so that the man would not miss work.

For several years after we started social service in the factories, the owners and administrators of these factories would thank the school. I always had more offers of jobs for social workers than I was able to train.

Then the same sort of social service was developed in the schools through the Ministry of Education. I developed at TSS what we called the Family Aid Service with the help of various donors. If a social work student found out that a child could not go to school because she had no shoes, we would give money to buy shoes. Our Family Aid Society was used tremendously for such emergencies. In most of the schools in the south of Teheran, we had social workers.

When people saw that professional social work was something that was helping people and the country, many would contribute money, especially to the community welfare centers in slum areas. Wealthy people would put money or a check right on my desk—sometimes large sums of maybe $20,000 or even $50,000 and ask me to go to the province, the city, where they were born and organize something like a welfare center for their own people. There were people who had the money, but to donate it, they needed someone and someplace they trusted.

I understand that you were also involved in changing a governmental facility.

FARMAN-FARMAIAN: By law, the mayor of the city of Teheran was responsible for people who were abandoned, destitute, physically or mentally sick, or beggars. In the south of Teheran, the city had an institution that was reminiscent of a Charles Dickens novel. Everyone was in it: prostitutes, children of all ages, and physically and mentally sick people. They received only custodial care and some food. There were no programs or treatment for those who were mentally or physically ill.

When I took a group of students to visit this institution, we were appalled. In fact, some of the students who visited resigned from the program, expressing their refusal to be in the profession of social work if it meant working in such an environment. However, there were still many students who did get excited and wanted to help.

We realized that the mayor was the only one that could bring change. Governmental corruption was widespread, the money budgeted to the institution was manipulated, and the administrative staff did not want us to make any changes.

We approached the mayor and insisted that he visit the institution with us (neither he, nor any previous mayor had, he said). Finally, we persuaded him. As we walked through its halls, my students who were behind him noticed that he became red; sweat was forming on his brow; and tears were streaming down his face. Finally, he said, "I want you to help me to help these people. I will be behind you, just tell me what I can do. I will be at your disposal." We were delighted. We gave him a proposal that included separate programs for the school-age children, the babies and toddlers, as well as specific programs for those who were mentally or physically ill.

The babies and toddlers at the institution were malnourished. Many of them were sitting on the floor just rocking themselves back and forth. We decided that this was beyond the scope of our expertise; we needed specific professional help for these children. We asked the mayor to get the UN Food and Agricultural Organization (FAO) to give us a nutrition expert. He did, and an FAO representative came immediately.

This woman lived with this group of children, and we provided student assistants, interpreters, and facilities. With our help, she created a program and diet for these children. Three months later, she came to the school of social work with a photo album of the infants she had helped. It included pictures of them before her intervention and after. We could not recognize many of the toddlers; they were fat, physically healthy, crawling, and, in some instances, even walking.

The program for school-aged children included a plan to relocate them to a dormitory-type facility in the city so they would have access to the local schools. However, when we tried to enroll them, the school rejected them, because they had no records.

All we knew were the names given to them by the mayor's workers when they entered the institution. They had no birth certificates and no knowledge of their parentage.

We asked the mayor to contact the census office of the Ministry of the Interior, the agency responsible for issuing birth certificates. We asked the agency to help us by issuing birth certificates for the more than 400 school-age children at the orphanage. The mayor helped, and two representatives of the Bureau of the Census arrived to work in the orphanage.

The students chose the name for each child's mother and father. A doctor assisted us in determining the approximate age of each child and a birth date. Once birth certificates were created and issued for the children, they were enrolled in a local school.

We also began to move many of those who were physically sick into hospitals for treatment. We did this with the help of the Ministry of Health and the mayor's office. The mentally ill patients were sent to an institution in a semirural area; at the time, we had no treatment programs for those who were mentally ill. So the mayor hired a psychiatrist from the University of Teheran to head the institution, and he began a basic treatment program. We were very happy with this particular appointment, because he immediately hired one of our graduates.

Many of the healthy babies and older children were put up for adoption. However, according to Muslim law, inheritance rights could not automatically be given to an adopted child. With the help of the Ministry of Justice, we were able to pass the Custody Law. This law permitted qualified families to apply for custody of these children. The qualified family was responsible for their child's care, protection, and education, but the child could not inherit either the name or the assets of the custodial family.

Then there was rehabilitation of the "Fortress." What was that about?

FARMAN-FARMAIAN: In the middle of the city was a walled-in area of 10 to 12 city blocks called the "Fortress." There was one entrance, just large enough for one person to pass through at a time. Within these thick, high walls was a city of 1,500 prostitutes, pimps, and madams.

The Fortress had no electricity, no clean drinking water, no paved streets, no showers, no public toilets, and an open sewer that passed through the community. We discovered, by counting at the entrance, that an average of 4,000 people entered or exited this area each day.

The smell and sanitation problems in the Fortress were overwhelming. We contacted the Ministry of Health, and they sent a representative to help with the sanitation problems. The mayor authorized the city to pipe clean water into the area, pave streets, and cover the open sewage area. We gathered all the madams together and told them that they must install clean water and showers. Slowly, we were able to clean up the area.

The average age of a prostitute working in the Fortress was 15 years. Our survey revealed that 90 percent of the girls had been kidnapped, primarily from the villages, and were held hostage by the madams and pimps. When they were brought to this community, they were penniless. Their pimps would give them money for clothing, jewelry, and bedding, causing the girls to become financially bound so they could never leave.

Like the majority of people in the country, these girls were illiterate. So we organized a center with literacy classes and tried to find ways to pay off the girls' debts. The Ministry of Justice helped us to raise funds to "buy" these girls from their pimps. Many of the younger ones who could remember where they came from left the Fortress with our help and returned to their families. The social workers helped the others to find legitimate jobs.

This project was instrumental in saving my life. During the 1979 Islamic Revolution, revolutionary thugs set fire to buildings in the Fortress. My students at the center contacted me. I immediately went and found that the fire had begun to burn the entrance. I tried to mobilize the police and fire departments, but they hesitated, wondering whether they should try to put out the fire or let the prostitutes and everyone trapped in the Fortress burn to death. They were unsure of which group would come into power, and they were hoping that by not acting they could remain in favor with the winning group.

I fought with the police and the fire fighters. I insisted that it was their duty to help those human beings trapped and in danger, regardless of what group won. So they came. But the entrance was so small, they could only fit in one fire hose. Finally, the fire was extinguished, and the women were saved.

A few weeks later, I was detained by the revolutionaries and taken to be executed. As I was standing at the wall waiting to be shot, the assistant to the Ayatollah Khomeini arrived and recognized me. He told the revolutionaries that I should not be executed, because I was instrumental in saving all those people in the Fortress from being burned. So I was released and my life was saved.

I'm sure there is more to the story concerning what led up to the threat to your life.

FARMAN-FARMAIAN: In February 1979, the shah was deposed and the Islamic Revolutionary group under the leadership of Ayatollah Khomeini took over Iran. Many students became active in this revolution, including students at our school of social work.

One morning when I arrived at the school, four Islamic revolutionary students of mine approached me with machine guns and forced me to go with them. At that time many government employees and university professors had been fired and some had been taken to prisons to be shot. Revolutionaries charged these people with working for the shah's corrupt regime, and thus, working against God.

The revolutionary social work students took me to Ayatollah Khomeini's headquarters to be shot with others on the roof of the building. At this school building they were occupying, there were conservative mullahs who knew of my work in prisons, in hospitals, and among poor people. They sent somebody to ask me questions about the charges the students had brought—that I had stolen money, that I had been a Central Intelligence Agency (CIA) agent, that I had killed people. They had worked up 10 or 12 charges against me. I had no lawyer, but they tried me anyway. The clerics claimed that the students were young and immature and that the charges were not based on anything. For example, the students who had turned me in gave as their reason that I was suspected of being a CIA agent and that I had sent students abroad to U.S. universities. The "tribunal" concluded: "These charges are baseless; you have served the country well; go back to school." But I knew that if I went back there, the revolutionary students, who were holding machine guns, were going to kill me themselves. Besides, I did not want to work in an atmosphere where I was thought to be a traitor.

How did your life change when you left Iran for an adopted land after your life was threatened?

FARMAN-FARMAIAN: I am grateful for the United States and that I have been able to survive. But I had to go through a lot of difficult times. My country was taken, my brothers were in prison, everything my family had was confiscated, and the women and children in my family had run away. Then the school was taken over, and my house was occupied. I had absolutely nothing left.

I left Iran with the clothes on my back, and I had to find a job to be able to survive. So I came here to the United States, hoping I could find a job.

When I got to the United States it was a bad time for social agencies to hire me because of the U.S. hostages who were being held by the Islamic revolutionaries in Teheran. Every place I went to get a job they would not hire me, because they thought perhaps I was one of the terrorists. The atmosphere was poisoned against Iran. I was stereotyped. Finally, social work friends with whom I had gone to school advised me to sit for the Los Angeles County civil service exam, and I did. I was able to get a job as a children's services worker for Los Angeles County, and I started working for them in May of 1980. Up until that time I was taken care of by my friends; somebody gave me a room, somebody else took me to lunch, and somebody else took me around for job interviews. I was fortunate to have such good friends. I worked in the county Department of Children's Services on child abuse until I retired in 1992.

The city of Los Angeles had changed a lot since I was last in the United States in 1954. I had never seen so much drug abuse or so much child abuse when I was getting my education. As a student, I do not think I had even one case of sexual abuse of children.

The work entailed long hours, especially after I became an investigator and had to drive an average of 80 miles a day just to find the parents of the children who had been abused or find the relatives or a foster home for a child.

The heavy demands of the job exaggerated the problems I had within myself. I was living here alone, my family was scattered all over the world, and my brothers were still in jail in Iran. I was also worried about my elder sisters and brothers who were still in Iran and how they were holding up financially, because everything they had had was confiscated, including their pensions.

Since you retired from public social service in the United States, I understand that you have been enlisted to speak at universities.

FARMAN-FARMAIAN: I am very interested in social work and social development, and I was asked by many organizations, even when I was working, to give talks about what became of Iran. Americans have been interested to find out what happened in Iran. Sometimes when I would give a talk they would say to me that they had not been aware of the truth. Now that I have lived among Americans for 20 years, I see the reason why. People do not seem to have the time or inclination to read the details of events in other countries. They get a sound bite on the television or they read the headlines of the newspaper. Many people never knew what the CIA was doing in Iran.

If I had come to another country, I might not have been able to survive. So I feel that I owe it to the American people to keep them informed about my country. I especially feel that it is important for students to know the truth from the point of view of a person who went through this.

When my book [*Daughter of Persia: A Woman's Journey from Her Father's Harem through the Islamic Revolution*] came out, departments of history, women's studies, and social work as well as other departments in the social sciences began to use it as a reference or as a textbook.

Your book can be considered not only a personal history but, in some senses, a social and political sourcebook.

FARMAN-FARMAIAN: *Daughter of Persia* was published in 1992. It is the story of my life and my beloved country, but it also includes the story of the establishment of the first school of social work in Iran and what the social workers were able to accomplish.

The hardcover edition of *Daughter of Persia* is out of print, but a softcover edition has been published and has been reprinted several times. It was translated into various European languages—German, Swedish, and Dutch. In Germany it was a bestseller for a couple of years. They are using it in many countries in schools of social work and elsewhere.

Aside from the gratification of having your book widely used, I note that you have received several awards and honors.

FARMAN-FARMAIAN: The county of Los Angeles gave me an award, the city of Los Angeles gave me an award, and the YWCA honored me with a leadership award. I have also received several awards from Iranian communities in the United States.

What do you envision now for Iran and for the social work profession in Iran?

FARMAN-FARMAIAN: From the political point of view, Iran, I think, is not going to stay in isolation, because it is strategically an important country. Because of the religious government they now have, they have been kept in isolation, but there is no doubt they have to come out. Iranians have thousands of years of culture. They have Persian art, Persian poetry, music, and literature. We cannot let Iran stay in isolation. I have a lot of hope for the future of the country. Moreover, the natural resources, in particular oil, are so important.

Unfortunately, the campus of the school of social work has been taken over. And I understand the women social workers who were in the government have been under duress. I receive many letters from my previous students, and I also get telephone calls from them. Life has not been the way they thought it would be. A lot of them have left social work and gone into other fields, such as business. Some have come to the United States or have gone to Europe or Australia.

The social work graduates who stayed in Iran know that they have to get social work education back. When the revolution came in 1979, the population of Iran was about 33 million; now, after 20 years, it has more than doubled to nearly 70 million. The city of Teheran when I left was only about 4.2 million, but, according to reports, today it is more than 12 million.

Contraception and family planning were outlawed right after the revolution. In recent years, they have finally recognized that they have too many unemployed people, a shortage of housing, of schools, and of health facilities. Three years ago they called on the UN to help them with the population explosion. Since then, I have received reports that they are promoting family planning once again, using methods such as vasectomies for the men.

They are bringing back social programs that we started. They have rediscovered the needs of the people. They are trying to train and hire social workers once again. Some universities are training social workers in departments of sociology, but I do not know if they are giving them fieldwork experience.

Just recently, I received a social work book that one of my students who had gone to France had published. He told me that he is trying to get the campus of the school of social work back. So it seems a lot of people are now recognizing the importance of social work training, and I hope that the future will bring all the helping professions back to Iran.

Have you ever wondered what would have happened had you been allowed to continue with the school during these past 20 years?

FARMAN-FARMAIAN: The United States is so advanced, but there are some programs that we had in Iran that are not readily available here, such as social services in the schools, in rural areas, and in times of natural disasters. In Los Angeles when the earthquakes come, I wonder where the social workers are. In Iran we would be there with the professors and students of schools of social work.

If we had been able to continue our work, social work would have been much more advanced today than it was when I left. In 1975, students were coming to us from neighboring countries. Our school would have been a training center for all the neighboring countries, at least until they could start their own.

We would have been able to do a great deal, especially in publication. We had developed so much research. The school had its own printing shop, and we published books that would have been useful for the people of Iran and the neighboring countries.

We haven't discussed your international social work leadership experiences up to this point. Please tell us something about those and also anything that you envision for social work worldwide.

FARMAN-FARMAIAN: I am very grateful to organizations like the International Association of Schools of Social Work (IASSW). From the beginning, in 1958, we received consultation and expertise from IASSW and also from the U.S. Council on Social Work Education. Dr. Katherine Kendall, the executive secretary of IASSW, visited us several times and gave us advice. We enjoyed IASSW's help a great deal.

While I was studying in the United States, I became familiar with the curriculum materials that were provided by the Council on Social Work Education and realized that the American curriculum would need to be modified to suit the situation in Iran. For example, all through my course of study in the United States, I never was taught about rural development or about community development in slum areas. The students from the Third World, the developing countries, and the poor countries needed knowledge related to their special conditions and problems.

The problem is not only the individual; the problem is with the whole community or the larger society. We need programs to concentrate on an entire area and its population. For example, children get sick and have diarrhea because there is no clean water. I cannot put a caseworker there to teach a mother to boil the water. In the first place, fuel costs a lot, and the mother does not have the money to boil the water, and besides, it is time-consuming if you have eight children. So we have to solve the problem from the root.

At a couple of points you have referred to family members who have been imprisoned. Could you tell us about their present circumstances?

FARMAN-FARMAIAN: My brothers have been released from prison because they were not found guilty. Some of them are not able to leave Iran, but the majority of them are living abroad. They are scattered all over the world.

We are a large, close family, and we miss each other, so once a year we get together in Europe. Those of us who live in the United States get together every Thanksgiving and share a turkey.

Do you have any closing thoughts?

FARMAN-FARMAIAN: I just want to tell you that with all that has happened, I am not sorry that I am in social work, because I know that we all have a responsibility to bring about a better life for one another, whether in Iran, the United States, or some other part of the world.

AIDA GINDY

Born in 1920, Aida Gindy earned a bachelor's degree in social science at American University in Cairo. For three years during World War II, she taught at the American College for Girls in Cairo and volunteered with other human service agencies. She earned a master's degree in social economy and social work at Bryn Mawr College in the United States, where she also did postgraduate studies.

In the late 1940s, as a trainee at the United Nations, Ms. Gindy worked with founders of the United Nations. She returned to Egypt to assume a position in the Ministry of Social Affairs, Social Research Division, from 1950 to 1952, where she served on a team that helped establish the Egyptian Public Assistance Law.

Ms. Gindy then began a 32-year career with the UN, becoming the first professional woman seconded to the UN Economic Commission for Africa. In 1963, she became Chief of the Social Welfare Services Section of the UN Economic and Social Development Department in New York. She returned to Africa in 1975 as the first woman director of the regional UNICEF office for Eastern and Southern Africa in Nairobi. Five years later, she was appointed as the first woman director for the European Region, headquartered in Geneva.

Upon retirement, Ms. Gindy returned to Egypt, but continued to serve as a consultant with UNICEF, UNDP, and UNFPA. She also has been active with Egyptian national commissions, committees, and projects of the Ministries of Health and Population and of Women, as well as with volunteer organizations. She has received various national and international awards and now lives in Cairo.

BILLUPS: *Could you please share your experiences of growing up in Egypt?*

GINDY: I was a happy child. My immediate family consisted of my parents, two older brothers, and three older sisters. I was very much a member of an extended family, with maternal grandparents. My mother was educated at the Assiut Girls College and Pressley Memorial Institute, a Presbyterian mission school.

My grandfather helped finance education for girls, and my grandmother educated us about the importance of the environment. She taught us a great deal.

When I was eight, in 1928, we moved away from my grandparents, into our own home. From the beginning, my mother and father stressed community service. I remember hearing my mother discuss important women's issues, for example, education for children and young girls, community participation, and political life. She was influenced by a great leader, Mrs. Hoda Shaarawy, the wife of the prime minister, who was one of the first Egyptian feminists. My mother was one of the first national presidents of the Young Women's Christian Association (YWCA).

What about some of those community and civic responsibilities?

GINDY: My sisters and I were very lucky to attend the American College for Girls. The Americans were the first to promote education for girls in Egypt in the 1880s. The government opened its schools to girls at about the same time. The American College for Girls included primary school, high school, and two years of college. The institution stressed the importance of civic and community responsibilities and the value of human development. I became a junior Red Cross girl and a junior YWCA member.

Helen Martin, principal of the college, influenced me. She loved Egypt and her "daughters," the students. She taught us leadership, teamwork, unselfishness, caring for others, how to develop self-confidence, and how to speak out on controversial matters.

Summer holidays, I brought poor children from the semirural neighborhood to my grandmother's garden to teach them personal hygiene, nutrition, reading, games, and so forth. My grandmother would drop in and would teach the children songs about gardening and fruits and the care of flowers; it was a beautiful experience.

When I was a teenager, I became a camp counselor. Since my childhood had prepared me for a career in human development, it was not difficult to make choices when I went to the American University in Cairo (AUC). The AUC was a great institution. Sociology was my main field of study. My thesis, which many people told me not to dare write about, was on the beginnings of the national debate on family planning and overpopulation.

What influenced you as an adolescent?

GINDY: My parents were liberal. I felt free. For example, having learned about first aid as a member of the Red Cross Society (now Red Crescent), I helped during national emergencies. I remember going out, a girl of 15, with members of the Red Cross to the areas surrounding Cairo that had been deluged by very heavy rainfall to help families and children in tent camps.

In late adolescence and young adulthood, I went to YWCA camps as a counselor and a discussion leader. These were coeducational camps outside Alexandria. Boys were not separated from girls during activities, only in the sleeping areas.

At camp, we discussed problems of Egypt's young population, such as their independence, their rights, and their family ties. These were fascinating. This age group was highly idealistic, and we would stay in stimulating discussions for hours. For two weeks, the camps at which I was a counselor also served poor and deprived children who were selected to participate either because of their families or because they had problems of malnutrition. Most of these children had never seen the beautiful beaches of Alexandria.

The Current Events Club at college impacted me as an adult when I and others wrote a play in 1941 on peace. The world was at war at the time. I played Joseph Stalin. The idea of world peace became an important part of my life.

Another leadership role you had early on was as Student Council president.

GINDY: I was elected at age 18 while in the American College for Girls. The council discussed problems related to extracurricular activities, discipline, staff-student relationships, sports competition within and outside school, and other subjects brought to our attention.

As a council representative, I was trained in public debates and public speaking, which helped to enrich my experience in understanding human nature and human relationships. Muslims, Christians and Jews lived and studied together. We studied each other's religions and their similarities and influences on one another.

Following your university studies, did you go to graduate school immediately?

GINDY: I graduated from the university in 1943. My junior college alma mater was short on teachers because some of the American teachers couldn't return from summer break.

Dr. Helen Martin appealed to some of us graduates to teach. I and two of my friends volunteered to teach from 1943 to 1945. Teaching is a wonderful profession. It is sharing knowledge with the younger generation, their aspirations, their interests, and their concerns. These useful and inspiring years gave me a lot of confidence.

Dr. Martin also asked me to help with extracurricular activities because these had been so helpful to me in my own development. Yet working with adolescent girls, who were confused by the war situation and with this terrible period of Hitler, was difficult. It was a period of enlightenment for me. Another memorable experience was when I was visiting refugee tent camps in the desert with other Red Cross girls. The Allied Forces and the Red Cross had put these camps in the shadow of the pyramids. The children didn't have any books to read or to color. We used pebbles for writing alphabets on the sand. Later we were able to provide copybooks and pencils. In the mid-1940s, I won a scholarship to study in the United States from the American Embassy.

The voyage to America from Alexandria was a great education. I called it the "Gripsholm School." We hated our rooms, so we used to go on deck and mix with these poor displaced children who had to be deloused before coming on the boat and who didn't know any English. They were still feeling the shock of the war.

The maimed children would appear after dark to breathe some fresh air. The Red Cross girls were on their own, enjoying their freedom and looking forward to returning home, but I was interested in learning more about the children. They were Greeks, Slavs from southern Europe, and others, very poor, with hardly any clothes. Many were from Jewish families who were going to relatives or others for adoption.

When we finally landed, we were met by a man from the U.S. State Department and one from the Egyptian Consulate. He said, "Miss Gindy, you are going to Bryn Mawr, and you leave tomorrow." So the following day somebody came with me to Bryn Mawr because I had no clue where it was.

The campus was beautiful. The Bryn Mawr Department of Social Economy was not yet relabeled the School of Social Work and Social Research; the curriculum emphasized social policy and social administration, with strong leanings toward social science, anthropology, statistics, and economics. We also learned social work methodologies.

I was very lucky to have as my educational adviser Dr. Hertha Kraus, who was from Germany. She had headed the Welfare Department of the City of Cologne before immigrating to the States. I was placed for field practice at a settlement house in North Philadelphia headed by Marion Lantz. She had worked in Ramallah, Palestine and she knew Egypt.

The settlement house had a lot of migrants from the Middle East, primarily second generation Arab immigrants, mostly Lebanese and Syrians, not Egyptians. The Egyptians tended to come later. I learned about how these immigrants adjusted as adults in Philadelphia, often starting as mechanics and tradesmen, and how the second generation often seemed to reject the traditions of the first generation, even the culture.

Dr. Kraus was a social philosopher and a social planner, a great woman with vision who helped train the founders of the UN Social Affairs Department. I was eager to specialize in community participation, organization, and development. I knew I would return to Egypt to be very involved with social policy, research, and administration. Dr. Kraus and other professors gave me full support.

In 1946, the United Nations was born. Dr. Kraus, who was involved with the UN from its inception, stressed its objectives in her teaching. In a very important course on international social welfare and social policy, she brought us the UN Charter to study. Mrs. Eleanor Roosevelt, as an American delegate to the UN, was getting involved with the discussion on the human rights declaration. Hertha Kraus kept us informed, sharing with us the summary records of the Social Commission, which debated the world's social issues and problems as well as the UN's role in social development and social welfare.

In a way I was born, or reborn, along with the United Nations. This was an area of professional interest. The objectives of the UN Charter, the advocacy for one world, peace, freedom, equality, and development, all merged in a course I was taking on international social welfare policy and development, though it concentrated primarily on the developed world.

Membership of the UN at that time was almost 50 states. Egypt was one of the signatories of the charter. Yet during this postwar period the emphasis was on what England, the United States, France, and the former Soviet Union resolved. (China was not yet a member.)

It was while you were still a student at Bryn Mawr that you gained your initial on-site experience with the UN?

GINDY: Yes. I asked Hertha, "Can I get to know more about the United Nations?" She said, "I'll try," and later she brought me the good news that I could go there for field training the second year of my master's program.

The UN was still at Lake Success, New York. I was supervised by the founders of the Social Affairs Division. Alva Myrdal was the head of the Economic and Social Affairs Department. Sir Rafael Cilento, an Australian, was a well-known social leader, and Julia Henderson was director of the UN Bureau of Social Affairs. It was an unforgettable experience.

At the end of my training period, Julia Henderson and Dorothy Kahn, chief of the Social Welfare Section, asked me if I would join the UN staff. I said, "No, no, no. I am very green. Besides, I must go back to Egypt." They responded, "You are the first Egyptian woman we've met in the UN, and we want to keep you." I said, "Wait."

I was torn because Hertha Kraus thought I should become a doctoral candidate. I decided to apply to the doctoral program and studied for one year. But then my mother died, and I had to return to Cairo.

So you went back to Egypt.

GINDY: Yes, and I didn't regret it because I went to work for the Minister of Social Affairs, The ministry served as a great educator, reformer, and leader within Egypt. The minister placed me in a poor urban area, Sayda Zeinab, in old Cairo. There was a small ministry office in the area, the Urban Center. About five or six workers, headed by a social worker, were providing basic individualized case services, interviewing poor families for the provision of relief. They also were involved with the problems of delinquent and vagrant children.

When I was introduced to the all-male staff, they looked at me with great suspicion, wondering: What in the heck is this woman doing here? I felt those bad vibrations, and I said to myself, "I better approach them delicately." They already knew that my English was stronger than my Arabic. I said very diplomatically, "I am coming to learn from you." That helped boost them a bit, and I said, "I would like to know what are you doing, how long you have been here, and what do you think of this community? Do you think there are problems beyond the individual and family problems, the children, the delinquents, and the vagrants?" They replied, "Oh yeah! It's a very poor community and it's a community without much sanitation or health services and we don't know much about the economic instability."

I said, "Maybe we should study the community and start looking into their needs first." So we started working as a team. We conducted a survey of our community with a sample questionnaire. I explained what this community organization and development is all about, and that only when the people started expressing their needs would it be possible to determine their priorities and respond. It took almost 10 months until we really started understanding each other.

The urban community development project was successful and was established as a model. At the people's request, we established a citizens' committee that worked closely with us. We also pulled in the local government, and we started seeing quite a bit of positive change. This is what we call community development. It's not the staff telling the people what they need, but the people telling us! It was a great lesson to me that you don't have to rush with the ideas that you come with from abroad. It seemed at times that I had to relearn everything from my home country, answering to myself how applicable were my overseas studies to the projects I undertook.

After that first year, the minister established the Division of Social Research, and he brought 10 of us who had studied abroad to work together. I was the only woman. They were wonderful to me. They were really great men. It was already 1950, and the minister said, "I'm getting two experts from the United Nations and, Ms. Gindy, you know how to deal with them. They are going to help us prepare the first Social Security Act for Egypt." I would be in charge of drafting a paper on social security coverage.

The team worked with the two experts a year and a half before the bill was drafted and passed as law. This was another great experience. In reality it was a public assistance act for helping poor people, widows with orphans, and elderly or disabled people.

In addition to my work with the ministry, I was asked by the American University to teach a course in sociology and a course on community development from 1950 to 1952.

Then came a return to the United Nations. Correct?

GINDY: Yes, at the end of 1952 I was invited to a YWCA conference in New York City because I was a member of the board of directors of YWCA Egypt. I stayed an extra week and decided to visit the UN. Julia Henderson was still there as a director, as was Dame Geraldine Aves. Dorothy Kahn was still the chief of the Social Welfare Section. I told them what I was doing, and Dorothy Kahn said, "Why don't you join us? We need you." I said, "I am an Egyptian civil servant." Julia Henderson, who was the big boss, said, "You should talk with the head of the Egyptian delegation to the UN and ask what he thinks."

So I went to Dr. Omar Loutfi, who was an expert in Egypt on human rights, and I said, "The UN wants me to work for them." He said: "You go ahead. We don't have an Egyptian woman there." And I continued, "Well, I have been a civil servant for almost three years." He said, "I'll send them a cable. I want you to be here in the UN. We have only one man in Social Development who is Egyptian." The minister's response was, "I'll give her six months' leave. After that, if she doesn't return, she loses her job."

At the time there were no rigid regulations on the probation period. Before the six months were over, Julia Henderson offered me a permanent contract

I started at the UN as a junior on the first professional level (P2) and was appointed as a child welfare officer. My chief was Dorothy Kahn, but my immediate supervisor was Dame Geraldine Aves from the United Kingdom, who was involved with displaced children, as she had been during the war. I'll never forget my first assignment; I had to write an article on the UN history of work in child welfare and delved into and researched the records of six years, from 1946 to 1952.

Martha Branscombe replaced Dorothy Kahn after her retirement. Martha, who had worked placing displaced children in England during World War II, was a great thinker, reformer, and rebel. She was so influential in broadening child welfare services to stress family welfare, community services, maintenance of family levels of living, training for social welfare, and so on.

I recall an Indian delegation asking, "Why isolate the children from the family in the Western way? You should place them back into the family, then look at the children within the family and assess what is happening." That was a great step forward that suited the developing countries. This emphasis gradually brought to light bigger problems between the industrially developed and developing world; you could see the broadened concept of "development" crawling toward becoming the role of the UN in the 1960s.

Another area of interest was the huge concern of the developing countries for training in social welfare. Their members said, in effect, "We 'inherited' certain educational programming from the British, the Americans, or the French, with an overemphasis in social casework. We want training to cope with much broader problems, and we want to train auxiliary workers as well. We cannot afford only highly trained professionals." That's when the UN became involved with training of multipurpose auxiliary workers.

The Social Welfare Division of the UN was providing very generous technical assistance programs in training social workers. We had to recruit a lot of experts to help countries do training in social policy and social administration and the like as governments were establishing new ministries of social welfare, family welfare departments, and child welfare divisions. We leaned heavily in the beginning on American assistance.

How to recruit and match international experts to priorities in the developing world became a major issue. Some people going into the field were overwhelmed by the complexities. The UN founded a "university" to prepare people who could advise governments. Part of my expanded responsibilities between 1952 and 1959 was to help with technical assistance programs, briefing experts on national family welfare and child welfare in particular.

Then you faced a new opportunity?

GINDY: Late in 1958, Martha Branscombe told me, "There are opportunities to go to the field. Would you be interested?" I jumped at this idea. I talked with the new executive secretary, Mekki Abbas, who was establishing the UN Economic Commission for Africa. A week later Julia Henderson announced, "Aida, you were chosen."

Working in Africa was the highlight of my career with the United Nations. I arrived in Addis Ababa at the end of 1959. The new leadership guiding African countries toward decolonialization and independence included Nyerere in Tanzania, Kenyatta in Kenya, Sengor in Senegal, Kawunda in Zambia, Nkrumah in Ghana, and of course, the emperor of Ethiopia, Haile Selassie, who was our host. I helped establish the Social Development Division of the UN Commission, the greatest challenge in my work in Africa.

We emphasized helping governments establish ministries responsible for social welfare, helping departments establish family and child welfare programs, schools of social work, training of social workers, auxiliaries, and so forth. UNICEF assisted cooperatively with us; it gave high priority to training in social work. New social work educational programs were established in Uganda, Ethiopia, Tanzania, Ivory Coast, and Ghana. Some were independent schools; others were university-affiliated.

In addition, UNICEF, in partnership with us, helped countries to promote programs for participation of women in development. Some needed drastic changes to work realistically. For example, women were being taught how to prepare fruitcakes and scones, so I asked, "Do the rural children eat scones and fruitcakes? Let us first find out more about the diets of the children and mothers." The British supervisor looked at me, but said, "Yes. We'll make some changes."

At the time, East African countries were not all independent. I learned a lot about community development that was so indigenous to African culture and traditional practices in countries such as Kenya. People readily helped each other through the movement called Harambee, a form of group work combined with community participation. The local government also participated.

Some trainers in Africa separated community development from training in social work. I tried to bring them together as one integrated social work methodology. Ghana and Ethiopia accepted this combination. However, the French were less flexible. They separated social work from community development, particularly in rural areas.

Your challenging days in Africa were becoming numbered, right?

GINDY: I returned to UN Headquarters in 1964 and became chief of the Social Welfare Section. The section had units for family and child welfare, training for welfare, and disabled people. I added units for youths and for elderly people. We served as the liaison office for the Social Affairs Division to UNICEF. We worked very closely with the UN Population Division, the Women's Division, and the Housing Department.

The role of the Social Welfare Section became increasingly more dynamic. We also contributed to the Economic Development and the Human Rights Divisions. Social welfare as it related to health was carried out in conjunction with the World Health Organization (WHO), social security with the International Labor Organization (ILO), and education with United Nations Educational, Scientific and Cultural Organization (UNESCO). This meant a continuous and dynamic rethinking of the role of social welfare to move with the demands of the world at the time. Either in my role as chief of the Section or with colleagues, we succeeded in branching out into broader areas of development. The section worked very closely with a large international membership of nongovernmental organizations (NGOs) active in the fields of social security, refugee work, family planning, and training for social welfare.

It was a very stimulating time to work with the UN team in New York. When I think of how many countries I visited on long- or short-term assignments, playing a leadership role on behalf of the UN in Asia and Latin America, Africa, and the Caribbean, they add up to about 120 countries in a career of 32 years.

In 1975, the International Year of the Woman, the female delegates on the executive board of UNICEF were angry because UNICEF didn't have a woman director in any regional field office. It was becoming an issue not only in UNICEF but also with all of the UN agencies. UN delegates were asking, "Where are the senior women?" I remember the Russians very well, supported by the Americans and many other delegates, asking personnel to give them statistical data on the matter. And I recall listening to the delegates sitting on the UNICEF board, where I was representing the Social Affairs Division.

After the last session of the board, Henry Labouisse, the executive director of UNICEF and one of the great men of the UN, came to me and asked, "Are you interested in joining UNICEF? We want you to become the first woman regional director." I said, "Yes." He said, "With your knowledge of Africa—we are going to have a vacancy in our Eastern-Southern Regional Office, which is based in Nairobi." I said, "I am very flattered, but I am committed to the Women's Conference until September." This was July. He said, "We will wait."

I imagine that your change in UN responsibility was to be quite a professional jump.

GINDY: Yes, I jumped from P5 to D2 level, the highest professional level. By December 1975, I was transferred to UNICEF and worked there through July 1984. UNICEF was my favorite of all the UN bodies, not only because it serves children but also because it works at the grassroots level. It is action- and field-oriented. UNICEF was at the beginning the United Nations International Children's Emergency Fund, established after World War II to respond primarily to the needs of the children of Europe who required emergency assistance. UNICEF today serves children mainly in developing countries.

Returning to Africa was like going home. There were a lot of people I knew in the fields of health, education, nutrition, and social welfare. Moreover, UNICEF had recognized from the beginning the importance of the role of women, as individuals and mothers. And although UNICEF started with limited programs of what the British called "mother craft and home craft," adopting the idea that women's work was mainly with home and children, this emphasis was completely transformed in the 1970s and 1980s. UNICEF assisted women's training in health and sanitation and in reproductive health, but women's role in community development and their contributions to income-generating activities became a new priority in the 1980s and 1990s. This transformation came about primarily with the demands of the developing countries.

The regional office in Nairobi was responsible to 20 countries. Each country had its own UNICEF office; thus UNICEF had flexibility to respond to the needs of a country in training staff or volunteers for programming in the field of basic education for children; for health, water, and sanitation in homes and in communities; and for health promotion for children, including programs for immunization and nutrition. Africa needed more schools, books, blackboards, desks, and the like. UNICEF responded. We had an adequate budget and we had capable national staffs that worked in partnership with the international staff. We also worked very closely with the representatives of WHO, UNESCO, and so on. They helped us in education, health, and training of personnel.

Henry Labouisse loved children. I remember his first visit to Africa in 1979. I would tell him I had prepared a program for him to meet the heads of states, prime ministers, or ministers. He always said, "Yes, but I want to go see the children." So in East Africa he became affectionately named "Chief Henry Labouisse," and I was called "Mamma Gindy." We traveled, along with his wife, Eve Curie, the daughter of the famous scientists. He spared three weeks, and we visited Kenya, Uganda, Zambia, and Tanzania.

I saw the famine and civil wars in Somalia, Uganda, and Ethiopia, and the famine in Tanzania and Kenya. I will never forget the families in Uganda when I was out in the bush. The children were so undernourished that one toddler about two years of age could barely walk; a slight breeze would make him fall. The toddlers were fed by eyedroppers because they could not digest any solids.

UNICEF's work is not limited to the provision of supplies and equipment. It also assists governments in development of programs, training, and monitoring and evaluation. National projects are usually for four- to five-year periods. UNICEF also assists in promoting some basic social research, advocacy, and communication programs.

After these years in Africa, you took on a UNICEF responsibility in Europe?

GINDY: Yes. After my five years in Africa, I was surprised to be informed by Jim Grant, the executive director appointed in 1980, that I would go to Geneva as director of the European office. The Geneva office was mainly to advocate for UNICEF, to coordinate with UNICEF in New York on fundraising, to work with UNICEF's 27 committees in Europe, and to cooperate with the UN and specialized agencies in Geneva. Jim Grant's said he wanted someone who would help interpret for Europe the needs of children in the developing countries.

I went to Geneva in June 1980. I was the first woman to be appointed to that post and the first who was not European. That was not welcomed by many Europeans. I said to myself, "Aida, you must be very diplomatic." So I used all of my diplomacy, and they gradually overcame their reservations.

After World War II, under the direction of its founder, Maurice Pate, UNICEF extended assistance to the war-torn European countries. Out of loyalty to UNICEF, almost every country in Europe established national committees to raise funds, to advocate for UNICEF's work, to adopt or team up with children's programs in developing countries, and to plan field visits to developing countries. The regional office in Geneva had a large division to coordinate with these committees. It also had divisions for advocacy, information and communication, and cooperation with international UN agencies and NGOs interested in children.

The administration in New York was surprised when I informed them in 1981, my second year in Europe, that certain countries in the south of Europe wanted UNICEF's assistance for their children's programs. Poor children, wherever they may be, suffer from ill health, bad living conditions, malnutrition, and poor sanitation. It was difficult to obtain funding from UNICEF headquarters (all Europe was considered part of the developed world). But I was able, to the surprise of many, to initiate a modest exchange program whereby the rich countries of the region, such as Sweden and Denmark, would extend technical supports or provide equipment not only to the developing world but also to other countries of Europe. For example, through our office, Sweden provided one social welfare expert on children's day care to Portugal, and Denmark provided spare parts for dairy equipment to Poland, which had undergone tremendous hardships in the 1980s. These projects proved successful.

Your responsibilities with UNICEF included the preparation of official reports and other publications. Tell us about those.

GINDY: With UN publications, you are an anonymous writer. The variety of publications is enormous, but almost all are published in the name of the secretary general. They are mainly policy-oriented documents, surveys, or comparative studies, usually requested by UN delegations. There are publications based on information received from governments at UN request, such as comparative studies on day care services or international adoptions. Then there are manuals for training personnel. There are policy papers based on social research to be submitted to expert committees for review. These works are written by professionals from within the UN or with the aid of experts.

Experts like Katherine Kendall and Herman Stein, Frank Paiva and Meher Nanavatty, and Dame Eileen Younghusband were involved from the beginning with the international training documents for social work. My role as chief of the Social Welfare Section was to coordinate with the writers and staff of these studies, briefing them on trends in the UN, preparing the questions in collaboration with colleagues and experts, and helping to analyze the data before publication.

Since your return to Egypt, what have been your principal activities?

GINDY: I returned to Egypt at the end of 1983, after 32 years with the United Nations and UNICEF. I thought I should come back to my roots, back to people I grew up with, so that I could contribute something to my own country. While I was with the UN and UNICEF, naturally, I visited Egypt every two years on what the UN called home leave. However, there were a number of changes taking place at the time I returned.

Mr. [Hosni] Mubarak had become president. At an alumni meeting of the American University in Cairo, I was asked to speak on my experiences with the UN. Little did I know that Mrs. Mubarak was in the audience as an alumna. After I finished, she sent someone to call me to her table. It was a big surprise. She told me, "You worked with UNICEF and the UN so many years; it's time you come and help us." Her organization was the Integrated Care Society, a multidisciplinary organization designed primarily for services to children. I accepted.

Mrs. Mubarak asked me specifically to think about how we could develop a model program for children with special needs, including mentally and physically disabled children. As a result, a group of 10 of us from various disciplines, including social workers, special educators, therapists, medical doctors, and psychiatrists, met regularly for 10 months of hard work to propose a plan. Now, a center for children with special needs has been functioning successfully for eight years. The Minister of Health and Population has said that he plans to replicate it throughout Egypt.

Another aspect of Mrs. Mubarak's activity in which I was involved followed the earthquake of 1990. This was the first catastrophe of this kind that we had experienced. The destruction was mainly in urban slum areas. Overnight, families were completely displaced. Children were dislocated. Schools were destroyed. Mrs. Mubarak asked 20 of us to volunteer to work with the victims in the transitional camps. Eventually some of these victims, who had originally been housed seven to nine individuals in one room, were provided apartments in which each family had about three rooms to live in and a separate kitchen, bathroom, and living room. This resettlement program was based on the urban community participation development approach whereby the people themselves became the decision makers, defining their priority needs and services. The resulting programs emphasized literacy for women and children who had dropped out of school because of the disaster; and provided credit for income-generating projects for women, club groups for elderly women, activities for street children and rehabilitation programs for mentally and physically disabled children. This project became one of the 40 urban projects that the Habitat Organization of the UN selected as outstanding models worldwide. It was given a special award during the Habitat Conference two years ago.

In addition to my volunteer work, I also sit on the National Commission on Women, which deals with women's problems in the labor force and industry and their legal rights, as well as issues concerning women and rural development, gender equity, and economic development. In March 1997, we had a conference on the role of women in rural development.

I am also a volunteer on the Board of Population and Development, a national commission established by the Minister of Health and Population as an outgrowth of the UN Population Conference convened in Cairo in 1994. NGOs were very strong advocates on population matters, family planning, reproductive health, and prevention of female circumcision—all issues addressed in the recommendations of the conference.

We would like to know something about some of the special recognition you have received.

GINDY: One of my international awards was given to me in 1983 by Jim Grant, former UNICEF executive director. On a tablet it reads, "For your contribution to the world's children." This was much appreciated.

A second award came from the UN Secretary General, a diploma with the medal of the UN that read, "For serving the UN for more than 30 years."

A third award came from the Italian UNICEF Committee, one of the leading committees in Europe. Interestingly enough, the recognition was for services to children in Africa. And I said, "Why in the world is Italy giving me this for my services in Africa?" and the chairman of the Italian committee told me, "We gave money for the children in Africa, and we knew how hard you have worked to help those children over there." I was very touched by the generosity of the Italians.

The African women, including the Kenyans and the Tanzanians, gave me an award for the services extended to rural women in Africa.

National awards came from Mrs. Mubarak for my services to the earthquake victims and from the minister responsible for population and family planning, who gave me a special award for helping in the preparation of the UN Population Conference in Egypt. Another award was from the American University in Cairo, a Distinguished Career award.

It is a good feeling to know that you have been appreciated. It is also wonderful to have served for a special purpose, for human development. This was my aspiration since I was a teenager. I have a feeling of fulfillment because I am now 79 years old.

As you look back, do you have any reflections to share with your present professional colleagues or with students of the profession?

GINDY: Having been accepted as a professional colleague by many of the outstanding professionals who helped me grow throughout my career, I wish to thank them. We shared common concerns and aspirations, and we supported each other, whether at international conferences or expert group meetings or through writing to one another or otherwise exchanging information.

I hope that students who are moving toward a career will hold onto their aspirations until they are fulfilled. How deep are their concerns for humankind? How are they inspired to work with commitment and with vision? Are there persons who are inspiring them like those who inspired me? Are the decision makers involving them in activities where they can learn from each other? Do they have potential that has not yet been recognized by their professors? Are the students challenged by their future careers?

I think a lot about these matters. Why was I inspired? Will I see the same degree of commitment from my grandnieces and grandnephews?

I always go back to the importance of family influences and schooling. To what extent do the families and schools of today give young people their support? Do they have time to spend with them? In particular, do the professors give time to share their thoughts with their students? What are the driving forces motivating students today—is it money, independence, materialism? Or are they human concerns—the quality of life—that count?

༄༅༄

HARRIET JAKOBSSON

Born in 1926, Harriet Jakobsson was educated at the University of Stockholm, the London School of Economics, and Western Reserve University (now Case Western Reserve University). She has devoted much of her life to pioneering efforts in social work practice, education, and consultation in Sweden and around the world. She has taught at the Universities of Lund in Sweden, Trondheim in Norway, and Tampere in Finland, as well as at her principal academic home, the University of Örebro in Sweden.

Perhaps the most notable of Dr. Jakobsson's professional endeavors has been her extensive work with the UN, Swedish Save the Children, and the Swedish International Development Agency, including the administration of refugee camps and aid efforts in Ethiopia, Eritrea, Djibouti, Sudan, Somalia, and Indonesia. For 4½ years she led a social work education program in war-torn Beirut.

Dr. Jakobsson has served as vice president of the International Association of Schools of Social Work and of the Swedish Scout movement, national president of the Business and Professional Women's Organization, and board member of both the Inter-University Consortium for International Social Development (IUCISD) and its European Regional Branch. In recent years, she has been called upon by the Swedish Defense College to provide human rights training for military and police officers of Nordic and Baltic countries preparing for leadership of UN peacekeeping missions in Bosnia and Kosovo, specifically about children's reactions to war and to being in refugee camps. She has received national and international awards.

BILLUPS: *You have been identified closely with social work throughout your professional career. How did you find your way into the profession?*

JAKOBSSON: I had planned for many years to be a pediatrician, but as I graduated in the "Spring of Peace" in 1945, I couldn't go straight into medicine. My father was getting old; he wanted me to reconsider and to choose something requiring a shorter preparation. So I went to a career adviser. I said I wanted to work with children, and she said, "Why not try social work?" My older sister was in social work training, so at first I didn't want to pick that up because she was doing it. But my father said it was a very good education for girls. I also think my choice of career had to do with my Scout leader, who was a devoted social worker.

One had to have one year of pre-field training before entering the University of Stockholm School of Social Work. That was very, very good for me.

Because I wanted to get into a hospital for pre-entry social work experience, I was put in a program for registered nursing. That was an excellent experience for me, especially when later in my career I would be out in the refugee camps.

My next training experience was with unmarried mothers who could not take care of their babies. They were in an institution. I learned a great deal about babies and about preserving food, baking, sewing, and so on.

My third pre-entry field experience was in a more general social work agency where I did a number of tasks. At that time, people had to have a special ration book to present in a special shop to buy wine and hard liquor. They could ask for an extra ration. Those applications had to be screened, and that was one of my jobs. I remember somebody writing, "I work at the railway, and it is so cold, so I want more hard liquor," or "My father-in-law has finished my supply."

I did other things, like interviewing teenagers about their drinking habits. That meant that I went on home visits to their families. The work with the kids and teenagers was fun because I was not that far from them in age.

Were these pre-entry field training experiences chosen by you, or were they assigned?

JAKOBSSON: The School of Social Work at the University of Stockholm recommended them. I am all for prospective social work students having pre-entry experience to help them to explore areas of interest and, more basically, to decide whether or not to enter the social work educational program.

Once enrolled, I had my first student field training at a special agency for mothers-to-be in Örebro, where my main task was to interview expectant mothers. I screened applications regarding dental work, clothing, things for the house, supplementary food, and extra assistance in preparing for the baby—all of this depending on income and social status. For most of these things, the women did not get cash. They had to have a piece of paper that the agency provided to be presented at the shops.

One of the bad things about the home visits was that to verify need I was expected to open the cupboards in the kitchen and see how many cups and plates and so on they had. In the bedroom you needed to see if they had enough blankets. Despite this harsh investigative approach, I had some very, very good home visit experiences.

The second field experience was in a prison psychiatric clinic, where all the certified murderers, thieves, and sex abusers were housed, in Långholmen, the state prison in Stockholm. My responsibility there was to obtain the prisoners' life histories and to call all the references, which meant, for instance, that I would call their teachers. They might say, "I have had many children to teach during my lifetime and can't remember" or "Oh, that was a lovely boy." I was also administering and interpreting the psychological tests, as we had no psychologists. The head of this clinic, a psychiatrist, was using the prisoners more or less to standardize the TAT (Thematic Apperception Test) and other tests.

At one point a judge called my father and said, "Do you know what your daughter is up to? Because that guy she talked to today is one that I am going to sentence to life in prison for murdering his wife." My father very confidently replied, "I expect her to know what she is doing. The university has sent her there. She seems happy when she comes home, so don't be worried."

We did all the other social service things prisoners needed: "Would you call my wife and find out how the baby is doing?" "I have heard that Jim has smallpox. Could you call and ask how he is doing?" "Could you reclaim what I have pawned? I have the money here."

My third student field experience was in the adult psychiatric unit at the University Hospital in Uppsala. Again, I was very lucky because they hadn't had many students from the School of Social Work, and one of the professors always invited me along on hospital rounds. That was very good experience. If there were special lectures or visitors from anywhere around the world, I was always invited to join them.

So, in addition to your course work, your educational program provided you with six on-site practice experiences?

JAKOBSSON: Yes. The training today requires only one semester of field training and one semester of a field-attached project. Today there is no compulsory pre-field training, although many students have it, or its equivalent, because today many students are older than before and may be experienced.

I feel that we had many more demands made of us than is the case today. For instance, we had both written and oral exams; students today usually have only oral exams.

Subsequently, you also took special courses, seminars, and conferences, not only in social work, but also in other subjects?

JAKOBSSON: In Sweden you were expected to take additional courses after you had been working a while. For example, all of a sudden the National Medical Board decided that all of us working in abortion services in a psychiatric setting needed to have a special course and a certifying piece of paper, so I went to a mental health seminar for a semester.

I had wanted to work with children ever since my interest in pediatrics, so I went to a program in Stockholm called Ericastiftelsen, where we were trained in child psychology and child psychotherapy. They took in a maximum of 20 students—two social workers, two psychologists, two teachers, two nurses and so on—which meant that we were exposed to an interdisciplinary team work experience.

Those two postgraduate training experiences occurred before my study at Western Reserve University in 1960–1961 in Cleveland.

I was accepted into what at that time was called the Cleveland International Program. When I was interviewed in Sweden, I didn't even know that they were considering me. They asked, "Have you ever considered studying in the United States?" And I said, "Oh, that's like going to the moon." About a week later, I got a phone call from the American Embassy to tell me that I had been awarded a Fulbright scholarship, and I asked, "You must be wrong because I have never applied for one." They said, "No, no, you only need to decide, because others applied for you."

Later I received some Swedish scholarships as well. I was asked by a governmental board if I could please go to Oxford and London for a course on juvenile delinquency. By that time I had been working in a school for delinquent girls. They wanted me to go because I knew more English than most. So I stayed in Oxford in one of the colleges for men. While there, every morning one of these old men they called a "scout" came to my room to ask, "May I put on a fire for you, *sir?*" "Would you like a cup of tea, *sir?*"

Then there were UN scholarships, a type of exchange in which I welcomed a social worker from England as a guest in Sweden, and in turn I would spend time in England with her as part of the work—including lectures, seminars, interviews, observations—for a month or so. I did that sort of exchange twice with colleagues in England and once each with colleagues in Holland, Italy, and Turkey. I also spent some time at the Maxwell Jones Clinic and participated in a number of other courses and seminars in England for up to a month or so at a time.

Tell me about your well-known special concerns for children in war.

JAKOBSSON: I took some of those Tavistock leadership courses, including some special psychology/analytical psychiatry types of training. One course offered by the Hebrew University in Jerusalem was held in the north of Israel. During that training, I met a very nice medical doctor from Boston. Her husband was on a sabbatical, occupying the Sigmund Freud Chair at the Hebrew University. He organized a special seminar on children of war, and I was asked to go back to Jerusalem to give a workshop. There I met some other people with this particular concern for children in war.

I thought for a while that I should write something special about children in war or refugee children, but so far I haven't managed to do more than small pieces.

Going back to the earlier part of your career that prepared you for your special work with children and their families, do you care to share with us a bit more about those early years?

JAKOBSSON: I did some short-term things after my graduation from university, like working in an abortion guidance clinic. I also did additional work with prisoners scheduled for psychiatric examinations.

Then I was a temporary social worker in a children's agency, supposedly for just one year while the social worker for whom I substituted was away for training. When the year was over she took another job, and I was asked to take the job permanently. By then, I was a specialist in work with teenagers, some of them heavy drinkers, some of them abused, some in very, very bad family relationships. This was interesting, but tough, especially as I worked in Helsingborg in Sweden—20 minutes by ferryboat to Helsingör (Elsinore) in Denmark. Many of the teenagers went across to Elsinore, so the Swedish police would call in the middle of the night, wake me up, and say, "*Your girls* are drunk. The Danish police are sending them by the next boat. Do you want us to bring them in to the police station, or are you coming to meet us at the ferry station?" So off I went.

At the same time, I was a kind of family supervisor with some families that couldn't cope. For example, instead of taking the children out of the family and into custody, the Local Welfare Board (equivalent to juvenile court) decided that a mother with three small children (and a husband out on a ship somewhere) needed special services because she couldn't look after the children. So a visiting nurse and I would alternate personal daily visits to her home and help her to learn how to look after the children so that they wouldn't be taken from her.

Once I went with the mother to buy clothes for the children. She had the idea to dress them like the royal children, the boys in air force uniforms and the girl with swan's down around her neck. This was not practical; the family was living in an area where children were playing in the dirt and garbage, and there were no laundry machines at the time. So, it was finally decided that the children should have sweaters, plastic coats, and rubber boots. The mother cried about this decision, and I felt very superior in a bad way. That was part of the job, as was teaching her how to cook. (Her husband was a good cook, the cook on a ship, but she didn't know how to cook anything.) Except for some decisions, such as the clothes for the kids, she was very happy that we were a support and taught her some things.

I took a year-long leave of absence from the children's agency for a position at a psychiatric clinic in Uppsala before I returned to work with children, this time in an approved school for delinquent girls. Among these girls were some that I had sent to this school from the agency where I had worked earlier. I was really worried, then, not knowing whether we would be friends or enemies, but we developed a good working relationship. They defended me any time anyone dared to say anything rough to or about me.

Some of these girls had experienced extremely traumatic life circumstances. One girl, for instance, had a mother who was remarried to a man who couldn't stand the girl. The family made this girl wait to see if there was any food left for her to eat after the family had finished its meal. So she went to stay with her grandmother most of the time, but her grandmother developed schizophrenia. Finally, the grandmother was in such bad shape that the neighbors called the police to pick her up and take her to the psychiatric hospital. When the girl came home they were carrying her beloved grandmother out the door. And they didn't tell this girl why. So she started screaming and fighting, kicking the police, and so on. She got arrested. They called me. When I got there, I said, "I want to sit down with her. You unlock that cell." They did. "Please give me a cigarette for her." They said, "She's too young." I said, "She wants a cigarette, and please bring some coffee and a big, big sandwich." They hadn't given her one thing, and nobody had told her why they had taken her grandmother.

Later the police were relieved when I took her along to see her grandmother. I had her placed in an approved school, but she later left for another school when she got pregnant. Years later, in a store in Denmark, someone was standing staring at me. I recognized her. She had two healthy looking children with her. She and I have since had contact over a very long time.

From these sorts of responsibilities and experiences, I went into a child guidance clinic. That was one of my most rewarding jobs. It was a new clinic that we started that was to be on the hospital grounds, but not part of the hospital. We were sent to Oslo, Copenhagen, and other places to observe their facilities while our building was being planned and built. We told the architects to do things that they said were impossible and we said were *not* impossible.

In Sweden, when constructing an official building you have to use 1 or 2 percent of the entire cost for aesthetic enhancements, for art and decorations. One artist was particularly creative. He constructed some special beds for children, toys, and unique equipment in addition to some beautiful decorations. While we may think our work is mainly with the patients, the physical environment is highly important.

The social ecology of the clinic was highly important, too. My main task was diagnostic work, administering all kinds of tests for the increasing numbers of children who were long-term patients, but I was also responsible for the teenage ward. We also started a special treatment home of a secure but supposedly more homelike environment for children who didn't need to be kept on the hospital ward any more. We expected the parents to come to the clinic to take their children for lots of outings and to have regular sessions with the staff. Most of the parents later agreed that their children had benefited from this innovative treatment.

We didn't need an administrator, but that was part of my responsibility. My title was Curator, and later it was First Curator. It meant that I was first in the sense of having had the most training for the child guidance field, and I could supervise the others on the staff. A doctor, a child psychologist, and I met every week for organizing seminars for all the staff members. For this purpose, I used some of the knowledge I had gained while in the United States, the United Kingdom, and elsewhere.

Did your time spent in training and in supervising others serve as a rather natural career preparation for your next 25 years in academe?

JAKOBSSON: Yes, but at the same time I never particularly wanted that sort of career change. I was asked by the person I had temporarily relieved in the child welfare agency, who at the time was on the faculty at the University of Lund, if I would fill in for someone there who was wanting to get away for a year of professional leave. I was hesitant because I loved my clinic and all the work with the children, the teenagers, and staff, but eventually I agreed to go for a year.

I was to arrange student field placements and provide training for field supervisors, but one of my former teachers and the dean persuaded me to teach in the classroom. Then I learned that the dean of one of the schools of social work was going to start a new school at the University of Örebro. He and I had been working together on governmental studies, investigations, and surveys. He said, "I want you to come with me to help start this new school."

During the first year there weren't enough courses for me to teach, but there was very much remaining to be done in Lund, so I was commuting 500 to 600 kilometers by train. I stayed in Örebro during the week and went to my home in Lund over the weekend.

That was another of those pioneering things. In my new capacity as professor and academic dean, we were developing courses and by that time teaching the three principal social work methods of the day: social casework, social group work, and community organization. At that time we had one lecturer for each method at each of the first five schools of social work in Sweden. We who were selected as representatives of the five schools tried to develop curriculum and training together and to help each other. We wrote case studies, translated professional literature, and so on.

Was this also about when you became internationally involved?

JAKOBSSON: It was about that time that I began to pick up on things international, learning more from outside than inside Sweden. I met two of the key figures in IASSW, Katherine Kendall and Herman Stein, at my first IASSW conference in 1966. They helped me a lot at that first conference and have ever since.

Some years later, about 1975, I was asked to come to Trondheim, Norway, because they were starting what they called a new higher social work education with an expanded amount of research teaching. Those who were admitted to that new master's program were very experienced social workers. Some had held chief positions in national government agencies or in hospitals and so on. Seven men, nicknamed "The Boys Club," were the first students. Ernest Witte, former executive director of the Council on Social Work Education, was the first professor. Later, Chuck Guzzetta of Hunter College in New York City came on. Both were very good people to work with.

Besides classroom teaching, I coordinated fieldwork, which some students didn't think they needed, with their experience. But after being placed, they enjoyed it and learned a lot from good supervisors.

I was the only one on the faculty with Scandinavian social work experience. This made life for me a bit hectic because I was invited to communities of Norway to give many courses, weekend seminars, workshops, and so on. But I enjoyed it.

I flew back to Sweden every month for meetings. Sweden was about to go through a systemwide university reform, and the social work education was going to be turned upside down. I was first an expert for, then a member of, the governmental committee making recommendations.

I also was on a special small planning committee, a group of 10, that worked with both the Department of Education and the National Board for Universities. We were supposed to look at the reform issues for higher education not from the view of our own university or our own special areas of interest, but from the perspective of the needs of higher education in the nation as a whole.

One of your international involvements has been your consultation with a relatively new school of social work in the Baltics.

JAKOBSSON: The Riga Institution, Attistiba School of Pedagogy and Social Work, asked the Nordic Council of Ministers for someone to consult with them, to evaluate their program, and to help them get accreditation. A colleague from Tampere, Finland, and myself made several visits, and we had many long discussions with the students, among others, who offered good suggestions.

We wrote a positive report for the Ministry of Education, but for the school itself we were rather critical. The dean at first thought we were trying to cut them out of funds, but finally she realized that through our candid critiques we were trying to help. They had no permanent faculty other than the dean, although they did have many visiting faculty for short periods of time. Also, there were too many students in the classrooms for everyone to be able to sit down. We recommended more full-time faculty and training for the staff. We thought that they had to build the school step by step and not all at once. So one of the professors of law has gone to Florida to get more training, and someone else went to the University of Gothenburg. The dean went off to Switzerland, Germany, Denmark, and England for study. The school finally did get its accreditation.

You have served as a consultant to an impressive array of other organizations. Could you tell us more about that, including the years you spent in Beirut?

JAKOBSSON: One of the universities in Beirut, at that time called Beirut University College (BUC) and now the Lebanese American University (LAU), asked Swedish Save the Children if they could have help from somebody who could develop a program in social work. I was asked to go there as a professor in social work. This was just after the massacre in the communities of Sabra and Shatila and the Israel military occupation. I was supposed to leave for Beirut in spring 1983, but I couldn't go until the fall. Even that was delayed because the airport was not open because of the war.

My salary and insurance were to be paid from Sweden, and the university was to provide me with an apartment on campus for what was to be a one-year assignment. As the conflict in Lebanon worsened, I had to fight my way with the Swedish authorities, especially our State Department, for they said it was too dangerous to be there. The UN had taken all its staff out of Lebanon. But I said, "If students are coming there to go to school, I want to be there. It's not more dangerous for me than for them."

So I went and stayed. While I was there I always had a ticket to come home, but the airport was often closed, so that didn't help very much. One could go out, I suppose, by boat, but you had to go right through the worst war zones between 9:00 and 5:00, crossing the Green Line where shootings always took place.

I had to be evacuated a few times, but it wasn't too bad for me. While there, I was even sent out on some missions—twice to Jordan for meetings about children at risk, and once to UNICEF in New York to work for a week with a small group concerning children in war and the UN Convention on the Rights of the Child (Article 38). I left Lebanon one other time to present a paper in London.

I stayed 4½ years, so the students graduated before my tour of duty was up even though because of "the situation" (that was what the war was called—"the situation") students frequently couldn't come to class, couldn't take their exams, and couldn't read because they had no electricity.

The students had little or no idea about democracy; they had no idea about voting or following up with what they had voted for. I tried to teach this in an indirect way. In a course called "Knowing the Client," a course that had been in the old catalog but had never been given, I asked, "What kinds of clients would you like to know?" I wrote on the blackboard, in the old-fashioned way, every suggestion they had. Then they voted and ended up with the aged, refugees, and street children. Later in the course, someone asked why we were discussing only these groups of clients, and I said, "I did not choose these; you did." Then they had to try to figure out among themselves why decision making in a democracy is important.

The students became extremely good in their coursework. For one assignment, I said to them, "Find the oldest relative you have, or if you don't have any elderly relatives in Beirut (because many of them had moved out), find the oldest person you know, and interview that person. Make up the questions yourself and report back here what you learned." One girl said, "Old persons don't remember anything, so why should I do this?" But after completing the assignment with an elderly relative, that same girl said at the next class session, "Could I please start? I know something different now. I never, ever before thought that she had anything to say."

Like this girl, many of the students came back to the classroom impressed with what they had learned. Other students who had interviewed street children said that they had been arguing with and shouting at street children, telling them not to do this or that, but from what they had learned they would never do so again. Afterwards, they even took the initiative to go to the Beirut YMCA program person to set up programs for these youngsters.

"The situation" must have had profound impact on the larger university and its surroundings as well.

JAKOBSSON: Yes. Our students could cross register in courses over at the old American University, and we received students from there. (They didn't have social work on their campus, and we had students who wanted to take psychology or other courses over there.) We were six or seven blocks away from each other, but during the fighting this was often a difficult area to traverse.

In principle, we were always open during "the situation." In practice, we sometimes had to close because the students could not leave their homes. Sometimes, we might open in the morning but have to close down after an hour or two because the students had to try to get home before things got worse, or soldiers might come and tell us to get out. We faculty members were advised always to give many tests so that students could receive final grades for the year maybe as early as March instead of June.

There was the threat of kidnapping going on all around us. Our university's Presbyterian minister was kidnapped one day when he was going out with his wife. After he was kidnapped, I received a letter from him written the week before, asking me to come to a meeting. That was a bit spooky.

It was trying, but still it was of great importance to do your work under these circumstances, even though you could not quite make it the way you wanted it. A major challenge was to send students out in the field. There were virtually no supervisors. One of my best students called me when I had already stayed on in Beirut beyond the time I was supposed to leave for my summer vacation. She had asked to do some Red Cross work in the coming academic year, but said she had just heard that the agency to which she was assigned had been totally destroyed by bombs. So I had to stay on a bit longer and try to find another placement for her.

On the Christian side of the Green Line there was a Jesuit university, and they had a social work program. In Beirut we couldn't cross the dividing line, but their faculty members and I could meet at international social work conferences. It was strange but good to meet abroad. Many colleagues who could not attend would send messages through someone. Maybe now, 15 years later, we can meet in Beirut.

I had helped to interview somebody to take over after I was to leave. She wanted to come, and I introduced her to the dean and said, "This would be just the person. She lives here. She knows much more about the country and local affairs than I do. She can speak Arabic as well as English. She has a degree from an American university." I think the real reason she was not accepted was that her husband was with the opposition political party.

While serving in some of the world's trouble spots, I understand that you have been required to have a bag packed at all times in readiness for departure. Could you tell us about that?

JAKOBSSON: It used to be that the bag was ready because I was on a series of contracts with the United Nations High Commission for Refugees (UNHCR) and Swedish Save the Children. Both called on social workers who had experience working abroad and who could take leave in less than 72 hours. The first time I went out was during the huge exodus of "boat people" out of Vietnam. In helping set up a new refugee camp (at the time the largest in the world), I was told, "As you are a member of the Scouts, we expect that you will be ready to live in a tent and to cook your own food, if necessary. So be prepared."

This was only the first in a succession of such assignments?

JAKOBSSON: Yes, but I never applied for any of these assignments. All I had to say was yes or no. In one instance, I was called by an older colleague who said, "I think you should go to Africa instead of me because I want to go to the Galápagos and see the turtles." The Swedish International Development Agency (SIDA) wanted a four- or five-month survey of the refugee situation on the Horn of Africa, including a written report. In Somalia there were 1.5 million refugees in 26 ordinary camps, plus a number of reception camps.

So I went to Somalia, Ethiopia, Djibouti, and Sudan to see about repatriation possibilities for the refugees of war and famine. To get into Somalia you had to go through Nairobi, Kenya—to get in by the back door. Once in Somalia, you traveled without roads, right through desert.

I had a wonderful 19-year-old driver. We had five flat tires in one day. There was no petrol. We finally were given some that looked like orange juice. It turned out later that it had sand in it, and the engine broke down. We couldn't phone anybody. I spent the night in a rustic military camp. The next day an officer flagged down an overfilled bus and made sure I was squeezed in. I had some goats blowing on my neck and a bag full of chickens under my feet. The bus driver had the gear shift held together with a small ribbon that had to be tied and retied as we went along. When I finally got to the meeting, much too late, and told the story of our adventure, they said, "Oh, you're always wanting to go places by local buses. Don't complain."

Another trip was by air from Ethiopia and up to Eritrea. We were not supposed to go to Eritrea, but the team of which I was a member did not give up. We waited for hours outside the ministry. Finally, we did get permission, yet they didn't think we would dare to use it, but we did. And we did figure out why they didn't want us to go. We saw 14 Russian MIG planes and near the landing strips there were big fox-holes where guerilla soldiers were dug in. All along the route we had soldiers in front of us searching for land mines.

The authorities lost track of us for a while. When we met with somebody, he drove us around in his car because, he said, "The walls have ears." But on learning of our whereabouts, the authorities moved us to a luxurious hotel. Soldiers were posted outside our doors at all times, and we couldn't go anywhere except accompanied by guards. When we were finished and were to return by air to Addis Ababa, they said, "Nobody flies out of here when it starts to get dark because then is when antiaircraft guns shoot everything down on the assumption that they are military targets." But, as you can see, we returned safely.

Were most of your responsibilities on these assignments concerned with refugees of war?

JAKOBSSON: Much of my work was with refugees, but other assignments had more to do with general international aid. Sometimes surveys and planning were combined with something else. Sometimes I have headed a team, and sometimes I have been by myself. I was asked to evaluate a Danish project in Mozambique. I was also invited by a Danish governmental group with European Union funding to help the new Albanian government, especially its Ministry of Social Affairs, by teaching some basic ideas about modern social work. We met with an interesting group of people who came to the seminars earlier and earlier each day and stayed late despite some difficulties in translation. It worked out well, I think. The report of our seminars and visits to mountain hospitals were to end up in a document in both the native language and English, but I don't know what happened because the trouble in Albania and Kosovo began shortly after our departure.

Then, too, because I have worked in the Middle East and had good contacts on both the Israeli and Palestine sides, the University of Örebro was invited by UNESCO to join a project called PEACE. The university asked me to go in as one of a group of three for meetings in Nablus on the West Bank. Yasser Arafat himself came and gave an excellent speech, and the minister of education as well as the personal adviser to Queen Noor of Jordan (formerly the minister of social affairs) were present.

There were problems for the Palestinian participants on some days because of difficulties in passing military checkpoints, but the universities are open again and want cooperation with Europe. I hope to be able to go to Jerusalem and Ramallah in the near future and help to develop a master's program in social work.

And another of your activities has taken you to France.

JAKOBSSON: I came back not long ago from an interesting week in Caen on the Normandy coast. In World War II, when German-occupied France was first invaded by the Allies, Caen was heavily bombed, burnt out, and destroyed. After the war, Sweden gave the city of Caen and some surrounding towns a total of 400 houses and some day care centers for children, helping with training and equipment for the latter.

It was the fiftieth anniversary of that Swedish assistance, and the French invited representatives from the board of Swedish Save the Children to join the celebration.

We met old child care staff members and some of the first children of the day care center, by now 55 years old. It was very touching to see an almost bald man say to us, "I'm one of the twins. Do you recognize me? We were the first kids in this place." There was a lot of laughing and crying. We also visited some of the Swedish-donated houses that are still being used, and we discovered that no family wants to move from them. The streets and road signs still bear names like Stockholm and Bernadotte.

Still another of your recent adventures has been with the Baltic military forces.

JAKOBSSON: While I was working in the Middle East, some of the UN observers who were attached to the Swedish Defense College asked me to share my experiences of war, especially working with civilians and children, as part of the international training of Swedish military officers and Nordic police being sent out on UN missions. I've been doing that for a few years now. That led to my being asked to join a small team of two military officers and a Red Cross lawyer to train officers in the Baltic countries, some of them former Russian officers, for peacekeeping missions.

My part was to teach the officers about human rights, especially those related to the UN Convention on the Rights of the Child.

In modern war, civilian casualties are much greater than those of military forces compared with World War I, when civilian casualties were about 8 to 10 percent of the total killed, and World War II, when civilians were roughly 40 to 48 percent. Now in some conflicts as many as 98 percent of the casualties are civilians who are massacred. This is because of modern weapons such as land mines and so on, but it is also due to the horrendous ethnic and religious conflicts and hatreds in Rwanda, Bosnia, Kosovo, and elsewhere.

A measure of courage must be part of the equation that goes into acceptance of some of these assignments.

JAKOBSSON: I have been fortunate enough to be very healthy, so I have been able to take a lot of stress. Of course, you get some small illnesses when you are out in the field, especially in the Global South, but I have never been terribly sick. I did have to have part of a lung removed after coming back from one of the African trips.

On one occasion, I had reported to the Swedish government that the United Nations High Commissioner for Refugess (UNHCR) was performing extremely badly in Djibouti. Somehow that report reached Geneva. I was asked to please go to Djibouti and write what I thought should be done and who should be recruited as staff. That meant going right out to work in two big refugee camps to help them to decide what was needed. While there, nobody wanted to drive me. The UNHCR drivers were extremely pleasant but said, "We will give you the best vehicle, even though there are no roads. Stick with the stones put out by the French Foreign Legion, and you will be all right." But I had a great protection officer, a young man from Belgium. He would come with me any time. It wasn't that difficult; it's just that nobody wanted to be out in the dirt.

Among the many hats you have worn, you have served as president, vice president, or chairperson of various groups. Could you tell us about those?

JAKOBSSON: I have been the vice president of the Swedish Scout movement for many years, which meant I substituted as necessary for the president, who was a member of Parliament. During that period, I was heading a Sea Scout camp with 10,000 participants of all ages from 20 countries. We had some wonderfully competent leaders—professionals serving as volunteers.

I am the president of a school for adult education that is owned by the Swedish Scout movement. That is a very special Nordic type of adult education called Folkhögskola. About 150 adult students live there, including some who have mental retardation. The latter receive training for living alone or in group arrangements. Other students have dropped out of school and have come back. Many were poorly educated earlier in their lives. We have a great board! Six of us have been appointed by the Scout movement. The others represent the local area, one from the commune and one from the county.

I was vice president of the IASSW (International Association of Schools of Social Work) for eight years after having served on the board for a number of years. I am one of 12 members on the board of Swedish Save the Children, which has 110,000 members.

I also belong to a lot of women's organizations, for example, the Soroptimists, and I was national president of the Professional and Business Women's Organization.

In addition, I have served on the boards of the Inter-University Consortium for International Social Development (IUCISD) and its European regional branch for a number of years.

Also, the Ministry of Education appointed me to lead an executive group to plan and develop group placement and practice settings for six or so social work students per agency, something we had never before had in Sweden. The resulting plan was adopted as part of a total national program. This required a lot of negotiations with labor unions and so on to determine who would provide the supervision, who would have ultimate control—the schools or the government, who would pay for the field training supervisors, and what would be decided about leaves of absence for the field trainers.

Among your skills I have had the pleasure to observe are your presentations of papers and your presiding at meetings. Am I safe in saying that you have learned some tricks of the trade?

JAKOBSSON: We have found out, you and I, that while there are many similarities on the two sides of the ocean, we don't conduct meetings the same way. We are so bureaucratic in Sweden that we learn as schoolchildren how to carry on a meeting. We expect the chairperson to have planned the agenda, have it written, send it out, and stick to it. That doesn't mean that we can't be flexible, because we always have at the end of the agenda other questions and special points. As elsewhere in democratic organizations, between meetings the president's duty is to have a small executive group to deal with policy decisions in the interim.

And what of your public addresses and presentations?

JAKOBSSON: In making presentations I think it depends very much on the audience. I try, if possible, to know if the people in the audience are knowledgeable about the subject; who are they? I talk to children one way if they are in the first grade and another if they are in the twelfth. I love to talk to the first graders because they feel no restrictions about asking questions.

I hardly ever write out full concepts. I only note key words. At conferences, neither the audience nor the interpreters want you to read a paper. They want you to speak. At first I found it extremely difficult, but I now feel more free about giving papers. I like very much to have audiovisual aids, but I don't like overhead projectors because you have to turn aside and write or point, and that is sometimes a distraction. Also, sometimes the technical part can get so messy that it doesn't add to the presentation.

What do you consider to be some of your major accomplishments?

JAKOBSSON: I have been very lucky to have been involved in pioneer work. That included helping a child psychiatric setting get built. Then there is the School of Social Work that I helped to establish at the University of Örebro and the master's program at the University of Trondheim. There was that first refugee camp in Indonesia, and later my work with established refugee camps where I helped to change things. Also, there was establishing a social work program in Beirut.

I assume that you have had a core philosophy underlying your pioneer work?

JAKOBSSON: I have had the motto "Never give up," despite all the difficulties. The more I have been in this field, the more I do not look for problems. I look for resources. Also, after all of these years, I have come to the conclusion that most people want to help themselves, and what we must do is to support them in doing so.

Have you had what you consider to be some failures or near-failures?

JAKOBSSON: Sometimes I use a whole session to share with students all of the things that went wrong in my practice, for that is a way to learn, too. Very many of those mistakes were in that first large refugee camp in Indonesia. I came from Sweden; I had a man on my team from England and one from California. I was working with a man from Ireland and off and on with a social worker from the Philippines.

With all this diversity we first tried to do things by the book. That didn't work. For example, we thought we should meet with the camp committee made up of refugees, and we called them and an interpreter, but nobody came. We learned later that the refugees thought while we had asked them to the meeting, they should have been the ones to ask us! We had made an agenda, which to them was absolutely wrong. If they were going to talk to us, they were going to make the agenda. These were seemingly simple things, but you can see how understanding cultural differences can play a key role.

Some nurses wanted to have a vaccination program in a refugee camp in Djibouti. They invited the refugee mothers and children to a vaccination day, but they weren't getting the mothers' cooperation. They asked me what to do, and I said, perhaps recalling the previous experience, "Have you talked with the elders, the older men with the beards, the top men in the camp? Otherwise, you won't get anything done."

The nurses asked the elders for a meeting, but the elders said that they would only talk to me. Actually, I shouldn't have been helping the nurses because they were from a nongovernmental organization (NGO), but I was the only UNHCR person present and was in charge of the camps, and so the elders wanted me there at the meeting (perhaps because they thought I was old enough to be a counterpart).

The three nurses were sitting next to me, and the old men across from us. The elders talked directly to me, I talked with the nurses, and then back to the elders. In 10 minutes we had it all fixed. The old men went out and told all the mothers to bring their children, and that was it.

We learn from our mistakes, many times the hard way. We could easily be upset if we do not know the local culture and language well enough. It can also be dangerous if you know only a few words. The people may then think you know the language. I have seen it happen. Then they ask you a question, and it's impossible to answer. But sometimes you can learn by exchanging; I give you one word and you give me one word. I have found that to be the case in talking with adults and playing with children. They teach you words, and they laugh their heads off when you can't pronounce them correctly.

Is there anything else you would like to say with respect to your greatest challenges or those that you see for the profession as a whole?

JAKOBSSON: We think that we can apply knowledge, and sometimes we can, but we have to prove that on a day-to-day basis. For example, in Beirut, four of my professor colleagues at the American University were taken hostage by Islamic militants, and I was in the room when they were taken away. Then, for almost a year afterward, I had to practice crisis intervention. I was the only person on hand who could help take care of the wives and other relatives of the hostages. Sometimes you get to use your knowledge in a way that you had never expected.

Social work training does not provide everything that social workers need to know. In the kind of social work that I have been doing, we must know much more about ecology, the environment, gardening, the necessity of clean water, and so on. We don't ordinarily learn very much about these subjects. However, when I went to social work school, we learned a great deal about garbage and sanitation practices. That has come in very handy in refugee camps. I knew how much a rat eats and costs in lost foodstuffs per day, and that if you have a certain disease you need a certain diet and so on. That was part of our social medicine course, which has now been cut from the curriculum.

A big challenge in many parts of the world is that our colleagues must teach with very few books and supplies. In Beirut, we copied as many books or parts of books as we could, and every time I went abroad I took books back for the students. Those are some of the things you have to do.

With all that you have done, could you share with us something about your honors?

JAKOBSSON: In 1987, the Central Association for Social Work, the oldest social work professional organization in Sweden, presented me with an award for "extraordinary inputs in the development of social work." In 1988, the International Association of Schools of Social Work (IASSW) presented me with a tribute for my courage, devotion, and contributions to international social work, social work education, and social development. In 1998, I received from the Swedish Scout movement a travel scholarship in appreciation for 30 years of human rights work, and in that same year I was recognized by the IUCISD with a lifetime achievement award for outstanding international service. Other recognition has included an award from the Danish Peace Fund and another from the Nordic Schools of Social Work. In 2000, I received the Katherine A. Kendall Award from the IASSW honoring a lifetime of distinguished international service to social work education. And, in 2001, Örebro University promoted me to an honorary PhD in social work.

Is there anything more that you would like to add?

JAKOBSSON: I have very many friends now among journalists. We discuss things such as how they quite often write about or show very, very poor children, those who are almost dying, and then when they have been showing them on television, they say, "We would like to have some money. We're fundraising." But I keep saying, "Tell about the children who might survive beyond next week if they receive aid. Because otherwise it seems so hopeless." Journalists are often very well informed and open to what is new, and you can get a lot of help from them.

You need your family and your friends and so on, but you also need the help of official persons in your own field and in related fields. It's good to consider these official persons as being not above your level so that you can talk to them and work with them. Diplomats often don't know the real situations. So many diplomats have said, "It's good to talk to social workers. They see things in a different way." So it is often a two-way street in being of assistance to one another.

ROBIN HUWS JONES

Born in 1909, Robin Huws Jones spent his early life in Corwen, a small town in North Wales. His mother died when he was three, and he spent most of his childhood in Liverpool with his father, a shop assistant. He left school at 15 and worked for 10 years in the Liverpool YMCA while taking evening classes. At age 25, he earned a bachelor's degree in economics with honors. He then earned a master's degree in social science at Liverpool University. His thesis on child nutrition earned him a prize from the Royal Statistical Society.

In 1939, Mr. Huws Jones became resident tutor in the city of Lincoln (United Kingdom) for the Oxford Extra-Mural Delegacy. In 1949, he was appointed director of social studies in the University College of Swansea (part of the University of Wales). While he was at Swansea, a special course of study was introduced, leading to the training of social welfare administrators, teachers, and practitioners from 60 developing countries. He was instrumental in organizing a creative and comprehensive interdisciplinary project to revitalize the industrially polluted Lower Swansea Valley.

In 1961, he became the first principal of the National Institute for Social Work in London, a center for training staff from social service departments to be responsive to changing needs of local communities. Mr. Huws Jones was president of the International Association of Schools of Social Work from 1970 to 1978 and received local, national, and international honors. He lived with his wife in York. They had one son, two daughters, and four grandchildren.

Mr. Huws Jones passed away in June 2001. He was a great age, 92, and died peacefully in the retirement community where he lived with his wife.

BILLUPS: *Could you please provide us with a glimpse of your childhood years or other influences in your early life that may have contributed to your decision to enter the human services field?*

JONES: I was born in Corwen in North Wales. My family spoke Welsh—not a dialect of English but a different language. In my parents' time, speaking Welsh was discouraged.

My mother died when I was three. My sister, less than a year old, was looked after by my aunts, and she looked after them later. My father took care of me. He was a draper, skilled but very poor. He soon left Corwen for Wrexham, in North Wales, where I picked up English. Later he sold cloth as a shop assistant in Liverpool.

We lived in a small, crowded working-class house. In Britain at that time, people used to accept lodgers.

At age 11, children took an examination that selected those who qualified for education until age 16. I was not considered promising enough even to sit for the examination. My first academic triumph had been to learn Welsh at the age of two, followed by my learning to speak English at age six, but years later I was still trying to apply to English the phonetic principles that govern Welsh spelling. My headmaster feared bringing discredit on the school by putting me forward as a candidate for high school. So I left school at 15 with no prospect of further education.

I got a job as an assistant librarian at the Central YMCA in Liverpool. I was really an all-purpose office boy. The working day lasted from 9 A.M. to 11 P.M., but included a lot of idle hours, which I used for reading. Later, my younger colleague and I organized discussion groups and summer camps for young dock workers, who were often unemployed. I made some good friends among the young men at the YMCA; 70 years later some are still my friends. Old men used to drop in to get warm and read the newspapers. On days off I sometimes visited them, desperate old men in cots in ill-equipped hospitals (This was 20 years before the National Health Service). I also visited young men dying in sanitariums; tuberculosis was prevalent.

Was it about this time that you were able to continue with your education?

JONES: Yes, by my late teens I decided that while still working for the YMCA I could take examinations leading to a London University external degree, a bachelor of science in economics and sociology. On my two or three free evenings I attended evening classes provided by the local Education Authority. By the age of 25 I had a bachelor of science degree with second-class honors.

Before this I had the fortune to meet David Caradog Jones, director of statistics at the University of Liverpool. He offered to advise me after I got my Bachelor of Science degree. This led to my enrollment for a master's degree in social science. He also helped me to find evening teaching to maintain myself.

The course lasted three years and involved fieldwork as well as research. The theme of my master's thesis was the nutrition of schoolboys, which during the mid-1930s was pretty terrible. Doctors working for the Education Authority used to visit schools and decide by looking at the boys which ones were undernourished and needed free meals. It was thought that a system based on physical indices, a combination of height, weight, and girth, might save time and money. My job was to test these indices, comparing them with the doctors' assessments.

In one school, I had to ask the doctors to reassess the children's nutrition data to test a proposed index. The reassessment showed a startling variation from the previous test. It seemed necessary to retest the doctors' assessment. I bribed the children with oranges (then a luxury for poor children) to come to school for a day in the holidays. Five doctors, experienced medical officers, examined a sample of 200 boys. One doctor said that 90 were malnourished, another said nine. The remarkable thing was that not all nine were included in the 90. The chief school medical officer said that such diverse results could not be published. I suggested getting other major local authorities to participate in the study. We obtained similar disparity in results from a considerably larger sample.

As a result of this research, I was invited to read a paper before the Royal Statistical Society. The results were quite sensational: Every British medical journal published an article on the subject. The Royal Statistical Society awarded me the Francis Wood Memorial Prize. I was then about 27.

I was invited to stay on for a year or two as part of the research staff of the University of Liverpool. I also served as a tutor at the International Labor Organization Summer School for Trade Unions in Geneva, twice during the 1930s and again in 1950.

Please tell us more about the early stages of your academic career.

JONES: In 1939, I was invited by the Extra-Mural Delegacy of the University of Oxford to become their resident tutor in the city of Lincoln. Oxford University had developed a tradition of teaching adult education in isolated industrial areas. The work of the Extra-Mural Delegacy included cultural activities and other programs helpful to the neighborhoods.

During World War II, Lincoln was surrounded by military airfields served by young men from all over the world. I was asked, in addition to my regular work in the city, to give talks to these men. I shall never forget my terror when the president of the University of Michigan sat in on one of my classes. They were on subjects I greatly enjoyed, especially the discussions afterward. For instance, the Beveridge Report came out with the proposals for a national health service. Again, one of my regular classes in the city made a local survey of juvenile delinquency. The survey, entitled *Who Has Offended?*, was published by the Workers' Educational Association.

Special lectures were booked from all over the world. Life for civilians was often very drab in wartime. The adult education movement in Lincoln brought in plays, art exhibitions, and concerts, where we listened to young performers in Air Force uniform who afterwards became world famous.

In 1943, I was sent by the Ministry of Information to travel on a submarine-infested Atlantic to North America to tell about war conditions here.

In 1949, a few years after the war ended, there was a change in my career. The University of Wales in Swansea approved me as director of the Social Studies Department, which gave the academic background for social work. This brought me in touch with people like Eileen Younghusband, whom I invited to become our external examiner, and Gertrude Williams, who was a distinguished writer on social affairs. Eileen Younghusband one day asked whether Swansea would be willing to start a special course for social welfare administrators and social work teachers and practitioners from developing countries. The idea was to help to promote the talents these men and women from around the world would need as they held or would hold positions on university faculties and in governmental departments. The request originated from the Technical Assistance Administration of the UN. I felt like I was caught up in a benign hurricane.

One additional member of staff was provided for, but we had little financial support. We had generous help from members of other faculties at Swansea and from staff at the University of Wales at Cardiff, including Andrew Lochhead, head of their department of social studies.

Eventually we had students from 60 countries—Portugal and Greece, North and South Africa, the Middle East, Southeast Asia and Japan, India, Pakistan, and Sri Lanka, and many countries in the Caribbean. I am still in touch with some of my former students.

Was this program the only one of its kind?

JONES: When it started it probably was the first and only. Many other educational institutions became involved later.

A few days after the students arrived in Swansea, they were taken in small groups to villages. They stayed for two weeks in the homes of skilled manual workers and shared the local life, attending political meetings, football matches, women's groups, and, if they wished, the non–Episcopal chapels then so important in Welsh life. One Saturday evening, a school caretaker put on his best clothes and took his student guest to hear a distinguished Cabinet minister speak about the legislation following the Beveridge Report. The Cabinet minister was the school caretaker's brother. Some of these village friendships led to correspondence and even visits many years later.

The students also went to London as a group, visiting the Houses of Parliament, meeting leaders from all political parties, and seeing innovations in social services.

In 1958, under the auspices of the Ford Foundation, I visited former students in the Middle East and Asia. I was happy to find that, as expected, many of these men and women had become leaders in social welfare and social work in their countries. These trips, to Burma, India, Malaysia, Singapore, the Middle East, and other places, were unbelievable adventures. I saw great beauty and terrible poverty. In the desert, I became aware as never before of the significance of water.

In 1955 you were appointed vice chairman of a British Ministry of Health committee.

JONES: Yes, it was a Ministry of Health Working Party on Social Workers in Local Authority Welfare Services, set up to consider staffing needs and make recommendations. Eileen Younghusband was the chair, so it was known as the Younghusband Committee.

A major finding was that local health and welfare services were complex, patchy, and inadequate. Eileen Younghusband proposed a staff college, which would train the trainers of local social service staffs. The term "staff college" I think originated in the armed forces, where staff were trained for special responsibilities, for instructing others not only in the subjects to be taught, but also in how to teach them and how to plan refresher courses to keep up standards.

When I read her proposal for the first time I thought that however desirable such a college would be, it would be too expensive to provide. How wrong I was! The day after the report was published, two foundations, the Nuffield Foundation and the Joseph Rountree Memorial Trust (now the Joseph Rountree Foundation) telephoned me in Swansea (Eileen Younghusband being out of the country) to say they were interested. Eventually they decided they would jointly promote organizing and operating the staff college, later called the National Institute for Social Work. It is housed in central London.

I was dismayed to receive a letter asking me to become the first principal of the National Institute for Social Work Training (as it was called at first). I was social policy oriented and did not have social work training. Also, I was deeply engaged in my work with overseas students in Swansea.

I believe that by this time another major project had emerged in Swansea?

JONES: Yes. On my frequent visits to London, the train passed through the lower Swansea Valley, one of the most appalling scenes of industrial devastation in Britain. This was one of the earliest sites where nonferrous metals had been smelted. There were great hillocks of toxic waste, poisoning the earth and the atmosphere so that not a blade of grass or even moss grew. This grim landscape was strewn with the ruins of industrial buildings. A lifeless river wound through the valley. Yet the valley was edged by fairly recently built houses for workers. Many attempts had been made over decades to revive the area but for various reasons, including the multiple ownership of the land, this proved too daunting a pursuit.

It seemed to me that an objective study of the history and characteristics of the area might lead to successful attempts to rehabilitate it. A proposal was put to the University College of Swansea to initiate an interdisciplinary investigation. The secretary to the government's Welsh office and the chief executive of Swansea Borough Council offered encouragement and my colleague A.V. S. Lochhead supported me throughout.

Ultimately, with financial and other support from central and local governments, the university, industry, and foundations, an extensive study and public education resulted from the collaborative effort of the Swansea Valley Project, and a major report was published. This extensive report carefully pointed to the multifaceted ways of redeeming and transforming the Valley physically, economically, socially, and aesthetically, while improving the surrounding poor urban environment. For example, one of many practical actions has been the planting of 130,000 trees and forest conservation educational programs.

At this point you were persuaded to leave Swansea?

JONES: Yes, but by this time a committee had been formed including representatives of the University College, Swansea County Borough, the Welsh Office, industry and the press. The project would go forward, though the process would be long and frustrating. At the end of the 20th century the slag heaps have gone, though some ruins remain as archaeological monuments. There are modern factories, sports grounds, and in some places woodlands and green meadows.

So now you are the principal of the National Institute for Social Work Training in London?

JONES: Yes. I started there in September 1961. When invited to become the first principal of the National Institute for Social Work Training, I talked about it with people at both of the funding organizations and refused. Eventually, however, I was reoffered the position and accepted it.

We aimed to train, much as the Younghusband report had recommended, to ensure that social work development would be relevant and responsive to the changing needs of local communities. We encouraged the local authorities to measure community needs and then to help social service practitioners deal with those needs. In addition, we offered both one-year and three-month courses for social service trainers and refresher courses for senior social workers.

We also produced teaching materials: Substantial books were published for us by Allen & Unwin and pamphlets mainly by the National Council for Social Service. One of our first publications attempted to evaluate the success of adoptions. Within the first decade of operation, 23 major works had been published, and in 1972 five more were prepared for publication.

One of the most important and rewarding things that happened was that Eileen Younghusband joined the staff of the institute as a consultant and served as adviser to a course of study set up for tutors of social service workers. Courses were generally held in the National Institute, but shorter courses were held in the North of England, Scotland, and Northern Ireland.

One of my special interests was to try to assess the value of social work to the client. I felt that this aspect was neglected. Miss E. M. Goldberg, OBE, who became our director of research, helped with this.

In addition to the major full-time professional responsibilities that you assumed over the course of your career, were there part-time civic and professional responsibilities that you assumed beyond the Swansea Project?

JONES: I sat on some important committees. From 1965 to 1968, I sat on the famous Seebohm Committee, set up by four government ministries to examine the structure and staffing of local government social services. Many of its recommendations became law in the early 1970s in spite of a change of government. I also served on the Minister of Health's Long Term Policy Group, the Minister of Overseas

Development's Advisery Group on Social Welfare, and the Colonial Secretary's Advisery Committee on Social Development. Nationally, I also chaired the Old People's Welfare Council Training Committee and the National Assistance Board Advisery Committee for a number of years. Locally, I served on a major metropolitan hospital board. In 1969 I delivered, at the invitation of the London School of Hygiene and Tropical Medicine, four Health Check lectures on "The Doctor and the Social Services." These were published by the University of London Press.

Didn't you also assume some professional responsibilities overseas?

JONES: Yes, in the early 1960s I consulted with the Indonesian Government, and I visited Vietnam for the British Council. Also, in 1964 I was a visiting professor and Hodgson Memorial Lecturer at the University of Minnesota in the United States.

Through your professional relationships overseas and through work with Dame Eileen Younghusband, you became involved with the International Association of Schools of Social Work, becoming its treasurer and later its president. What do you recall as some of the highlights of your involvement with the IASSW?

JONES: Naturally, our special course in Swansea for men and women from low-income countries put me in touch with schools of social work throughout the world, and I was given a great welcome when I visited many of them. My first direct contact with the IASSW was at its international conference in Munich less than 10 years after World War II. When I was finding my way about the city, the evening before the conference, I heard two people speaking English and asked them the way. One of them was Katherine Kendall. I have been asking her the way about the IASSW ever since.

Soon after the conference, I was asked to be chairman of the membership committee. Later I was asked to become treasurer. I was not a financial expert (though I was told later that I excelled as a beggar with charitable foundations) but it appeared that others would do the real work; I needed only to pronounce principles and see they were adhered to, and present reports. Meanwhile Katherine saw that the coffers were full. Finally, I became president.

During this period, what were the main issues for the IASSW?

JONES: One of the biggest issues while I was an officer and a member of the executive board of the IASSW was the government policy of apartheid in South Africa. Some of the countries, especially in Scandinavia, held that South African schools should be excluded from membership until apartheid was no more. Others among us thought that schools in South Africa that accepted black people as their students and faculty should be allowed to join IASSW membership. But the Scandinavian countries were determined, and I'm afraid they were so determined that it strained relations.

I also learned how difficult it was to be an executive board member and later president of an organization that was so far flung.

In choosing speakers for international conferences, we could not always rely on their addresses being relevant when they came from remote places with meager educational resources. I could certainly be blamed for some mistaken choices. Katherine Kendall, however, usually came to the rescue. There was nothing she couldn't do, really. She knew everybody and she'd been everywhere. Katherine always made it easy for people to be at their best.

In the late 1970s, it was decided to move the central administration of IASSW from New York to some other center. Europe seemed most appropriate. A number of fascinating venues were offered, but the final choice was between Vienna and a town near Brussels. In Vienna we were greatly helped by Dr. Maria (Dorli) Simon, who had just resigned from the directorship of the Vienna School of Social Work. She was indefatigable in arranging meetings with industrialists, financial wizards, and especially governmental ministries and civil servants. In the end, I had the honor of signing an agreement on behalf of the IASSW in the room with seven doors where the celebrated Treaty of Vienna had been signed.

Perhaps the high spot of my presidency was the Golden Jubilee of the IASSW, held in Jerusalem. It was, of course, a controversial meeting place, but we were received graciously and renewed and established many friendships.

One of your contributions was to encourage popular education in family planning. Could you please speak to that?

JONES: At that time Herman Stein, I think, was the president, and Katherine Kendall won the support of an American government organization concerned with population policy. It was hoped that social work teaching could help to get across the importance of population policy, because it did not advocate particular proposals or methods for restricting population. But we can't (and this is my own phrase) have death control unless we have birth control.

This, of course, is controversial and led to fierce opposition from political and religious interests. But a vigorous and stimulating meeting of an interdisciplinary advisery committee to the IASSW was held in the United Nations building in New York in January 1972. I enjoyed chairing this meeting for six years.

I believe you were invited to visit schools of social work across the world to see what they were achieving in relation to population policy?

JONES: Yes, and the task was formidable. The whole purpose of population policy was interpreted differently in different countries. Sometimes (for instance, in Iran) the restriction of population growth was alien to prevailing religious and political codes. In some other countries there was ready acceptance of the need to raise the age of marriage and limit the number of children. This series of visits was the most difficult task I undertook for the IASSW.

I have heard of the artistry that characterized your chairing of IASSW meetings, your ability to defuse a tense situation and your skill at turning a phrase with humor while striving for the highest goals and standards.

JONES: As chairman, I think my first rule would be constantly to look out for people who wanted to contribute. I would jot down their names and make sure that everybody who wished to do so would get a chance to speak. That's an essential part of chairmanship; I hope we now take it for granted. Sometimes I felt I failed, but usually the members would come to my rescue.

The great thing, really, is to have interest in the subject, get to know the people on the committee, greet them at the door to the committee meeting or before (in a way that they don't feel it is simply your duty to do so), and finally let them see in the meeting that they are going to be given a chance to speak.

You have been honored with not only the Francis Wood Award of the Royal Statistical Society but also with an Honorary Doctorate in Law. Would you care to share your reflections on these honors?

JONES: The first award was called the Francis Wood Memorial Prize. Nobody knew who Francis Wood was, and when I did inquire, nobody seemed to know. It just goes to show how very difficult it is to get a permanent memorial. It was a prized statistical studies honor in those days.

The honorary doctorate was presented to me by the University of Wales. The citation referred to the regular social science courses at the University College of Swansea, to the research studies started there, to the United Nations course, and of course to the Swansea Valley Project.

Still another honor, this for a lifetime of outstanding accomplishments with the IASSW and for your outstanding international service to social work education, was your receipt of the Katherine A. Kendall Award.

JONES: It is the only one that I publicly display, partly because of my great affection and admiration for Katherine.

On the subject of aging, do you have any reflections?

JONES: Well, I am 90 years of age, very old for a man, and I don't like it. That wisest of men, William Shakespeare, often said how awful age is, and I agree. These days when so many of us live to be old we don't even have those things that he said should go with age: "honor, love, obedience, troops of friends." Alas, when you get to be my age, the troops become straggly. But the one good thing I think that can be said about living to an old age was said by a distinguished Frenchman: "On the whole, it's better than the alternative."

A person with the considerable accomplishments that you have experienced ordinarily has a strong support system of some kind. Is that true in your case?

JONES: I had very faithful secretaries both in Swansea and London. I am lucky to be still in touch with both. One is in her mid-90s. Of course my wife comes immediately to mind for a variety of things for which she has been particularly supportive: her tolerance at my unavailability when she needed me; her not very willing tolerance of my bad temper when I was overtired; her readiness to give innumerable parties for students and colleagues from all over the world, the British ones as well. And especially when I was doing drafts of papers, many times she would agree to read them and help me with them.

Are there any closing thoughts you would like to share with members of the profession or for the students who are to follow?

JONES: I would like to say that if social work is to become fully and unquestionably a profession as is medicine, it must seek to establish clear evidence of the effectiveness of its achievements. We have to introduce more rigor into the profession.

KATHERINE A. KENDALL

Born in Scotland in 1910, Katherine Kendall traveled with her family to live in Chicago in 1920. She completed her undergraduate education at the University of Illinois, and after a few years in England and Spain, she returned to earn her master's degree from the new school of social work at Louisiana State University. Interrupting work on her doctorate at the University of Chicago, she served as assistant director of the international unit in the U.S. Children's Bureau and as a social affairs officer at the United Nations.

In 1950, her doctorate granted, Dr. Kendall was appointed executive secretary of the American Association of Schools of Social Work and in 1952 helped launch the Council on Social Work Education (CSWE). Over the next 20 years, she served the CSWE as educational secretary, associate director, executive director, and director of international education.

In 1950, Dr. Kendall was appointed to the board of the International Association of Schools of Social Work (IASSW). Elected honorary secretary in 1954, she served 17 years as a volunteer in this capacity. In 1971, she became the full-time secretary general of IASSW, until she retired in 1978.

Dr. Kendall was the first Moses Distinguished Professor at Hunter College. She also was a Carnegie Visiting Professor at the University of Hawaii, and taught at Howard University. She recently completed a monograph on the international beginnings of social work education. She has received numerous national and international awards and honors, including four honorary doctorates, and continues to give volunteer service to CSWE and IASSW. Dr. Kendall lives near Washington, DC.

BILLUPS: *What prompted you to take up a career in a helping profession?*

KENDALL: My motivation may have been a bit different from that of many people entering social work. The story begins at the University of Illinois in Urbana, where I did my undergraduate work in Romance languages, history, and philosophy. That is where I met my future husband, Willmoore Kendall, my Spanish professor, who became my fiancée. Although he was only a year older than I, he was already an assistant professor, working on his doctorate. We traveled in a young, rather Bohemian faculty crowd, much more interested in literature and art than in anything political or social. My firm intention was to become a journalist, a foreign correspondent.

That all changed when Ken won a Rhodes scholarship and spent three years in Oxford. When I finished my degree, I followed him to England. Again, we found ourselves involved with an interesting group, young student leftists and some rather special professors, mostly neo-Fabians. Everyone seemed to be left-wing in Oxford in the 1930s. We were in Paris at the time of León Blum and the famous sit-down strikes. After Ken and I were married in London, we lived in Madrid, where he was a foreign correspondent for the United Press. I tagged along, trying to learn all the things he was learning, first at Oxford and then in his work.

What was your life in Madrid like?

KENDALL: We were in Spain before the Civil War and became very involved with the supporters of the United Front that elected [Manuel] Azaña. We saw this as a triumph of democracy, and Ken decided Spain would no longer be very interesting. He wanted to return to academia, and a teaching fellowship offer from the University of Illinois prompted us to leave Spain in 1936.

What I saw and learned in Europe completely changed my goals. My exposure to the social movements of the 1930s and the causes they supported colored me "pink." I needed to do something about all that was wrong in the world around us. It was always understood in our marriage that I would have a career, and by 1936 I knew that it had to be something "social." But I had no idea what until I found social work.

How did you discover social work?

KENDALL: It took a little while because Ken, who was working on his doctorate in political science, had one of those teaching fellowships that barely keeps a graduate student alive. To keep us going, I worked two part-time jobs, one on the local newspaper in Champaign-Urbana and the other in a sorority house, where I was recruited as a tutor.

After Ken finished his doctoral work, we moved again, this time to Louisiana State University (LSU). Charles Hyneman of the University of Illinois, one of the well-known imports, was recruited to head the Government Department, and he brought Ken and me to LSU with him. At last it was possible for me to start my career, as we had a salary on which we could live comfortably. But what should I do? Law had been uppermost in my mind because, as a lawyer, one could certainly attack injustice. But law was not an attractive option in Louisiana, where the Napoleonic Code would have made it difficult to practice elsewhere.

Was that when you found social work?

KENDALL: Yes. Ken came home after his first day at the university and said: "Katherine, they're starting something new here, right in our building. It sounds like what you've been looking for. It's called social work. You had better look into it."

I did, the very next day. Louisiana was fortunate in starting pretty much from scratch in establishing its Department of Social Welfare. Relief had been handled by the parishes (counties) under old poor-law provisions that were readily abandoned after the passage of the Social Security Act. A number of first-rate, highly qualified social workers were imported to help set up and administer the new department, and one of the first things they asked for were qualified social workers. This led to the establishment of the social work program at LSU.

Runo Arné, the director, interviewed me. Classes were starting the next day, so he decided to let me in immediately.

I must have been a frightful pain because my passion for social action kept me on a soapbox all the time. I had decided the real job for social workers was to put ourselves out of business by changing the social and economic conditions that led to poverty and injustice.

That was what I proclaimed until I was placed in fieldwork. I soon discovered that unhappy and impoverished relationships can create every bit as much misery as inadequate social institutions. By the end of the first year, I became really convinced that social work had, and would always have, a helping as well as a social reform function. Perhaps only the rare person can function equally well both as a reformer and as a helper, but the profession can and should make room for both.

So you became a caseworker as well as a reformer?

KENDALL: That was certainly true in my first year in practice. As the first qualified social worker in the East Baton Rouge Parish Department of Public Welfare, I was given a specialized caseload (one hopes to demonstrate the value of professional education). It was a great responsibility and a marvelous experience that really helped to pin down the course of my professional life. It was a small caseload drawn from all the assistance categories. What the clients had in common was a perceived potential for a return to independence. I learned so much from them about living conditions, relationships, what happens to children, about resilience—most of all the ability of people to use help and resources. When I hear the discussions now on workfare and welfare reform, I remember that caseload. Good social work with adequate resources and sustained professional support on the road to independence is better than any answer I have yet heard.

Then you went on for your doctorate?

KENDALL: One of my professors, Henry Coe Lanpher, convinced me that I needed to study under Edith Abbott and Sophonisba Breckinridge at the University of

---

Chicago. There was a question of whether my master's degree would be accepted. The LSU program was accredited only for the first year. As I was the only student, my second year was highly individualized, with tutoring and special arrangements for fieldwork. I took extra courses in the social sciences to fill in gaps in my earlier education. It worked because of the personal attention I received from the social work faculty.

Edith Abbott accepted me for doctoral study, with the condition that I would do more fieldwork. Later, I was fortunate enough to serve as one of her research assistants. Working on the doctorate was pretty wonderful. With Sophonisba Breckinridge and Charlotte Towle in the classroom and Lois Wildy as my field instructor in child welfare, I was very happy.

Could you tell us something about the international responsibilities you assumed over the years following your doctoral studies?

KENDALL: I felt very much at home overseas. I have always enjoyed getting to know people in other countries and working with them.

My knowledge of Spanish started me on my international career. In the 1940s, the United States became involved in exchange programs with Latin America. The Children's Bureau, then in the Department of Labor, set up a special unit to organize study and travel experiences for the Latin American visitors. Elizabeth Shirley Enochs, who was an extraordinarily talented woman, headed the unit. She needed an assistant, and Edith Abbott suggested me. So I delayed my work on the doctorate for an exciting period with the Children's Bureau, working first with Latin American social workers and later, after the end of World War II, with social workers from all over the world. We organized educational programs and provided consultation and other services under the Truman Point IV Program.

By that time, Ken had gone to Hobart College in upstate New York. This was the beginning of my living in one place and his living in another. Sometimes I tried to follow him, and once he tried to follow me, but that didn't work. In time, this was a factor in ending the marriage, but not our friendship.

Tell us about your work at the United Nations.

KENDALL: It was a great. One of the first studies they commissioned was about the training and exchange of social welfare personnel, and I was recruited to do it. I turned it into a survey and analysis of training for social work all around the world.

In 1947, the UN was shining new and idealistic. We were located at Lake Success in a barn of a building that had produced material for the war effort. Now it was a peace factory. The people there were so imbued with the promise of the United Nations that there was no question in their minds that the world would become a better place, with no more war and maybe even no more poverty.

The UN then was not so bureaucratic; communication flowed easily. I got to know members of the Social Commission who helped in locating the best people to provide data. I was able to go directly to government agencies and practically every-where for information. Later, such requests had to go through departments of state or foreign affairs. As a result, I got to know, at least by correspondence, leading social work educators in almost all countries where there were schools of social work. Then, in 1950, at the first International Congress of Schools of Social Work after the war, I became involved with the IASSW—the International Association of Schools of Social Work.

This was my first congress, but I had been in touch with officers and members of the IASSW in connection with the UN study. The report had just been issued, and I was invited to be the keynote speaker to the congress and to comment on the report's findings. I was pretty scared. The speech itself created a flap because I was making the case for university education for social work before an audience made up primarily of Europeans. Except for the United Kingdom, social work education in Europe was under nonuniversity auspices.

After the Congress, Dr. René Sand tapped me on the shoulder and said: "You are on the Executive Board of the IASSW." That was how board members were "elect-ed" in those days! René Sand was one of the greatest people I have ever known. He was truly a Renaissance man, a medical doctor with a social mission and who was knowledgeable about everything from art and architecture to the furthest reaches of science. He founded the International Conference of Social Work (ICSW) and, with others, the IASSW. He initiated social work education in Latin America and was a key figure in WHO and other international organizations. He believed in social work and professional education.

You began your administrative responsibilities with the IASSW as its elected secretary. Could you tell us how that came about?

KENDALL: Well, in a way it was René Sand again. As a member of the board, I became fascinated by the organization and the people in charge. While I was still with the United Nations, I persuaded Sir Raphael Cilento, the assistant secretary general in charge of social affairs, to sponsor an expert group meeting of social work leaders to advise the UN on its social welfare activities.

This was right after World War II. A number of outstanding leaders were on hand, and great efforts were being made to restore communication. Both the ICSW and the IASSW were in a state of disintegration and shock. To help revive them, the National Conference on Social Work sponsored an international conference at the time of its annual conference in Atlantic City.

René Sand attended as the major representative of the ICSW and also as president of the IASSW. He was invited to speak at the end of a business session of the American Association of Schools of Social Work. Because of a slipup of some kind, there were only six people in the audience to hear him bring a poignant and beau-tiful message from "the schools of the old world to the schools of the new world." He was visibly shaken and very angry. He thought the American schools were turn-ing their backs on their international colleagues. I, too, was angry and made a vow that I was going to make American schools aware of the IASSW if it was the last thing I ever did. This was a little like my social action days back in my youth. The IASSW became a cause.

Not long afterward, the American Association signed up its entire membership as members of the IASSW. My becoming executive secretary of the American Association may have had something to do with that.

René Sand died in 1953. Dr. Moltzer of the Netherlands was doing his best as secretary, but he knew it was time for a change. He said, "It's not for us now. Younger people have to take over." I was offered the job as president or secretary. What they needed most was someone who would do the work, so I opted for secretary. But I had to be sure it was okay with my boss, Ernest Witte, because by that time the Council on Social Work Education had been established. I was the educational secretary, and Ernest was executive director. How I loved that man! He provoked some people, but everyone admired him.

I was in charge of accreditation, curriculum development, consultation, and all the educational services. We were understaffed and very busy. Ernest said, "You can do it, if you do it on your own time and it doesn't cost us anything." "Okay," I said, "I'll take that."

You really had two jobs, one with the Council and one with IASSW?

KENDALL: In a way, yes. Because of all the people who were working with me, it worked out fine. That was the joy of it. The new president of IASSW was Jan de Jongh, director of the Amsterdam School of Social Work, the oldest school of social work in the world. He was also the Dutch representative on the UN Social Commission. Dame Eileen Younghusband of the United Kingdom, one of the greatest of our forebears, came on as vice president. Then there was Charles "Chick" Hendry of the University of Toronto, who took over as treasurer. The team, including myself as secretary, was elected in 1954 at the second postwar International Congress of Schools, held in Toronto.

We started doing all sorts of new things, some of which our old friends in Europe were a little worried about. Remember, we were all volunteers. They wondered how we could possibly manage to run the organization with a secretary in the United States, a treasurer in Canada, and the others, including most board members, in Europe. Up to that point, almost everything had been European. We immediately began to involve the developing countries, all the new nations that were producing their own leaders. Latin Americans had been somewhat involved, but only peripherally. We got them in up to their necks. That led to the establishment of the Latin American Association of Schools of Social Work. As more and more schools and educators in Africa became involved, we helped them create the Association for Social Work Education in Africa.

It was in Asia that we probably had our most far-reaching influence. One outcome of our family planning project was the creation of the Asian and Pacific Association for Social Work Education.

Those were some of the accomplishments in the years when I was the secretary, due without question to the many outstanding people who gave volunteer service to the IASSW.

The IASSW has been fortunate in its leadership.

KENDALL: Indeed it has. After Jan de Jongh, Eileen Younghusband served as president for eight years. She stayed with us as honorary president until her death in an automobile accident in 1981. For me, it was a tragic personal loss as well as a loss to the field. Then, Herman Stein continued the tradition of great leadership. I had worked with him on countless projects at the Council on Social Work Education, so it was a tremendous joy to work with him as president of the IASSW after I had become its secretary-general. The last president with whom I worked was the delightful and talented British educator and internationalist Robin Huws Jones. The presidents had much in common. One delightful feature they shared was a marvelous wit and sense of humor that saved the day when board members got tied up in knots.

When did you become executive director of the Council on Social Work Education, and what was the arrangement with the CSWE and with IASSW?

KENDALL: I was with the Council from the beginning in 1952. As executive secretary of the American Association of Schools of Social Work (the graduate schools), I was one of the midwives at the birth of the Council. Betty Neely (the assistant secretary of the American Association) and I were the first staff members. My job was educational secretary. In 1958, Ernest Witte decided he needed an associate executive director, and I was appointed to that position. When Ernest left in 1963, I somewhat reluctantly agreed to serve as executive director. I said I would try it for three years, as I much preferred working on educational questions. Ernest had done a splendid job of fundraising and administration, and I knew it would be difficult for anyone to match his talents in those areas. However, I did enjoy it and was able to keep a hand in the IASSW through the employment of Alix Szilasi as an administrative assistant for international work. She was a lifesaver, with her command of many languages and exceptional administrative talents.

From the beginning, the council had a strong international outlook. Ernest Witte had carried out a number of overseas assignments. Mildred Sikkema, who early on had been added to the staff for accreditation and other educational services, was deeply interested in cross-cultural studies. She helped enormously with the IASSW. Betty Neely had close connections with a variety of international organizations. Arnie Pins, who joined me as associate executive director, was also very international. So, I was not alone by any means.

At the IASSW, we had revamped the bylaws to introduce some democracy into our operations. There was a clause limiting terms of office to four years with the possibility of reelection for another four years. An exception for the position of secretary was introduced when my name kept coming up every four years for reelection.

It became rather farcical to think of this as an elected office. But in 1966 I had to make a decision.

The IASSW board, looking towards the possibility of an independent secretariat, changed the elected office of secretary into a staff position as secretary general. Jane Hoey had left the IASSW a little money, which enabled us to work on plans to raise money. This was the period when President Johnson had declared strong support for international education. The U.S. Congress in 1966 passed, but unfortunately never funded, the International Education Act.

John Gardner, one of my favorite people of all time, was U.S. Secretary of Health, Education and Welfare (HEW). He was given authority to administer the act and set up a center in HEW for that purpose. Money was to be made available to educational institutions and associations. He was a good friend of the Council, and all of us saw this as a beacon of hope for financing international activities. The Council Board established a Division of International Education. Universities all across the country were doing the same thing.

I had to make a choice. The IASSW wanted me to take over as secretary general. At the Council, we had already added an amendment to the bylaws to affirm our interest in international cooperation. I left the post of executive director of the Council to become its director of international education. It was pretty much understood that I could also serve as secretary general of the IASSW. In other words, we split the difference, using whatever resources were available from the IASSW to add to CSWE resources for the new Division of International Education. Herman Stein was president then and with Arnie Pins taking over as executive director, I had strong support for our international work. It was great while it lasted.

I left the Council in 1971. With a huge grant from the Agency for International Development (AID) and additional support from the Swedish and Canadian counterparts of AID, the IASSW was able to set up an independent secretariat. We remained in New York near the Council. I not only had a full-time job as secretary general, I had a staff in this country and regional representatives in Asia, Africa, and Latin America. We recruited educators from each of the regions as our representatives. This helped enormously in our work.

The funds were given to promote social development and family planning. It was the right moment. Both were emerging as new responsibilities for social work education, particularly in the developing countries. The projects made possible all sorts of good things—seminars, advisory services with consultants from every region, books, and teaching material. It was a great period and lasted until my first retirement in 1978.

What about CSWE? Did it continue its international work?

KENDALL: Toward the end of the 1960s, the international emphasis began to fade. This was the time of student and faculty uprisings. There was a whole new look at minorities and their position in social work and social work education. When I moved into full-time work with the IASSW, the international emphasis was no longer as significant in the American schools. They had too many other things on their minds.

Years later, colleagues such as Werner Boehm, another committed internationalist, began agitating for an international committee at the Council. He finally succeeded. Lynne Healy, Terry Hokenstad, Chuck Guzzetta, and many more good colleagues got behind the movement. Now there is a Commission on International Education, which is doing a great job. Lynne Healy discovered what was being done in the schools; she found there were more faculty members interested in international work and content than we had realized. It was a matter of bringing them together. The commission has done that.

What would you say are the highlights of your career?

KENDALL: It was an exciting experience to be in on the birth of CSWE and to be the key staff member in launching its educational services. For about five years, I traveled the United States and Canada as a consultant, working with the graduate schools on curriculum building. This was the period of changeover from the Basic Eight to the generic curriculum. For many of the schools, the CSWE consultation visit was the first time the total faculty along with field instructors devoted a concentrated period of time to looking at objectives, working over learning experiences, and thinking about evaluation. It was an exhilarating assignment for me, and it was apparently also very helpful to the schools, even the oldest and the most exalted of them.

Then, of course, there were the six years of the family planning and social development project with the IASSW. So many splendid things came out of the consultation visits, the seminars, the work groups, and the interdisciplinary involvement that I can only say it was the experience of a lifetime to be in charge of the project. I had a great staff and an advisory council of nationally and internationally renowned leaders in both social work and population activities. We had representation from the UN and use of UN facilities for our meetings. Using regional staff and consultants from other professions as well as social work, we were in close touch with schools in the developing world, particularly in the Middle East, Asia, and Africa.

These activities also led to good work on indigenous curriculum development. We would all sit down together as colleagues to figure out the best way to produce quality social work graduates, ready and eager to meet new challenges.

What are some other highlights of your career?

KENDALL: It was my work with the United Nations that made it possible for me to have all those wonderful experiences later. It immersed me in social work education around the world and put me on the track for the rest of my professional life. At the time, too, it was important for the profession, particularly for social work beginnings in the developing world. As a result of favorable discussion of my report on training for social work, the Social Commission sent a significant resolution to the Economic and Social Council and the General Assembly, where it was adopted in 1950. It says:

That social work should in principle be a professional function performed by men and women who have received professional training by taking a formal course of social work theory and practice in an appropriate educational institution ... and that these courses, whether provided in universities or special schools, should be of the highest possible quality and should be sufficiently comprehensive to do justice both to the variety and the unity of social work (United Nations, Social Commission Report 1950: 3).

That sounds like the United Nations calling for social work education.

KENDALL: Indeed it did, and social work in the newly independent nations took off, maybe not like a rocket, but [the resolution] certainly gave it a boost. What it did, in effect, was to establish social work as a profession that required special preparation. That had not been thought of much before in the work of the United Nations. So in providing social welfare advisery services, the UN gave high priority to training programs. That meant starting work or improving schools of social work. UN and UNICEF programs also included international and regional seminars, expert groups, and fellowships as well as technical assistance. The IASSW was a partner with the UN in all those activities.

So the study did have quite an impact in the beginning. I guess it could be rated as an accomplishment. I remember particularly having a great time with a collection of definitions of social work. They ranged from social work as alms-giving in Saudi Arabia to the advanced professional services of the United States and the United Kingdom.

As an exercise, I played around with the international definition of health in the constitution of the World Health Organization. It was amazing that with a few word changes, it could have been a definition of social welfare, broadly conceived. The Social Commission members were mostly ministers or heads of social welfare programs in their countries. It was lucky they were so well-disposed toward professional training. The commission asked for a follow-up report at four-year intervals. Eileen Younghusband did the *Third International Survey of Social Work Training.* It was much more significant than the first one, because it got into the nuts and bolts of professional education. For many years it served as the bible for curriculum building in new schools. Much of what she defined as the core still holds true. I believe there were five studies before the Social Commission and the Economic and Social Council became less and less social and more and more economic in their activities.

Training for Social Work: An International Survey *was published by the United Nations Department of Social Affairs in 1950. Didn't it later become the basis for your doctoral dissertation?*

KENDALL: Actually, in effect, this was it. Helen Wright, the dean of the School of Social Service Administration at the University of Chicago, was my adviser. We talked about the study as a possible dissertation before I took it on. She wondered whether there would be enough depth and analysis to make it viable as a dissertation and kept that question open. We worked together on the questionnaires, and I made frequent trips to the university for her guidance; there was nobody at the UN who could work with me on this. As the data piled up and the study took shape, it was obvious that all the requirements for analysis, depth, creativity, and the like, could be met.

The New York School (Columbia now) placed a foreign student with me for fieldwork. She was Swiss and practically lived with me throughout much of her second year. Our methods were pretty primitive. Everything had to be sorted by country and then by subject. We had all these little piles of information about the individual schools and about social work. When we ran out of space on desks, we sorted on the floor. When we ran out of space at the office, we sorted on the floor of my apartment in Great Neck. Most of the material was in English, French, or Spanish with a little in German. I knew French and Spanish, and my student knew German as well as French. Between us, we could handle translation of the data.

The translation of the questionnaires and the final translations of the report were done by professionals at the UN, and therein lies another tale. When the questionnaires were sent to the translation service, I asked for a Russian version. That could be done only if authorized by the USSR delegate to the Social Commission. I buttonholed him, told him about the study, and asked for his help.

He would have none of it. He said the USSR didn't need social work because there was no poverty. Also, he was sure that what came out of the study would be American propaganda. Well, I answered, he knew more than I did because I wouldn't know what would come out of the study until I had the data. If he wanted to outdo the United States, he should be sure that the Soviet point of view was represented. For that, we had to have answers to the questionnaire. Well, he agreed to talk to me in my office, but only for 30 minutes.

I had pictures of three of my godchildren on my desk. When he came, he looked at them and asked if they were my children. I said: "No, they are my godchildren." He looked puzzled and asked: "What are godchildren?" I explained as best I could and then asked if he had children. He did, and they lived in Brooklyn. We talked about his children and how they were doing at school, and so on.

Then, I asked about children in the USSR. Were they ever abused, neglected, or abandoned? Most countries have problems like that. Yes, the children in Russia sometimes had problems. Then I asked how they were handled and learned about the special cadres to take care of such things. And did they have special training? Yes, they did. Well, we went through the whole range of Charlotte Towle's common human needs and problems—all, that is, except poverty, which I carefully avoided. The upshot was that they did have ways of dealing with social problems but, as you would guess, they were not the ways of the West.

He stayed for almost an hour and agreed to have the questionnaire translated and sent to Moscow. That was the last I heard of it. Although it was foolish to think there would be a reply from the bureaucracy in Moscow, it was a disappointment.

What have been your greatest personal challenges?

KENDALL: Of course, we are constantly being challenged in social work. That seems to go with the territory. It was sometimes hard for me to juggle jobs, the Council and the International Association. It did mean long hours. It also meant I always used weekends and vacations for IASSW business. Almost all the trips I took, lots and lots of them, I had to do on my own money and the only money I had came from my salary. But then, I don't live expensively so that didn't matter too much.

Time was perhaps more of a problem. I did a lot of writing at the Council— speeches, reports, policy statements. There was a lot of traveling as a consultant on curriculum building. On the plus side, I had wonderful help. I was blessed with first-rate assistants and, as the years passed, a great many dedicated IASSW volunteers. That was certainly one of the most satisfying aspects of my work with the IASSW. There were so many committed colleagues, I can't begin to name them all.

Are there other personal challenges you recall?

KENDALL: There are indeed. One of the major challenges, particularly at the beginning, was to make the IASSW truly an international organization. Until 1954, it was called the International Committee of Schools of Social Work. It had started in Europe in 1928, and after World War II Belgium, France, Germany, Switzerland, Holland, Italy, and the Scandinavian countries dominated the scene.

Before the Nazi period in Germany, the schools there played an important role. Alice Salomon, one of the founders of the IASSW and the first president and secretary, came from Berlin. She has been called the Jane Addams of Germany. Her family had lived in Germany for many years. When it was discovered that she was Jewish, Alice was expelled in 1937 by the Gestapo. She became a refugee, and it broke her. She had always had a red-carpet welcome wherever she had gone. As an exile, her life was very different. Many people tried to help her, but the adjustment was too difficult. In 1948, she died a lonely death in the United States. Fortunately, Alice's truly remarkable contributions are now being brought to light in research by German social work educators, notably Joachim Wieler. (That was a detour, but I had to say something about Alice Salomon. We don't pay enough attention to the contributions of our pioneers.)

To get back to the challenge: Parts of the world other than Europe were represented in the IASSW, but only peripherally. At the beginning, there were some Canadians and a few from the United States. Also one or two from Chile and Brazil, where René Sand had so much influence.

We worked awfully hard to identify schools and individuals and get them involved. The UN study helped. All the schools and the leaders who had contributed data became interested in continuing some connection with international colleagues. The new schools were eager to join an international organization, so it wasn't too long before the membership increased by leaps and bounds. This made it possible to hold our Congresses in parts of the world where we had not been before. Now, of course, the influence of the West is no greater than the influence of any other part of the world. In fact, it may be less.

The ongoing challenge that all social welfare and social work organizations face is the challenge of finding money to do the job. It's not at all ennobling to be poor. It's a pain. And it keeps us from doing what really needs to be done.

Those are professional challenges. What about the personal side of your life?

KENDALL: There have also been physical challenges. I sometimes describe myself as a bionic woman with ersatz ears, corneal transplants, and a rearranged interior. In my early twenties, I learned that I was losing my hearing. Hearing aids took care of that; again, I was lucky. I had excellent bone conduction, so the aid I used the rest of my professional life was tucked away behind my ear. Very few people knew I used one. Now, I flaunt hearing aids in both ears. For a brief period I was legally blind, but corneal transplants came to the rescue. Finally, I had the good luck of having stomach cancer discovered early. I lost the stomach, but survived with no great continuing problem.

These were all challenges that were inconvenient, although not in any way a hindrance, except when I wanted to go overseas during World War II. I was with the Red Cross, but couldn't pass the physical exam. Thanks to modern medicine and my Scottish genes, I am in good health and perhaps might even be called well-preserved.

And indeed you are. But have you ever experienced what might be considered failures in your career? Or let me put the question this way: Has there been anything you would have liked to have done differently?

KENDALL: There is one area in which I fear I failed. At one time, I thought that the real answer for social work education consisted of producing graduates who were first well-educated and then well-qualified through professional preparation. It was my idea to put together the social studies they had in Britain, before it changed, with the graduate training we had in the United States, before it changed. In other words, I wanted our undergraduate education to achieve what the British saw as social work education. This was a broad social science curriculum with an emphasis on economics and political and social theory, together with some social work subjects and practical training.

A professor in Britain, Roger Wilson, once said something I have never forgotten. I can only paraphrase it. He said that social workers get such a bellyful of life in working with people that they have to know a tremendous amount about society, economics, politics, and so on, in addition to what they know about people and how to help them. It seemed to me that building on such a base would prepare students to make good use of the more rigorous social work preparation that characterized our graduate programs in the United States. Our undergraduate programs do some of what I had in mind, but not nearly enough.

Of course, there were other things I wish I had done differently. I wish I had been more aggressive about some things, and sometimes I wish I had been less aggressive.

It's hard to find a happy medium. There was evidently a suspicion at one point that those of us who worked so enthusiastically for the IASSW were a tight little group. I don't think that was true, but you can see from my frequent references to certain people that we were close. Jan de Jongh and Eileen Younghusband and Herman Stein and Robin Huws Jones—we were friends as well as colleagues and did spend a lot of time together.

There may have been a perception that we were too Western oriented. In fact, I think we were rather good in making an almost exclusive European organization into a broadly international one. We did more than most Western educators I know in encouraging indigenous curriculum development. I think the schools with which we worked in non-Western societies would agree.

What are the issues that you think are likely to deserve, if not demand, increasing amounts of time, thought, and energy in the near future?

KENDALL: This is a time of great crisis for the people we serve and for the profession. In the social professions, whatever they are called, we face a strong backward movement. We see it even in Scandinavia. Of course, they are still way ahead as a welfare state, but they are rethinking their "safety nets." They can no longer do all that has been done before. They have to restructure. We have to restructure in this country. Canada is questioning what they can afford. One could go on and on for one country after another. And where does social work fit in all this restructuring?

Before we get too pessimistic, let us remember there is one place where social work is a bright and shining discovery. In the countries of Eastern Europe, programs of social work education are going well. I'll never forget a letter I received from one of the Hungarians who attended an IASSW seminar in this country and then became qualified as a social worker in Australia. He was so full of enthusiasm about this new way of helping people. He is now one of the leaders in social work education in Hungary.

I think we have to start looking seriously at ourselves, examining what we teach. This is a different world from the one in which many of us functioned as practitioners and educators. The Great Depression and the New Deal gave us our first big chance to make a difference. You found social workers in leadership roles in all the public services. Then we were out front in the war against poverty in the period of the Great Society.

It was the same on the international front. After World War II, when the UN began promoting social welfare services and sending advisers to all the new nations, some sort of social welfare provision was always included in their constitutions because that was what one needed to do to be a decent country. You had to look after people. Some of the developing nations are now going backwards, just like so many of the countries in the industrialized world.

Where do we go from here? I think we must do a lot more thinking about community, not in the sense of community organization, but rather in community renewal. We need to work with others in developing the forces and the resources that will help us get back the feeling that ours is a compassionate society. One of my heroes, John Gardner, is working on this in a movement called Alliance for National Renewal, which is gathering significant support across the country.

A new century is upon us, and new ways of dealing with social problems are needed. I don't have answers, but I do think that whatever we do in social work has to be more community, internationally, and globally oriented. This would certainly have implications for social work education.

The IASSW, the International Federation of Social Workers (IFSW), the ICSW, and the Inter-University Consortium for International Social Development (IUCISD) have all organized their international conferences around themes of social development and socioeconomic development for a number of years now.

KENDALL: Social development involves other disciplines as well as social work. One of the new ways of doing things would be to become more interdisciplinary in social work education. We have become too insular. I worry a lot about private practice and how that affects the curriculum. If private practice is the major purpose and end result of our professional preparation, I am not sure that we are doing the job that social work was created to do.

We were born out of a need to help everyone have a reasonably decent standard of living, a decent life with dignity. Remember what Franklin Roosevelt proclaimed: No one should be ill fed or ill-housed. Look at the nation today and the world around us. Despite the strong economy, too many people are hungry and homeless. I know we are working on such issues, but it isn't as obvious as it should be that social workers are the frontline troops in battling the reasons for that kind of misery.

We have lots of introspection in our field, but it has been related more to ourselves than to the purpose of social work in society and the world. We are not here to serve ourselves or our narrow, special interests. We are here to serve our own society and others in the global village in a particular way.

What are some of your current activities?

KENDALL: I'm still very much involved with the international work of the Council on Social Work Education and the IASSW. They both had the bad judgment to make me an honorary life member of their boards of directors. That means I attend all the meetings. So I expect to totter in at the age of 98 and in a quavering voice say, "Now, this is how we used to do it in the olden days. We tried that and it didn't work." Thus far, they have been very patient.

I participate in the IASSW Congresses. At each one since my first retirement, I have said: "This is it. This is the last one." Then, I keep turning up, mostly because I have heard that this old friend or that one will be making a speech or getting an award. Or it's in a country or city I love and want to visit again. I always have an interest in the subject matter, but now I'm afraid my interest is more in meeting old friends. I do help out the IASSW in any way that I can, now that it's once again managed by the officers and volunteers. The secretariat in Vienna had to be closed because of financial difficulties. Fortunately, the current officers are doing a fine job in putting the IASSW back on the track.

At the CSWE, besides being on the board, I'm active with the Commission on International Social Work Education. Until 1999, I also handled, as a volunteer, the Council's work on foreign equivalency determination. Actually, I started that job way back, soon after my retirement from the IASSW in 1978. It's a fairly complicated job, as the workers come from many different countries with many different educational systems, so it's not a matter of finding content identical with that offered in the United States (if that were true they would probably be dysfunctional in their own countries), but of assessing the overall comparability of subject matter and learning experiences. I was often conflicted. Because of my firsthand knowledge of so many competent social workers emerging from programs different from ours, maybe my calls on equivalence tended somewhat to the generous side, but I also realized standards must be maintained.

I understand there is not only a currency to your activities, but also an interest in preserving the historical record.

KENDALL: I sometimes think my major role these days is serving as the institutional memory for both the Council and the IASSW. For some time, I had been working on a history of the first 20 years of the Council to document the facts with little reference to all the interesting people who were associated with the Council. That makes it a dull history. Perhaps that's why I can't seem to stay with it. Well more than 50 percent is done, and I must do the rest.

At the moment, however, I have completed a historical record that I find so fascinating I just had to finish it. You will remember that we celebrated the centennial of the profession in 1999. The hundred years was based on the beginnings of social work education in the summer course organized by the Charity Organization Society (COS) in New York in 1889.

Well, in Britain and in Holland, there were a number of developments that either predated or went on simultaneously with the birth of the profession in this country. Octavia Hill, for example, started training volunteers in 1873 with objectives and principles of individualized service, which Mary Richmond once announced as the start of training for the profession. The University Women's Settlement in London and the London COS organized courses in the 1880s and 1890s similar to the course offered in New York. In fact, the impetus in New York probably came from the experience in London. It was exciting to find that a significant International Congress of Charities, Correction, and Philanthropy was held in Chicago in 1893 at the time of the Chicago World's Fair. The charity reformers were all very much in touch with each other. The very first school of social work in the world was established in Amsterdam, Holland, in 1899 with a two-year program and a curriculum we would recognize. It occurred to me that we needed a monograph on our international beginnings. I have just finished it.

Congratulations on the completion of this book [which has since been published].

KENDALL: This has been my life—always lucky. Elliot Richardson, my dear friend who had been living here at Collington, arranged for me to have a study room in the Scholars Program in the Library of Congress. I went down there at least three and usually four days a week. It was an unforgettable experience to work in those surroundings. The Library has every conceivable book and document on what I needed. The great problem was when to stop reading and start writing.

The approach I took in the book is a little different than the usual historical account. What I tried to do is to have all the reformers and pioneers tell the story in their own words. Using quotes from original sources, I let them say who they are, what they are trying to achieve, and how they are going about it. For me, at least, that makes it all come alive.

It is amazing how many parallels I found with present-day welfare reform. They were fighting pauperism, not poverty, and their main objective was to get people off the poor law dole or weaned from handouts. Some of the quotes I cited in my book could have come from our current crop of welfare reformers, particularly Republicans.

I understand you have also been close to the Social Welfare Archives at the University of Minnesota.

KENDALL: All of the CSWE archives have landed there. When I retired from the IASSW, I sent the archives everything from 1929 to 1978. When the IASSW secretariat in Vienna closed recently, another batch of material was shipped to Minnesota. It arrived in scores of cartons and David Klaassen, the curator, must have thought: "Good heavens, what am I going to do with all this stuff?" He was very relieved when I offered to help. I have been there twice, spending a week each time, sorting it out.

What a fascinating archive it is! I wish I were years younger so that I could write a history of the IASSW. I hope some ambitious young scholar will do just that. My papers and all sorts of letters are also filed there in an archive.

Through your career you have collected more than archives. You have collected a number of honors and awards. Tell us about them.

KENDALL: My colleagues have been very good to me. A substantial number of the awards have come from the Council on Social Work Education, starting way back in 1964 with an Outstanding Service Award. Now there is a Katherine A. Kendall Program Fund that was established in 1995.

Louisiana State University has also been very generous. In 1972, the University Alumni Association selected me as Alumni of the Year, the first time a woman had been so honored. To cap it all off, I was awarded an honorary doctorate in social work in 1987. The University of Chicago, another alma mater, honored me with a

Professional Achievement Award conferred by their Alumni Association. Ten years earlier, in 1971, the School of Social Service Administration gave me its Distinguished Alumni Citation.

The University of Illinois also awarded me a Honorary Doctor of Social Work degree, in 1989. The University of Pennsylvania gave me a Honorary Doctor of Social Welfare and Syracuse University also awarded me a honorary degree.

Other honors include a honorary diploma from Paraguay in 1960; the establishment in 1991 by the International Association of Schools of Social Work of the Katherine A. Kendall Award for distinguished service in social work education worldwide; and a number of appointments as honorary president and lifetime member of boards and commissions. Whatever pride I take in all of this needs to be shared by many other people who worked with me through the years as staff, fellow officers, and volunteers.

I understand that you have an active social life.

KENDALL: Yes, I get teased as the Pearl Mesta of social work. I like to get to know people outside of conference rooms. Asking delegates from the UN and UNICEF home for a drink and dinner made it possible to explore all sorts of things that helped to make cooperative work easier. Also, I liked to have board members at the Council get to know each other, especially when there were new members, so the first night of a board meeting, I would have them come to my house for cocktails. It may have made a difference. I don't know, but I liked doing it.

Another social activity of sorts that was great fun was putting on skits at the Council's annual meetings. We stopped writing skits when everyone became so tied up with protests. Social work had lost its sense of humor.

You did a lot of serious writing as well on social work and social work education. Fifteen of your articles and addresses were published as Reflections on Social Work Education. *Are there any current reflections you care to share?*

KENDALL: I fear we have entered a period when we are not highly valued. It is very important that we continue to value ourselves, what we know and what we do, and try to overcome the obstacles in our way. Of course, the current social and political climate is not in our favor.

How do you think we should view our international involvement?

KENDALL: We should be more careful in our judgments on international matters. I want international solidarity. Of course, we must build on the local, national, and regional, but too often social workers get stuck on their own narrow vision of the world. I see a lot of that in the United States. I suppose it is understandable, considering the severity of the problems we face at home. Yet I keep hoping for more give and take, so that we can appreciate the whole while working on our special interests.

FAITHFUL ANGELS

Despite all the cultural differences, we have many goals in common throughout the world. We may have different conceptions of the role of social work, but you can't get away from the fact that there are common human needs and common human and social problems. At the IASSW international congresses, I have seen many a conversion as participants from different countries get to know one another.

International experiences also produce new ideas. Social development, in which you have such a strong interest, is one such idea. Way back in the 1950s, it was known as community development. Then it was rural development. Then it became developmental social welfare. The UN and UNICEF were probably the most instrumental in getting the idea of social development into social work. Now it is being explored in scholarly publications, but we still haven't quite discovered how to make it more clear as one of the objectives of social work education.

This brings us again to interdisciplinary collaboration. Social development will never be ours alone. We may be missing the boat a bit by not having more to do with other disciplines working in this area. There are some colleagues who are active on this. David Cox of Australia is one; Jim Midgley of the United States is another. Your own Inter-University Consortium for International Social Development is a chief proponent of this approach as well.

The IASSW has just published a new directory of some 1,500 programs called social work or social "something." Now, we have to find or discover what social work is and what the social "somethings" are. Social development is in there somewhere, as there is definitely a resurgence of interest in it as a field of practice for social workers.

❦

JOHN LAWRENCE

Born in 1931, John Lawrence is a graduate of the Universities of Adelaide and Oxford and of the Australian National University. Australia's first professor of social work, Dr. Lawrence headed the School of Social Work at the University of New South Wales for 14 years (1968–1982), chaired the university's Faculty of Professional Studies, was a member of the University Council, and was central to the development of the university's Social Policy Research Center, a national center directly funded by the Australian government. He taught social policy for 30 years, with special interest in the ethical justification of policy and of professional intervention. He is a former president of the Australian Association of Social Workers and served on its National Ethics Committee.

For eight years, Dr. Lawrence was elected to the executive board of the International Association of Schools of Social Work. He has held positions in the governing bodies of community agencies, including the vice presidency of the Australian Council of Social Service (ACOSS). A firm advocate of international experience, he spent almost seven years away from Australia studying, researching, teaching, and acting as a consultant in England, the United States, Canada, Thailand, and Sweden. Among his achievements were a Rhodes Scholarship, Fulbright Senior Awards, the Moses Distinguished Professorship at Hunter College in New York, and a Canadian Commonwealth Fellowship. He is a member of the Order of Australia. He is married and the father of two sons and a daughter.

BILLUPS: *Could you share with us some of the early life influences or experiences that helped steer you into social work?*

LAWRENCE: I was guided into social work by Trevor Jones, who was a psychologist on the staff of St. Peter's College, the private

Anglican school that I attended in Adelaide for the final five years of my secondary schooling. After a year at a state high school, I was admitted to St. Peter's. My schooling at both state and private schools gave me an awareness of class and religious differences, prejudices, and opportunities, although Australian society was obviously not as socially stratified as societies in the Old World. The headmaster of St. Peter's was Colin Gordon, a rather enigmatic Englishman whom I came to respect, especially in my final year, when I was the captain of the school. He helped me with my high jumping and later urged me to apply for a Rhodes Scholarship to Oxford. I had no clear career ambition while at school. According to a family story, I once answered the question "What are you going to be when you grow up?" with "I don't have any ambition; I'll just go into the bank like dad." My father entered the Commonwealth Bank at the age of 16 and left at 65.

My brother and I were born in Mount Gambier, a small country town. After transferring to the Adelaide branch of the bank in 1934, my father became notorious in bank circles by refusing all further transfers until his children were educated. This took a considerable length of time, my younger sister finally graduating in economics in the early 1960s. Neither of my parents was university educated, but all three of their offspring became academics.

My parents were basically decent, responsible people who loved, encouraged, and supported their children. I can remember my father saying when he heard that I might choose social work as a career, "You won't earn a lot of money, but you should have work when others are out of work!" His mother had been an active member of a Ladies Benevolent Society. My brother and I recall being excluded from the room in their house in South Melbourne where she placed cakes, pastries, and other perishables she distributed to "the poor"; she had collected them from shops at the end of their trading week. Apart from Grandma Lawrence, I was not aware of any particular welfare tradition in the family.

As well as being the first vocational counselor to be employed by an independent school, Trevor Jones also happened to be on the board of the social work course at the University of Adelaide, so I was obviously extremely lucky to discover social work as a career option. I was, in fact, the first male student recruited straight from school to this particular course. At the time, only the Universities of Sydney, Melbourne, and Adelaide had social work courses or programs. Trevor Jones suggested I combine the diploma in social science (a social work qualification) with an arts degree in history and political science. (I topped the state in history in the Leaving Honors examination, which served as matriculation for university study.)

Studying modern greats, or PPE (philosophy, politics, and economics), at Oxford helped me to decide to seek social work employment on my return to Australia, partly because the field was still small and I could be part of its development.

What was the nature of your education for a career in social work?

LAWRENCE: My combined diploma in social science and honors BA in history and political science at the University of Adelaide (1950-1953) included four field placements: at the Catholic Family Welfare Bureau, the state Child Welfare Department, the Australian Red Cross, and a Commonwealth Government Repatriation Department hospital. My time as a sergeant psychological examiner in a unit of the Citizens Military Force under the command of Trevor Jones was also counted as relevant. My honors thesis for the bachelor of arts was a historical study entitled "Australia—Wide Old Age Pensions."

At Oxford, I attended Magdalen College, following in the steps of other Australians, including Malcolm Fraser, a future Australian prime minister. Bob Hawke, another future Australian prime minister, was a fellow Rhodes Scholar while I was at Oxford, but he chose the postgraduate route. I might also have undertaken a postgraduate degree but was well advised that postgraduate study at the university tended to be a rather isolated and lonely experience, and I would get more educational benefit from further undergraduate study.

PPE covered six compulsory subjects and two electives. The compulsory subjects were general philosophy from Descartes to the present, moral and political philosophy, theory and working of political institutions, British political and constitutional history since 1830, principles of economics, and economic organization. My electives were British social and economic history since 1760 and the political structure of the British Commonwealth.

I was secretary, then president, of the Raleigh Club, a club of Commonwealth students who met to discuss social and political affairs, often with an eminent speaker. The focus was on the emergence of independent nations from their former colonial status.

One curious aspect of the Oxford experience was the virtual absence of sociology as a recognized discipline. Amy Wheaton, the director of the University of Adelaide social work course, had already given me some sociological education, but the first full chair of sociology in Australia was as late as 1958. For someone like myself with a developing interest in social structures and social relationships, this was a matter of concern.

Tell us about your first professional practice responsibility.

LAWRENCE: On my return to Adelaide, I was employed briefly as a social worker by the Family Welfare Bureau, which helped ex-servicemen and their families. My next employer was the Commonwealth Department of Social Services, which under the direction of Lyra Taylor had developed a nationwide social work service connected with Australia's social security system. Our state social work director was Madge Forsythe, who had a master's degree from Case Western Reserve University in the United States. She provided excellent supervision, which I certainly needed and appreciated.

I provided casework service to beneficiaries in Adelaide and for a residential rehabilitation center. Lyra Taylor organized for me a study tour of the Central Office of the department, which was still in Melbourne. I remember vividly the head of the tiny research unit warning me that I would lose my academic soul if I worked with him, because his research topics and what he could say were heavily circumscribed by the government.

Generally, I could not have wished for a better setting for my early professional practice. We had good professional leadership and supervision, staff development programs, staff conferences, and a national social policy framework we were expected to understand and contribute to.

During this period, I became secretary of the small South Australian branch of the Australian Association of Social Workers (AASW) and was the organizing secretary for the Sixth National Conference of the AASW. Through the conference work, I became familiar with colleagues in other states and with leaders in the field, most of whom attended the conference.

Am I correct that this practice experience was followed by doctoral study?

LAWRENCE: Yes. My early practice experience, including my experience with the professional association, convinced me that social work was likely to be a worthwhile long-term career. By 1958, social work education in Australia had been developing for three decades, and many of the pioneers were still around. No history of Australian social work had as yet been undertaken, so my next career move was to do just that. A doctoral research scholarship in the History Department of the Research School of Social Sciences at the Australian National University in Canberra made this possible. I was only interested in the scholarship if I could do this topic.

The Australian National University (ANU) began after World War II as a completely postgraduate research university. Distinguished scholars were recruited back to Australia from overseas to head its schools. Historian Keith Hancock led the Research School of Social Sciences. He had been the general editor of the official civil history of Britain in World War II and had invited Richard Titmuss to write the volume on the social services, despite his lack of academic qualifications. That volume is said to have led to Titmuss's seminal appointment to the Chair of Social Administration at the London School of Economics.

Hancock suggested Titmuss as an examiner for my PhD thesis; the other examiner was W. D. Borrie, a notable social historian and demographer who had taught in the University of Sydney social work course in the 1940s. My thesis supervisors were Robin Gollan, a labor historian; George Zubrzycki, a sociologist; R. S. Parker, a political scientist; and Borrie.

My historical study of the development of professional social work in Australia was well supported by my social work colleagues. The research process was often tedious, hampered by inadequate or no archival policies and poor recordkeeping. When I could locate a document, I often had to copy it by hand like a medieval monk. It was, however, a rare opportunity to study a nascent profession with the collaboration of most of the main participants.

The ANU Press published *Professional Social Work in Australia* in 1965. Regrettably, it is still the only general historical account available. I updated it to some extent in 1975 and in the early 1990s.

I understand that you entered into an extended period as a lecturer and, later, professor of social work, as well as an administrator.

LAWRENCE: During my research for the doctorate, my wife and I had lived in Sydney, Melbourne, and Adelaide. We were particularly attracted to Sydney as a place to settle because of its cosmopolitanism and natural beauty, and because of the range of challenges and opportunities offered by its size. I was interested in the possibility of a community work position where I could make greater use of my educational and research preparation than in a casework position, but the only job available was assistant to the executive director of a state council of social service. It was a very poorly paid position with no obvious career prospects.

By this time we already had two young children, with a third on the way. Instead of returning to agency practice, I took an academic appointment in the social work school at the University of Sydney. The director of the department was a British urban sociologist, Tom Brennan, who was familiar with the British postwar university development of a subject rather misleadingly called social administration. I was to undertake teaching and research in social administration, the first such appointment in Australia. I was responsible for Social Theory 2, a final-year degree subject that combined social philosophy, the analysis of social welfare problems, policies and provision, and organization theory. This was compulsory for social work students, but also could be taken by arts students. One of those was Charles Perkins, one of the first aboriginal Australians to graduate from an Australian university. Charles was to become a controversial aboriginal leader with fluctuating fortunes. At one stage in the 1980s, he headed the Commonwealth Department of Aboriginal Affairs.

My colleagues included two founders of Australian social work, Norma Parker and Kate Ogilvie. Kate was a key figure in the development of medical social work and the New South Wales Council of Social Service. Norma was the outstanding first president of the Australian Association of Social Workers (AASW) and played a large part in the founding and early development of the Australian Council of Social Service (ACOSS). Kate had strong links with British medical social work. Norma had a master's degree and social work qualification from the Catholic University of America and maintained a particular interest in social work in North America. She was, however, very much an internationalist in her belief in the need for the profession to be operating appropriately in all societies where intelligent, informed, professional help could assist people. Norma has been a special friend and mentor throughout my professional life. In 1969, I compiled and edited a book, *Norma Parker's Record of Service*, to mark her retirement, and was delighted when this contributed to her receiving an honorary doctorate from the University of Sydney.

Although my teaching and research responsibilities were focused on the social, political, economic, and institutional context of the social work profession, I continued to be an active member of the AASW at the state and federal level. I also recruited others to the profession.

My appointment in 1968 to the University of New South Wales to fill the first full chair of social work in the country gave me a rare opportunity to shape a social work curriculum and to develop a full range of postgraduate educational opportunities: master's by research and by coursework, and doctorate by research.

In 1981, shortly before I ceased being head of the school, we had 423 students enrolled in the four-year BSW degree, 19 in the MSW (by coursework), seven in the MSW (by research), and four as doctoral students. Some of the early undergraduate teaching was done in other schools. In the early 1970s, the social reform Whitlam federal government offered funding for Australian schools of social work to increase their intake. I believed this was likely to be "soft" money, that social work should grow in open competition with other career options, and that already our school had achieved a reasonable size. Two of our academic staff did, however, benefit from a special scholarship scheme to improve their academic qualifications.

All our BSW students learned about the various dimensions of their profession—casework, group work, community work, administration, and research—with some degree of specialization, a major and a minor, and social welfare or social policy subjects, as well as human behavior and the social and behavioral sciences. Field education and classroom learning were integrated. The school employed a political/moral philosopher to teach two semesters of social philosophy, one a general introduction to ethics or moral philosophy, the other an introduction to political philosophy, especially democratic political philosophy, to attempt to give normative or value coherence to the various components of the course. We produced the first doctoral social work graduate in about 1983. Since then many have followed, both in our own and other Australian schools. My successor as head of school in 1983, Tony Vinson, was particularly successful in stimulating the school's research degree program.

Were you much involved in the life of the university as a whole?

LAWRENCE: Yes. The University of New South Wales developed soon after World War II as Sydney's second university. By the time of my retirement from the chair of social work in 1991, when I was appointed an emeritus professor, the university was rated as one of the best in the country, with a developing international reputation, especially in the Asian and Pacific region. It has been a pleasure to see it mature and to have been part of the process.

My membership of the Professional Board and on selection committees for the academic staff of different schools, such as law, history, philosophy, accounting, and community medicine, helped to keep my own discipline in a broader perspective and gave credibility to a newish venture like social work education.

I felt a responsibility towards the university as a whole, not just to my neck of the woods. In the mid-1970s, I took the initiative in the Professorial Board to establish a Resources Allocation Committee to monitor the university's allocation criteria. From 1979 to 1981, I was also a member of the governing council of the University.

When I joined the university, social work education had briefly been in the School of Sociology, but had then been established as a separate school linked with the Schools of Education, Health Administration, and Librarianship in a highly centralized Board of Vocational Studies in which the academic staff had no part.

I was responsible for negotiating a full academic faculty structure under the name of the Faculty of Professional Studies. I was its first chairman and chaired it again later. In 1985, I edited the faculty's joint and united submission to a university review committee, fending off an attempt to dismantle the faculty and lob social work back into the arts. The schools of our faculty were all professional schools preparing people mainly for work in the government and not-for-profit sectors of society. They had a common interest in the nature of professionalism.

In 1997, under financial pressure from the federal government, the university finally dismantled the faculty, with social work being relocated in a swollen faculty of Arts and the Humanities. Although there is considerable ambiguity, education for a particular profession and education in a particular subject or scientific discipline, though intertwined, are distinct. Professional education and research must be informed by the values and purposes of the profession in question, while discipline or subject education is informed by knowledge transmission and development. Academic structures have considerable influence on content and on educational outcomes.

During much of this same period, your professional responsibilities were hardly limited to your school or to your university alone.

LAWRENCE: True. While at Sydney University, I was the first secretary-treasurer of an association of teachers in schools of social work and was actively involved in the founding of the Australian Association for Social Work Education in the late 1970s. We already had formed the national Standing Committee of Heads of Schools in 1975. I represented this group in a joint committee with the AASW to review AASW accreditation criteria and procedures when relations between some of the schools and the AASW had become particularly strained.

When I was elected federal president of the AASW (1968 to 1970) education issues were paramount. Eligibility for AASW membership—following completion of an accredited education program—is the only nationally recognized qualification for social work practice. With a round of new social work programs in the late 1960s and early 1970s, some of them in colleges of advanced education, the professional association had to think through its attitude to the many program proposals coming forward. Because many of us in social work education were also active members of the professional association, the association managed to act as at least a minimum standard setter for the profession.

The overall entry standard was raised to four years of degree-level education, with various other requirements, and Australian social work was spared a proliferation of small, inadequate social work programs. All the same, in roughly a decade (1965 to 1976) Australia moved from four to 13 schools of social work, four in colleges of advanced education, and the rest in universities. The late 1980s saw the beginning of another round of new schools. By federal government decree, the system of colleges of advanced education was abolished, so all social work schools were now in universities, at least in name.

I understand that a national center with which you have been closely associated is of special importance.

LAWRENCE: Throughout my academic life, I have never lost my dual concerns for social work education and for social policy as a subject in its own right. For the past 20 years, my social policy concern has been reflected in a national social policy research center at the University of New South Wales. The current university leadership has referred to it as "a jewel in the crown of the university." It has published more than 140 research monographs, and its biennial national conferences have become a focal point for scholars, both national and international. Australia's Prime Minister addressed the 1995 conference, which attracted more than 500 people from government agencies, academia, and community organizations.

The Social Policy Research Center (SPRC) has stimulated social policy debate through seminars. It has built up a network of social policy research scholars, and has links to social policy centers and scholars in North America, Europe and an emerging a network in Southeast Asia.

The center's model has allowed all relevant disciplines, as well as government and nongovernmental agencies to contribute to the work. With a staff of about 30, the center's resources are, of course, still modest. It is, however, a significant movement in the direction of serious social policy scholarship and making social policymaking processes better informed.

However, the center's future is uncertain because of government withdrawal of care funding. If the center loses its breadth of mission, I believe Australia will have lost its only chance in this generation to develop social policy as a coherent subject or discipline. My own involvement with the center dates from its inception in the late 1970s. As head of the social work school, I chaired the steering committee of the Family Research Unit from 1972 to 1980, a national government research project financed through the Department of Social Security. In 1976, Max Wryell, a senior public servant on our committee, told me the Fraser government was going to establish a social welfare research center fully funded by the national government at the University of New South Wales. I became a member of the center's advisery committee, chaired its research management committee, and presided over its management board from 1990 until 1996, when I retired. I helped select the center's director in 1978 and again in 1986.

When I retired from the center, I was pleased to receive letters of appreciation from each of the successive directors, and also from the head of the Department of Social Security through which our funding came. In helping with this institutional development, I hoped I was making a far greater contribution to the long-term development of social policy as a serious subject than I could ever have made with my own individual research and writing.

I have never been a reluctant academic. I have positively enjoyed the degree of personal autonomy and intellectual freedom and interchange of a genuine university context.

What have been your primary areas of academic interest and scholarship? Have these changed over time?

LAWRENCE: Throughout my academic life, I have taught social policy, initially at the undergraduate level, then to postgraduate students in the 1970s. In the 1960s, I developed a social welfare framework that provided coherence to my teaching, research, curriculum design, and involvement with the SPRC. Its main components are charting the population, identifying their common social goals and means to their attainment, examining special population categories and their means for goal attainment, and examining outcomes of policy interventions. My social welfare framework provided a basis for comparative analysis, which, I argued in a paper to the SPRC in the early 1980s, is essential to the growth of the subject of social policy.

Now that my general book on professional ethics is behind me, I think my next project must be to write on social policy as a university discipline. My active interest in the history of the social work profession has been only spasmodic since my doctorate, although my conviction about the importance of historical study remains. It is often hard to give it priority in the face of the profession's contemporary and anticipated problems. On my "retirement" agenda is helping to establish adequate archival systems for both social work and social work agencies.

My doctorate stimulated my interest in the study of professions generally, and so did my involvement with the Faculty of Professional Studies and interactions with people from a wide variety of occupations. My book on ethics and professional conduct is now complete.

Can you tell us a bit about the book?

LAWRENCE: *Argument for Action: Ethics and Professional Conduct* was published in April 1999 by Ashgate, an international publisher in the humanities and social sciences. The specialized expertise and power of professions and professionals make it both difficult and pressing for them to identify and justify their contributions to society. That is the central concern that gave rise to the book.

The book is in two parts. In the first, the concepts of "ethics" and "professional conduct" are discussed through examining the relevant literature and constructing conceptual models for each. In the second, the model of ethical choice is used to discuss ethical justification of professional conduct in the various forms, locations, and stages provided by its social setting. The work concludes with a proposal for a national standing commission on the professions.

I have not lost my interest in social work, but rather have chosen to give priority in recent years to these broader intellectual grounding ventures, stimulated by my social work concerns and experience. For me, ethics or moral reasoning is the most significant human attempt to provide justification for human action. It should be central in all our educational and professional ventures.

Interspersed with your years in social work education in your homeland, you have had a rich variety of study leaves, visiting professorships, and teaching exchanges. Can you recount something about those experiences?

LAWRENCE: My first study leave, at the University of Michigan in 1967, made a lasting impact on me. It was the university's sesquicentenary, and there was a lecture series of "great minds of the century" that included people like Gunnar Myrdal, Raymond Firth, and Jean Piaget. In the first Younghusband Memorial Lecture at the international social work meetings in Montreal in 1984, I argued the world's general need for a reflective universal morality. The School of Social Work was large and flourishing, although some of its faculty were on soft money. I taught or co-taught three courses, or subjects, and monitored others. A faculty committee, which I chaired, made curriculum recommendations on social philosophy and professional ethics. And I was used as a consultant by Roger Lind, who was special adviser to the UN for the 1968 international conference of ministers responsible for social welfare.

In the summer, many of the American cities blew apart in race riots, including nearby Detroit. The extremes of wealth and poverty and the attitudes toward those who didn't "make it" in American society horrified me. Yet the year provided enormous professional stimulus, and my family greatly benefited from it.

We have maintained contact with some of our Michigan friends ever since that memorable year. I organized national residential seminars led by my Michigan colleagues Paul Glasser in 1974 and Rosemary Sarri in 1978. Rosemary's seminar was on the evaluation of social welfare programs. She and I produced a book from the case studies presented at the seminar. Senator Peter Baume, who chaired the Australian Senate Standing Committee on Social Welfare, was a participant and found it especially helpful, because his committee had a reference to report to the senate on the adequacy of Australia's health and welfare services.

I wrote for advice to the executive director of the Council on Social Work Education, Katherine Kendall. She channeled my letter to an excellent service in the U.S. Department of Health, Education and Welfare, which assisted overseas scholars to be most appropriately placed. That service sent my details to the six schools they deemed most appropriate; four were interested, and their correspondence was then sent on to me.

Having me was an experiment for the Michigan school. The school was on a roll; its morale could not have been higher. I recall Dean Fidele Fauri getting into trouble with the faculty because he told the university's president that perhaps Columbia University's School of Social Work still ranked ahead of Michigan's. Only up-to-date local knowledge in the United States would have identified Michigan as one of the best places for me to go for my sabbatical.

My second study leave was in the second half of 1974, in the Department of Social Administration and Social Work at the University of York in Britain. This allowed me to observe the rather troubled relationship between social administration or social policy and social work in that country. I found British social work fragmented. It did not have the same university standing as did social administration, and it had neglected management education, partly because of the educational ambiguity of the social administration courses. (In recent years, a number of the Australian schools of social work have tacked "and social policy" onto their names. This seems to me to court educational confusion, but it is easily done when a country has no independent schools of social policy teaching and research.) On our northern summer break in 1974, the family toured in Europe in a camping van, retracing some of the terrain my wife and I had covered in the summer of 1954.

My wife and I returned to the United States for another full year in 1983, at least partly for me to get out of the hair of Tony Vinson, my successor as head of the school at the University of New South Wales. This time, on the suggestion of Werner Boehm, I was a visiting professor at Rutgers University in New Jersey for the first half of the year and, on Terry Hokenstad's suggestion, at Case Western Reserve University in Cleveland for the second half. Werner and Terry were both former deans of their schools. In both places, I taught regular courses, made presentations to faculty and university colloquia on social policy and on the teaching of ethics, and visited other schools. The year was particularly notable because my wife, Trish, discovered she had a talent for sculpting, which she has developed seriously ever since.

I was the Moses Distinguished Professor at Hunter College in New York for another full year in the United States in 1987 and 1988, mainly working on my book on ethics and professional conduct.

For three months in 1990, I was on a teaching exchange at the University of Stockholm teaching a course on professional ethics. Before going to Sweden, we had two months at Wilfrid Laurier University in Canada, where I helped establish a social work doctoral program, did some teaching and consultation, and made presentations to a number of Canadian schools. I have greatly valued these opportunities to develop comparative knowledge, to see one's own country and programs in a broader perspective, and to build an international network of professional colleagues who share similar values and concerns. If I had my way, I would build into many people's existence periods of working and living in other places. Adequate professional knowledge can know no national boundaries.

During most of your career you have also been heavily involved in local, state, interstate, and national activities. Which of these activities received the most of your attention?

LAWRENCE: I have already mentioned some of my involvement at a national and interstate level in relation to social work education. My professional social work commitment has led to a substantial engagement in the social welfare institutions of my society. ACOSS, as the nation's peak social welfare body, has been of particular interest, and I had a range of involvement with it in the 1960s and 1970s when it was establishing a significant influence in community and government circles. The foundations for its present high profile in social and economic policy debates were laid then.

In the mid-1960s, I prepared the ACOSS contribution to the Terminology Project of the International Council on Social Welfare (ICSW) and edited the proceedings of its national conference. I gave plenary session papers at three successive ACOSS conferences and helped it to review its constitution in the early 1970s, and to pro-

vide a report to the National Poverty Enquiry in 1973. For five years I was an elected member of the Board of Governors, and was vice president for two.

In 1969, as federal president of the AASW, I gave two days of evidence in the first
"work value" case for social workers in the Commonwealth Public Service. The case
was an industrial milestone for the profession. For the first time, social work salaries
were aligned with the salaries of other professions with degree-level education. The
arbitrator was clearly a sympathetic listener to the social work case. At one point in
informal conversation, he disclosed to me that if he had his time again, this would be
the field he would enter. The successful pursuit of this case clearly gave lie to the
myth that social workers couldn't explain what they do.

Another national involvement I valued was being a member of a planning committee for annual national seminars run by the Urban Research Unit of the
Australian National University for four years in the early 1970s.

In 1979, the International Year of the Child (IYC), I gave the final overview at the
IYC National Conference in Canberra, edited the proceedings, and was appointed
to chair the conference follow-up group by the Commonwealth Minister for Social
Security. The follow-up group ensured that all of the relevant community bodies
were made aware of the content and the extensive recommendations that emerged
from the conference.

In 1986, on the suggestion of David Cox, I was invited to chair a New South
Wales committee of management and to be a council member for International
Social Service (ISS)–Australia, whose headquarters were in Melbourne. During the
next nine years, I helped ISS, an organization based on professional social work
capacity, to try to begin to fulfill the great potential I believe it has, especially in a
country of high migration like Australia. When I left we had a new national director operating with a three-year rolling plan, but lack of substantial funding was still
a major problem.

In 1992–1993 a group of us, including Alan Borowski, my successor in the chair
of social work at the University of New South Wales, induced the AASW to rethink
its handling of the so-called competencies project. This was a federal government
project emerging from the technical training sector that would cover preparation for
case aides and other professional support staff in social work. Its focus on skills reflected shallow, managerialist thinking. As the government tried to extend the project into
the university-educated professional sector, it ran into inevitable conceptual and
political trouble. Induced by federal government pressure and money, the AASW had
entered into a contract with outside consultants to identify social work skills. There
was no regard for the essential trilogy of values, knowledge, and skills that character-
izes professional practice.

I joined the AASW national standing committee on ethics when it shifted to
Sydney in 1993 and played an active role in developing the program and effectiveness of the committee as part of a nationwide system of ethics committees. We
revised the bylaws on ethics, set up a systematic recording system, carried out a survey of ethics teaching in schools of social work, and developed a kit on ethics especially for members of branch ethics committees. In 1995, I resigned with some

sense that my professional association was beginning to take more seriously its ethical responsibilities.

One occasion that I found particularly gratifying was an invitation in 1986 to speak on future directions for social work education at a seminar celebrating 50 years of social work education in South Australia, my state of origin. In the 1960s I was on committees of the Council of Social Service of New South Wales and the NSW Old People's Welfare Council (as it was then called). At the invitation of Hal Wootton, the founding dean of the law faculty at the University of New South Wales, I joined the council of the Aboriginal Legal Service at its inception in 1970 and stayed on it for five years, seeing it develop as a model for legal services in other states and moving to aboriginal management and control.

In 1977, I joined the board of the Benevolent Society of New South Wales, which took great pride in being Australia's oldest registered welfare organization. It ran the Royal Hospital for Women, a teaching hospital of the University of New South Wales, but its various welfare programs badly needed review and professional leadership. In my nine years on the board, I managed to help the organization to become progressive in its welfare programs and planning procedures, but I failed to achieve a change in its inappropriate 19th-century name. It was feared the organization would lose fundraising capacity if it lost its historical identity; changing the name that was enshrined in legislation required parliamentary action, and this was hazardous.

In 1982, I was given the difficult task of undertaking the first official child abuse inquiry in Australia. I was commissioned by the Minister of Youth and Community Affairs of New South Wales to inquire into the department's handling of a particular case and to make policy and procedural recommendations. My report, printed as a parliamentary paper, led to the appointment of additional appropriately qualified staff. Though the report made it apparent that the department required structural change and professionalization of its work, these have still not been achieved. Meanwhile, the department stumbles from crisis to crisis, with dire effects on its services to the public. I am distressed by the extent to which public welfare services are now so heavily concentrated on child abuse, rather than on child and family support systems.

You have been involved with a wide-ranging group of international organizations as well. Could you tell us about the major issues and concerns that you helped to address, and some of the outcomes?

LAWRENCE: As chair of the preconference working party for the 15th Conference of the International Council of Social Welfare (ICSW) held in Manila in 1970, I was thrown into the deep end of international conference discussion and politics. In the course of a week, something like 16 of us, drawn from different countries and international organizations, were expected to provide a report on the conference theme, using national reports. It was a remarkable, taxing exercise.

Together with Rifat Rashid from Pakistan, I served as consultant for an Economic Commission for Asia and the Far East–UNICEF seminar on developmental aspects of social work curricula in Bangkok in November 1972 and acted as chief reporter. My early interest in rehabilitation social work was rekindled when I helped in the planning of the 12th World Rehabilitation Congress, held in Australia in 1972. I helped to plan and chaired a seminar on social planning for physically and mentally disabled people that preceded the congress. We invited the distinguished African American social worker Jim Dumpson to be our main speaker. I served the Australian Council for Rehabilitation of the Disabled (ACROD) as a consultant on social planning.

In 1973, I was an active corresponding member of an ICSW committee looking at objectives of international conferences. It worried me that so much of the experience and talent represented at such conferences did not seem to be used effectively, and there did not seem to be ongoing work on particular topics. In all, I attended five ICSW congresses. Each immediately followed an IASSW congress.

My major sustained effort internationally was as an elected member of the executive board of the IASSW from 1974 to 1982. I served on steering and program committees for its congresses. In all, I attended seven of its biennial congresses. One of the lively issues was the emergence of the Inter-University Consortium for International Social Development. I attended the meeting of the consortium in Brighton, England, in 1982 before the main social work and social welfare meetings. I was not impressed by attempts by the consortium to nab speakers ahead of the other bodies or by any notion that the consortium was a legitimate substitute for the meetings of the social work and social welfare bodies.

I remember Katherine Kendall toying with the idea of changing the name of the IASSW to embrace developmental concerns, but I firmly believed that social work was the established international term for our occupation and that we had a responsibility to keep it progressive and developmental. I can recall Eileen Younghusband enthusiastically shaking me by the hand when I expressed this viewpoint. The last two presidents of the IASSW sounded me out about the possibility of running for the presidency, but I have declined and it is now too late. I couldn't get the funding that would be necessary for the travel, there were health considerations, and being a white male from a so-called developed country would not have been a political asset.

One aspect of the organization always worried me, and that was the low financial support provided by member schools. For many of the schools in more affluent countries, especially in North America, this represented for me an unacceptably low commitment to the profession at an international level. As head of a school, I was aware that membership dues were in the petty cash category for many schools.

In 1996, I resigned after 10 years on the editorial board of *International Social Work*, the official journal of the IASSW, the ICSW, and the IFSW. The editor invited me to write a guest editorial reviewing the journal, with comments on its future. This appeared as a discussion article in which I suggested the journal should become a specifically international journal for the social work profession, and the ICSW should establish its own journal.

Along the course of your career you have received several distinctions, awards, and honors. Could you share with us the nature of some of those?

LAWRENCE: For my university education, I was the fortunate recipient of a number of awards. A bursary for my Leaving Honors results paid for my time at the University of Adelaide. A Rhodes Scholarship for South Australia—there is one for each Australian state—enabled me to study at Oxford University. It took me overseas and, I am sure, permanently influenced my view of the world and my place in it. It did help me to realize that Australian academic standards were reasonable in comparison with those in other places. I have already mentioned my receipt of the doctoral scholarship at the ANU. This was government funded; I could not have paid for the degree from my meager social work salary.

Senior Fulbright awards supported my travel to the United States in 1967 and again in 1983. A Canadian Commonwealth Fellowship made possible my time at the Wilfrid Laurier school in 1990.

The year in New York, when I was the first non-American to be appointed as the Hunter School's Moses Professor, was especially memorable, because I could freely interact with all the faculty, which included Charles Guzzetta, whom I already knew well. Regular sessions about my book on professional ethics with Harold Lewis, the outstanding dean of the school, were a particular delight.

In 1997, I was made a member of the Order of Australia "for service to the discipline of social work internationally, and as the first Professor of Social Work in Australia, to the development of social policy research and to community agencies." Since 1975, I have been an honorary life member of the AASW.

Do you have any thoughts for the next generation of social workers and social work educators?

LAWRENCE: The present generation is far better educated than we were. It needs to be, not only to cope, but to improve life chances and life opportunities. We seem to be losing ground against the forces of commercialism, parochialism, and selfishness. Only by sustained organized action can the profession compete with what I might dramatically call the "forces of darkness"; the organization must cover all levels of human existence—local, national, and international. The idea of a profession needs to be better understood and welcomed, provided it is underpinned by moral reasoning that justifies our continuing place in human society.

❦

ESINET MAPONDERA

Born in 1925 in what was formerly Southern Rhodesia, Esinet Mapondera was educated in Zimbabwe, Botswana, and South Africa before receiving her advanced diploma in social work in 1964 at the Oppenheimer College of Social Work in Lusaka, Zambia (now the Department of Social Development, University of Zambia). She earned her master's degree in social work at Yeshiva University in New York in 1969.

She became one of the pioneer industrial social workers in her part of the world, first in her work at large copper mines and then at a large cement factory. In addition, Ms. Mapondera has been a successful market gardener and cattle farmer. She combined her skills and experience as a social worker and a business executive to found the Zimbabwe Women Finance Trust (ZWFT), serving later as its president. Her leadership at ZWFT has helped thousands of women learn new socioeconomic skills, promote their own credit opportunities, become skilled founders and entrepreneurs of their own businesses, and sustain themselves and their families within a part of the world that historically has experienced some of the harshest of socioeconomic circumstances.

Active on national and governmental boards, commissions, and committees in Zambia and Zimbabwe, as well as in international organizations such as Women's World Banking International, the International Ecumenical Loan Fund, and the Inter-University Consortium for International Social Development, Ms. Mapondera has also played a role in the liberation struggle that led to the independence of Zimbabwe in 1980. In recognition of her many contributions to the socioeconomic development of women and her other social welfare-related activities, she has received awards from business, church, and international social development bodies. She has four daughters and a son.

BILLUPS: *Were there particular early-life experiences that contributed to your decision to enter the helping professions?*

MAPONDERA: I was born in a rural village with an extended family. There was so much love in the village, like all other villages in rural areas of Africa where people live in clusters of kinship groups. It did not matter who fed or looked after me when my mother, father, or grandmother was not in the village. That helped me to grow up as a loving person caring for other people.

My paternal grandmother and my father, like my mother, worked very hard. When my father was a young man, he got a job with one of the gold mines where he herded oxwagons, earning two shillings and sixpence of British coins (equivalent then to about 25 cents) per month. He would give the money to his mother. My grandmother used the money to prepare for his wedding, buying a plough and gradually building a herd of cattle.

When my father got married, my grandmother had money to buy her first European clothes, rather than wearing traditional clothing made of animal skins. By 1940, she had become a rich woman by rural standards. Her grain bins were always full, and she had more than 20 head of cattle. At the age of five, I was given a cow by my father's cousin, and, by 1940, I had five head of cattle. This gave me the pride of owning property and built my self-confidence.

My mother lost her mother when she was six months old; her maternal grandmother looked after her until she was 10. When her father married another woman with four sons, my mother found herself a slave in her father's home, where she did all the housework and much of the fieldwork. She would sleep on bare ground without a mat or blanket. She became a hard-working woman and made me work hard as a child, both in the field and home. "One's hands are one's masters. One can never go hungry using one's hands," she used to say. In 1935, when she got seriously ill, I was not even 10 years old but I was prepared when I had to do the grinding of millet on stone grinders, make peanut butter, pound corn, cook, fetch water, and look after my younger sisters and brother until my mother got well.

There were very few secondary schools in Southern Rhodesia (now Zimbabwe), so when I was ready, my parents sent me to Inanda School in South Africa. During the holidays, I was a domestic worker for the Senator Edgar Brooks family at Adams College. I assisted his 85-year-old mother with great care. The way I looked after her was quite different from the other domestic workers. She told me, "Esinet, you are going to work with people."

I grew up being taught to face life realistically. I always tell people that I am a bush woman. There is nothing a rural woman does that I have not done. When I see girls and women struggling, they are reminders of my own life.

You also have happened to live in very interesting periods of history and early social work development in Africa.

MAPONDERA: Yes, in the late 1940s and 1950s, Africans wanted their freedom. Soon after Ghana's independence, Africans in the South started political movements.

In 1950, the African National Congress was rallied by the mighty African Mine Workers Union, which was highly organized because of the large working population in the copper mines. My husband was one of the leading men in the union. From 1954 to 1956, the union leaders organized labor unrest in Northern Rhodesia (now Zambia). In August 1956, all leaders were rounded up at night as "troublemakers." My husband and other leaders were imprisoned for six months and then restricted to remote rural home areas, where I joined him. This meant my leaving a nonprofessional social work job and going back to my rural life. I once again tilled the land, fetched water, pounded cassava for meal, and did all the housework and chores.

The restrictions were lifted at the end of 1959, and I got a job as a domestic science leader with Kitwe City Council and became involved with church work at Mindolo Ecumenical Center, Mindolo Kitwe, Zambia. Before and after this job, I had worked for the copper mines in Northern Rhodesia as an untrained industrial social worker from 1951 to 1956, and then from 1960 to 1961. I worked in areas that had more to do with teaching housewives and girls how to do housework, keep their homes clean, and keep family members in good health, but I aspired to become a qualified social worker.

One day, I was asked to address a meeting of white managers from all the copper mines on how productivity could be improved. I spoke on the importance of miners having literate wives trained in domestic science to enable them to look after their husbands and children. Hygiene and the proper feeding of husbands who were working hard underground was of importance, but some of the in-the-home deficiencies weakened the strength of the miners. My idea was that the managers of the mines would establish workers' centers for miners' recreation and the training of their wives in domestic science and housework. This was one of my social work initiatives even before I formally became a trained social worker.

Also, I became one of the first members of the Zambia Young Women's Christian Association established by Margaret Hathaway and Eunice Muparutsa. I also met the late Reverend Kitagawa, an America citizen who was working for the World Council of Churches in Geneva and who came to Kitwe for church conferences. I told him about my dreams. He consulted Margaret Hathaway, who told me that Reverend Kitagawa had told her to help me fulfill my dreams.

Then Billy Williams, who had been in Cyprus, was transferred to Lusaka, Zambia, to head the government's Social Services Department. He and other government officials decided to establish a school of social work in Lusaka. Harry Oppenheimer, the biggest funder of the school, was honored by having the school named after him.

Margaret Hathaway learned about these developments, so she mentioned them to me. I had never heard about plans for this school. (For the most part only blacks working in government offices and big establishments and as mine officials had ready access to newspapers.) Margaret got me two application forms. I gave her one copy to rush to Musonda Kalyafe, who faced the same dilemma as I did. She also did not know what she was going to do with her life and she also had become very active in the YWCA movement. By God's grace she got her application form before she boarded the plane to go to her rural home, where she was going to continue as a saleswoman in her father's little shop. We were among the first students admitted to Oppenheimer College.

I had four dresses, one pair of cheap shoes, and six cents in my pocket. The college provided us with bedding and toiletries, but I had no soap to wash my clothes. Musonda provided me with my needs. She had pocket money from her grant.

When I was accepted at Oppenheimer College, I was at first awarded a corporation scholarship. A week before the school opened, the copper mine company withdrew the scholarship because of my husband's involvement in the 1954–1956 rolling strikes.

A telegram from the college informed me of this while I was waiting to board a train to Zimbabwe to leave my five children with my parents. When I told my husband the news, he said I could go ahead with my trip. We got into Mr. Mattison's car and went to his house, where we were going to wait for the evening train. When I told Greta Mattison, his wife, about my tragedy she said, "Esinet, before you go to Zimbabwe, go to Oppenheimer College and find out why the scholarship has been withdrawn." When I got to Lusaka, I left my children at the house of my friend, the Reverend Munyama, my father's classmate and friend from Methodist training days. I asked the Munyamas for their daughter to accompany me to Oppenheimer College. When I got there, I met the registrar, introduced myself, and told him that I had come to find out why the scholarship had been withdrawn. He said, "Your case was very painful to board members because you were one of the best students to be admitted." Without further discussion, he went to his office and immediately brought two sets of forms for me to apply for a scholarship from two Catholic agencies. I dashed to the home of the president of the Methodist Church. He endorsed the forms. Like a bird with wings I dashed to the college to hand in the forms. Again with God beside me, the registrar told me to come back and start classes with other students early the next week.

I got my children and went to the roadside to wait for any means of transport, as buses had already left in the morning. After some time a transport for goods stopped and allowed us to enter the truck at the back. I had a Primus stove that I used to cook some food for my children when the truck stopped at some points. We spent the night on the truck. The following day we got to Harare and then went on to the rural areas where my parents were stationed.

The next day I returned to Harare, where I boarded the bus for Lusaka on Tuesday morning. On January 2, 1962, I got to Lusaka and found the driver waiting for me with a bicycle, as the car had broken down. To me this was more than enough. We walked to the college. The mountain had been conquered; I was going to start classes with other students, money or no money. I thanked the Almighty for this privilege.

Please tell us something about your experience at the college.

MAPONDERA: The college became my life and my family's salvation, for otherwise I imagine I would have lived in poverty all my life. I worked very hard. As a result, most of my papers were distributed to my fellow students.

I first met Professor Richard Parvis and his wife, Kaye, who are still close friends of mine at Oppenheimer. Professor Parvis trained us in group work and community development based on his experiences in India and other places where he had been on UN assignments. He became our inspiration, and both he and Dr. Mort Teichner from Wurzweiler School of Social Work at Yeshiva University taught us to be independent thinkers.

While British lecturers expected us to repeat what we had read in the books, the Americans expected us to analyze what we read, and we were expected to contribute our own thinking.

At that time, our people would say things for the sake of pleasing the white researcher.

While you were at Oppenheimer College, some interesting student practice and future employment opportunities were materializing.

MAPONDERA: I wanted to go into the rural areas for my final student fieldwork practice. My mind was set on the rural areas. Meanwhile, the Chilanga Cement factory near Lusaka had labor problems and had asked Oppenheimer College to help deal with them. One second-year student had been sent there, but they needed someone else to attend to the strained relations between management and employees. The employers were from the African National Congress party while the employees were all from the United National Independence Party. There was chaos.

Professor Parvis called me. He explained the situation at Chilanga Cement and told me that the college had deemed me the most suitable student to succeed the one who had just finished his fieldwork there, since I understood the political situation and the labor movement. I had successfully done my first fieldwork assignment in a difficult squatter compound in 1962, and I had already worked as an untrained industrial social worker. Chilanga was my destiny.

I stayed in the townships. This was the opportunity to identify myself with the people and to hear and talk with them. The community had formed its own welfare committee to discuss community problems. It was during these meetings with different groups of men, women, and youth that I stumbled on information that youths in the community were preparing petrol to bomb the factory. I called the youths to my house, and I asked them if it was true. They admitted that it was. They told me that they had decided to bomb the factory because management was not employing them because of their political affiliation. My role was to be a mediator, so the next day I went to the office and discussed the matter with the personnel manager. I explained that management should not mix its work with politics; they should employ the youths of the fathers who had been employees of the company for so many years. After some consideration, management agreed. With a smile, I called the youths to my house and told them the good news. The following day, 20 youths were employed at the cement factory. I became the hero of the day to both management and workers, as well as the Chilanga community.

I started women's programs in domestic science and the growing of vegetables. There was one family with a stove. I used this stove to teach women how to bake bread and cakes for their families. This program became very popular.

With the Community Welfare Committee, we started addressing other identified needs, particularly a serious need for adult education for both men and women, including most of the labor force at the cement factory. Also, education was available only for very few children who happened to live near mission schools, and there were not many in the early 1960s. There were no recreational facilities; only a beer hall had been built. All of this was reported. After my three months of student fieldwork, the staff, management, and employees agreed that I be offered a permanent job after my graduation. I asked them about employment for my husband. Management said there was no problem. They offered him a job as an industrial relations officer.

It was about the same time that I got a job with the Anglo American Corporation's Nkana Branch to carry out a population survey during a school holiday. They wanted the survey information to create recreational facilities in the townships. I did such a good job with the survey and recommendations that they, too, were quite impressed. Besides, they discovered that I was soon going to graduate. This, of course, was not that long after the company had withdrawn my scholarship once they knew which Mrs. Mapondera-Mwendapole (my married name) had been given it. Nonetheless, soon I received a letter from this company offering me a full-time position to take effect after graduation. Again, I gave my conditions. The toughest was for them to employ my husband. This request was a bitter pill for them, as he was still working for the African Mine Workers Union, which was giving them sleepless nights.

As usual, life is full of surprises. Anglo American Corporation management had never replied to me when I stated that I would take the job they had offered me on the condition that they offer a job to my husband. Yet, on my graduation day, a "top brass" official timed his visit to come pick me up to take me to the Anglo American copper mines. Meanwhile, Chilanga Cement's top team had also come for my graduation to take me back to Chilanga and with them was the general manager. I had already "cemented" a close working relationship with Chilanga during my final student fieldwork, and since I had received no reply from Anglo American Corporation, I went to work for Chilanga in July 1964.

At Chilanga, my husband and I settled down very well. I started putting my plans together to meet the needs of the community by carrying out a survey on education requirements. One afternoon we had a management meeting, so I mentioned the two major educational needs of the community—children who were out of school, and female and male adults who wanted to further their schooling or attend adult literacy classes. My statement shocked the works manager. He could not believe that poor laborers aspired to improve their educational qualifications. He said that what I had said was nonsense. I did not argue with him, as my survey report was still being typed. The following afternoon I sent a copy of the completed survey to the general manager. After reading the report, he said I should go ahead with the education program.

In mid-1965, the Commonwealth Development Corporation appointed a new general manager. He was Polish, married to an English woman named Helen. God has always sent his messengers to me in many ways. Helen and I became close sisters. She and her husband arrived at the right time, when I was at the point of implementing my ideas about community development. With Helen, it became easy for me to get funds for the construction of the school, which opened its doors to children at the beginning of 1966. In addition, we began adult education classes in the morning, at noon, and in the evening, to meet the needs of different shifts of the employees and homemakers. We employed our own qualified teachers, and the welfare hall was turned into classrooms during the week.

A few years after Oppenheimer, you furthered your social work education overseas, is that correct?

MAPONDERA: Yes, in 1967 I left for the United States to work toward my MSW degree at the Wurzweiler School of Social Work at Yeshiva University in New York, where Dr. Teichner had resumed his post as dean. At Yeshiva University, I gained quite a lot of valuable experience, not only from the classroom, but also in the field and from the people, particularly in east Manhattan, the Bronx, and Harlem, where I worked during the summer holidays of 1968.

In the States in the late 1960s, much emphasis was put on diagnosing problems, causes and effects, and applying remedial helping processes instead of helping people to stand on their feet with respect. Many of the large programs were simply giving financial handouts.

In Africa, my training was generic social work—grassroots self-help, social services, and especially group and community development. I see my task as a social worker to identify problems with the person, group, or community concerned. We sit down together as a team. This, to me, is the best way to solve most social and economic problems.

I can imagine there were times in your social work career when you have cried.

MAPONDERA: I do cry sometimes. In most cases I resort to prayer. This closeness helps me to work together with the people concerned. Comfort, love, and sincerity work wonders in difficult situations.

When I was in Zambia, there were cases of people who had lived all their lives in urban areas, cutting themselves off from their families in rural areas. They had not made any provision as to where they would go after retirement. Their pensions were not adequate, and they had no other means of sustaining themselves. In such cases I always ask myself, "If I were in their situation, how would I want to be helped?"

I went to a nearby rural area and asked the chief if he could provide land for people who were about to retire as Chilanga Cement employees and would be leaving company housing. The chief was very sympathetic; he offered to give them the land. Those who had vision started building their homes before they retired and are now quite comfortable, with land to grow their own food. Some had no vision at all. To them, I was just bothering them. Today they are feeling so sorry for themselves, living in shantytowns with no proper sanitation, not even a piece of land to grow one row of vegetables.

Another example of situations that can make one weep occurred one day when I was selling my potatoes at one of the townships. It was about 7:30 in the morning. I saw four women standing opposite the turnoff from my road into the highway. I thought they were waiting for someone. I went my way. At 10:30, I found them still standing there. I took the next load of potato bags at 12 noon. At around 5 P.M., after delivering my last lot, I was on my way back home to rest. Still those women were standing at the same place. I turned into my road from the highway, then my conscience nagged at me. I decided to go back and find out what they were waiting for the whole day. When I got to where they were, I asked them for whom were they waiting. To my shame and dismay, the women told me that since morning they had been trying to get transport to take them to their home, which was 25 miles along the highway. No bus was prepared to take such short-distance travelers. I felt so bad, cursing myself for having been so insensitive, because I should have asked them during my first, second, or third trip. It was getting dark when I drove them to their home.

You certainly have had a diverse career—nursing, industrial social work, market gardening, vegetable selling and exporting. Is there anything more you care to share about these activities?

MAPONDERA: I became a market gardener selling vegetables at the same time that I worked as a social worker at Chilanga Cement. I had all these activities planned. After I had assigned my workers different responsibilities, early in the morning I would either drive to the market or deliver vegetables to hotels and colleges. We started work at 4 or 4:30. By 6 A.M., I would be at markets in Lusaka or on my way to Kabwe, which was 85 miles away, or Kafue, 25 miles away. When not delivering to those cities, I would be out to the market selling the vegetables by 8 A.M. I had no free Saturdays. On Sundays, I went to church in the morning. In the afternoon, if I did not have enough tomatoes or other vegetables on my plot, I would drive to nearby rural areas to order vegetables that were in demand at the market or hotels.

I did this from 1971 to 1976. I then quit my job at Chilanga Cement after realizing that I could make more money by becoming a full-time market gardener.

Despite all my different activities, fundamentally I have always considered myself a social worker who has the welfare of other people at heart. Nowadays we need social work practice that looks seriously at the broad social and economic needs of the people and the importance of helping the masses to become self-reliant, as most of the social ills stem from poverty.

As a social worker, one has to set an example for others. I tell people that my background has been one of poverty. Then I go into the details of what I did to become what I am today. Through this I have influenced many women in both Zambia and Zimbabwe. I acquired all the good things not just to please myself, but also to be a role model.

Because of my experiences as a businesswoman, I have a better understanding of women's problems when they come to the Zimbabwe Women Finance Trust (ZWFT) seeking loans. When I established ZWFT, I would say, " See what I have achieved; you can do it too. Let us join hands and work together." These messages presented in person, in print, or on the national television and radio have inspired many women.

I understand that in addition to the many other interesting facets of your life, you and other family members have been heavily involved in national independence struggles. Could you tell us about that?

MAPONDERA: My grandfather, Mapondera Kadungure, was a national hero for whom the Zimbabwe High Court Building was named. Before the whites came, he used to be called on to settle disputes among other tribes and their chiefs. He helped Mozambicans fight against the Portuguese, and after the British settlers first came to colonize Zimbabwe in 1890 in an uprising against colonial rule by the indigenous people during 1899–1903, he became a noted freedom fighter.

It was very difficult to capture and arrest him, but then one of his colleagues betrayed him. He gave himself up to save the lives of his large family of more than 20 wives, 49 sons, 50 daughters, and their spouses. He died in prison. Some say that my grandfather Mapondera was sick, but others believe that he was poisoned.

When my father, one of the youngest sons, became a minister of the Methodist church, one of the white district officers could not believe that my warrior grandfather could have had a son who would become a minister of religion. Yet when the struggle for liberation from the British was raging for 15 years in the 1960s and 1970s, my father, working as a prison chaplain, secretly served as the go-between for political detainees and their families, carrying letters or verbal messages.

My father and I also became the underground messengers of very sensitive messages. I would be given small notes by freedom fighters in Zambia, inserting them carefully at the base of my handbag where no one could suspect that I hid such dangerous messages. When I got to Harare, my father delivered the notes.

Each time I think of it I shiver, because one day I was almost caught. I was driving from Lusaka to Harare. Two police officers had been to my place in Zambia, the Mimosa Farm, pretending to be freedom fighters. On their way back to Zimbabwe they reported me, saying that I was providing the training ground for freedom fighters, so the contents of my car were turned upside down. My bag was searched inside and outside, but by God's grace the note was well hidden. When they were searching my car I was busy engaging in chitchat with the police, acting carefree on the surface, but with butterflies inside. I was held at the Chirundu checkpoint for more than two hours.

When I got home, I was told that the Central Intelligence would like to see me the following Monday morning. As usual, I did not wait. I immediately dashed to the central police station. When I got there, the white policeman I was supposed to see had just left. One of the white policemen present heard my name and said "Yes, the famous Mimosa Farm!" Then I knew that I was in trouble. Nevertheless, I did not allow fear to control me. I responded with the same words "Yes, the famous Mimosa

Farm." At my sister's wedding that weekend, a number of Central Intelligence officers were on hand to see with whom I was talking.

Monday came. I was dressed to the nines in my African print dress. I was with my brother, who had come from Britain for the wedding. We were escorted to the white officer's office with a black policeman whom I had met several times at Chirundu. We all sat down. The white officer asked me about the political activities at my farm To start with, I told him that I had nothing to do with what were at the time Southern Rhodesian politics, as I had left the country more than 20 years back, but my farm home welcomed all Rhodesian freedom fighters because most of them were my relatives; some were friends with whom I had gone to the same schools; others I knew through the church where my father was an evangelist teacher and minister. I told him that there were many Zimbabwean blacks at my farm because they had nowhere to go; most of them were black Rhodesians who had been retrenched when the Zambian government decided to create employment for their own people.

The door was now open for me to tell them what was on my mind. I asked them who was really responsible for the fighting going on? I pointed out their faults as causes of the trouble. First, when advertising for jobs, the whites only hired whites when there were blacks who were even more qualified. I also went into salary differences. I went on, ending by telling them that many black Rhodesians wanted to come back home but were afraid of the treatment they would get. The listeners were so convinced that I had nothing to do with Rhodesian politics that they ended by giving me their names on letters of introduction, and added that I should assist all those refugees who wanted to come back home from Zambia. This arrangement did help many.

Many Zimbabweans were able to return home with letters of introduction, but I never dared come back for I knew my "sins" were not over.

I thanked the Almighty God and my ancestors' spirits for taking me out of the jaws of the lion. After this encounter, I never came back to visit in Zimbabwe until August 1975, and not to live permanently until 1979. I had been locked up at the Central Police Station in January 1971 on suspicion of political activities, but had been released because my father was still a prison chaplain.

I accommodated more than 50 girls and young women combatants with their babies from Zimbabwe African People's Union (ZAPU) camps, brought to my farm by Aunt Jane Ngwenya, for she had nowhere to put them.

The life sacrifice made by many Zimbabweans has been the greatest motivation for me to fight for political and economic liberation.

During this same period, you became a part-time lecturer at the Institute of Public Administration and began the first of a number of responsibilities on behalf of the Zambia Government, as well as the United Nations. Please tell us about that.

MAPONDERA: In 1970, when I came back from the United States after acquiring my master's degree, because of my academic record in Zambia, I was asked to lecture at the School of Administration. I gave lectures in community development and social services to students who were the first secretaries of the Urban and Rural

Councils so that they could formulate social service policies for their councils. I feel so proud each time I meet some of them, introducing me to others as the person who helped to make them who they are.

When the Zambian government was going to celebrate its tenth year of independence, I was appointed to serve on the Social Welfare Ad Hoc Committee, which was to examine the success and failures of the government during its first ten years. In 1977, I was asked to serve on the United Nations and Inter-Ministerial Commission charged with examining youth needs in Zambia and coming up with a policy statement that would address them.

In subsequent years, you served on a growing number of commissions, boards, and committees.

MAPONDERA: When I came back to Zimbabwe to live, it was my intention to go into market gardening. Unfortunately, I had no collateral. I applied for a job as a social worker at the Ministry of Social Welfare. Three times I was rejected for being overqualified. For 10 months I had no job. This was the most trying period of my life in Zimbabwe. I felt helpless. The money I had was dwindling as I still had children in school, both in Zimbabwe and abroad.

I prayed to God and my ancestors day and night. I developed a nerve breakout (a rash) at the top of my head. I was so morally and spiritually low but kept on hoping for God's intervention, so one day I decided to volunteer at the women's wing of the Zimbabwe African National Union (ZANU) offices. I offered my service to Mrs. Sally Mugabe, first lady of Zimbabwe, to assist her with the rehabilitation of female ex-combatants who had left the country and returned with little or no education. The ZANU party had bought a farm at Melfort for the young women, and I was to have a look at the farm and then make recommendations on how it could best be used. After examining all the facilities, I recommended that the farm be developed into a national vocational skills training center for women.

I was then asked to organize an all-women's nongovernmental organization (NGO) conference as a follow-up to the Women's Decade Conference that had taken place in July 1980 in Copenhagen. The conference was held in October 1980. Afterward, I submitted a report through the first lady to the government recommending that they establish a strong women's desk in one of the ministries. In response, the government decided to establish a Ministry of Women's Affairs.

During that same month, the government of Zimbabwe appointed me to serve on the Riddell Commission, which was looking into prices, incomes, and conditions of services in both private and public sectors in urban and rural areas. The commission was to make recommendations to assist the government with its social and economic policies. I was one of the two women on this commission.

At the same time, as most of the senior positions in government were occupied by whites, the government decided to appoint an increasing number of blacks. Having been an industrial social worker, I was the only woman appointed as an employee welfare service manager of the Post and Telecommunication Corporation (PTC). I was responsible for PTC employee services nationwide.

In January 1981, the government decided to establish the Zimbabwe Mass Media Trust, which was going to be responsible for establishing the school of journalism. I was one of two women appointed to its board, on which I am still serving. I have also served on a number of industrial boards countrywide with the Ministry of Labor and Social Welfare.

Let's turn to the international scene and your work in this area.

MAPONDERA: It has been a blessing in my life that I have been able to share my ideas and experience on social and economic development, in particular my concern for women's advancement, internationally. I have been presenting papers from the time I was in New York. I addressed a UN workshop on women in development held in Zambia in 1972.

From 1965 to 1977, I was a member of the Zambia Council of Social Services and presented papers on economic and social needs of people in Zambia and Central Africa. I have been to Canada three times, one of them at Queens University, where I presented a paper on innovations in organizing grassroots women. One of the conferences I addressed in Canada was organized by a group of women who wanted to find out how they could work most effectively with women in Third World countries.

I also participated in a Women's World Bank workshop in Holland in 1984 concerning the problems of women in Zimbabwe getting credit from financial institutions. I became an executive committee member of the Ecumenical Church Loan Fund in Geneva, representing the African region, from 1991 to 1997. In 1985, I headed the Zimbabwe NGO delegation to the 1985 Women's Decade Conference in Nairobi, Kenya.

In 1990, UNESCO organized a conference at Ife University, Nigeria. I was invited to present a paper on the training needs of women in science and technology. In November and December 1991, I went to India for the Asia Ecumenical Church Loan Fund (ECLOF) workshop.

In 1992, I was invited to Southern Illinois University to address faculty and students on social work practice from an African perspective. I talked about my own experiences and the way I applied my social work training as a person who worked in two developing countries, Zambia and Zimbabwe, comparing that with my educational experiences in the United States.

Finally, from 1986 to date, I have attended the International Symposia of the Inter-University Consortium for International Social Development (IUCISD) in different parts of the world. In addition, I was an IUCISD African region representative from 1990 to 1994 and an elected board member-at-large since then.

Could you please tell us something more about the Zimbabwe Women's Finance Trust?

MAPONDERA: I was at the first organizational meeting of the Zimbabwe Women's Bureau's (ZWB) in Harare in February 1981. The meeting was supposed to be addressed by a minister's wife, Mrs. Tekere. I was asked to address the gathering, 200 to 300 women. I spoke on the advancement of women in economic and social development. I gave examples of women in Zambia and in the United States. I gave myself as an example, reflecting on what I had achieved in Zambia. I was elected vice chairperson of the Zimbabwe Women's Bureau, which was the only women's organization to give evidence to the Riddell Commission on the problem of granting credit to women.

After writing to Women's World Banking (WWB), I was invited to attend its Biannual Conference in Holland in 1984. On my return, I told my fellow women about WWB. By that time, I was president of Zimbabwe Women's Bureau, an organization that was already working with grassroots women in both urban rural areas and that had produced a document of its research, "We Carry a Heavy Load." I asked the executive of ZWB that we establish an affiliate of WWB and that we invite other women's NGOs.

At first, the idea was well-received. The problem came when I said that we would first have to raise funds from our own pockets to be an affiliate. By the end of the next two to three meetings, the rest of the women had dropped out. Nevertheless, by February 1985 I had raised money on my own and registered a company, Zimbabwe Women Business Promotions, Ltd., meeting all the requirements of the WWB.

In October 1986, the WWB regional director from Kenya came to assist me in introducing the organization to financial institutions and the Reserve Bank. The governor of the Reserve Bank invited managers of different banks, and all the managers promised to work with us. We opened an account with Barclays Bank. We set a target of Z$100,000. Of this we managed to raise Z$20,000, and we wrote to WWB about this. They said that we should raise 25 percent and ask our bank if it could also contribute 25 percent. Then WWB would contribute 50 percent. Our bank said "No." Some of the women who had contributed started to withdraw their money.

It was not until 1987 at the WWB conference in Canada that I was able to present this problem in person. The WWB response said it would provide us seed money of US$5,000. Unfortunately, this promise to African affiliates was never fulfilled. We carried on.

In 1988, the Foundation for International Training in Canada gave us CD$15,000. This fund was supposed to be for the construction of a training center in one of the rural areas. In 1989, we reviewed the situation and priorities with the donor and we both agreed to wait.

I decided that we should establish an NGO to enable us to get funds from donors who had refused to assist us because we were registered as a company. At the end of 1988 we formed the Zimbabwe Women Finance Trust (ZWFT). We applied for NGO status to the Ministry of Labor and Social Welfare, but we received a regret. This was another setback, but I vowed that ZWFT was going to be registered, so I wrote an appeal and collected all the documents pertaining to the WWB movement and what women had done in Africa and worldwide. I decided to hand carry the letter and present my case. We continued to struggle. In November 1989, the Foundation for International Training arranged for our ZWFT Manager to go to

Bangladesh to study the Grameen Bank for eight weeks. She was back after four, saying the country was very dirty; she could not stand it. I was so annoyed and began to wonder if she and I had the same vision.

In June 1990, I was in Atlanta for the WWB Biennial Conference. When I got back to Zimbabwe the very women who had tried to block the registration of ZWFT, including this ZWFT manager, had decided to oust me from ZWFT.

Meanwhile, that manager was chosen to work for an NGO in the Netherlands on a six-month contract. To find a competent, experienced person as manager, I had to ask someone in England.

The new manager took her appointment in October 1990. I felt quite relieved. She worked hard. As no major donor was coming forth, we decided to start the ZWFT program on a trial basis, serving as a broker organization for women to secure bank loans. I approached the Barclays Bank general manager, Mr. Takawira. He agreed to the arrangements, which were for ZWFT to recruit members for a fee and to work with these women to help them make reliable plans and proper preparations before making application to the bank for loans, increasing their chances of success. Our responsibility was also to make sure of the repayment. It worked.

After we produced our first annual report, at the end of 1991, some donors gave us money for a revolving loan fund and a few staff salaries. We then had five staff members. As we continued in 1994, we got a loan from the Ecumenical Church Loan Fund in Geneva at 15 percent interest for a sum of Z$80,000. By this time, a number of donors believed in what we were trying to do.

The most recent ZWFT manager is Stanley Meda. He has a bachelor's degree in commerce from the University of Delhi and has worked for the Zimbabwe Ministry of Finance, where he rose to commissioner of insurance. He and I have the same vision and commitment for the economic development of poor people.

So, after all of these trials and tribulations, ZWFT was under way.

MAPONDERA: The way donors started coming to rescue of the ZWFT was a miracle. In 1993, at the WWB Biennial Conference in Italy, we met an Austrian government representative. We told him about our difficulties, exchanged addresses, and submitted our project proposal. Funds were made available to four affiliates in Africa: Uganda, Zimbabwe, Namibia, and Gambia. That meant ZWFT received US$250,000.

But the trials and tribulations weren't over. When WWB headquarters in New York heard about it, they intervened by saying the money should go through them. They would do the distribution. WWB New York had never communicated such requirements to us. Meanwhile, we had signed the agreement documents with Austria. When Austrian representatives knew that New York WWB had not routed the money through them, they called a meeting of the four affiliates and the African region representative based in New York. WWB was supposed to send a ticket for the ZWFT manager to attend the meeting but did not. We had no money in the organization to purchase the ticket, so I used my own personal money for our manager to attend. In

1994, we asked for the money. We were told that we had to give loans to 200 women before they could release it. In 1997, when we had given more than 1,500 loans and reapplied, we were told that the period for getting the money had expired.

In recent years I understand there has been much progress at ZWFT.

MAPONDERA: From 1992 to 1995, ZWFT had only given 385 loans, but one of the donors provided us with a consultant who introduced a new group lending methodology similar to that of the Grameen Bank. As a result, in 1996 alone we gave 786 loans and more than 1,500 in 1997, to the surprise of many.

We now have a portfolio of more than 5,400 individual members. Our target is to reach 10,000 by the year 2000. Consequently, ZWFT has made a name for itself nationally and internationally. Requests for our services are so great now that we cannot meet the demand.

We are also working with Zimtrade, a government institution that is promoting exports from Zimbabwe. We would like women to start exporting and to participate at national, regional, and international trade fairs. We are getting an export license for ZWFT members.

And of course there are your plans for the vocational skills training center, about which you have held a vision for so long.

MAPONDERA: The vocational skills training center has been one of my dreams since the conception of Zimbabwe Women Finance Trust. That is the reason we had to buy the five acres of land in 1990 on which our offices are now located. I realized that running microfinance credit services alone would not be adequate to enable women to participate fully in the national economy.

When we look at the types of businesses women are involved in—trading, raising poultry, fattening cattle, and clothing manufacturing—the markets are becoming saturated. With the skills training center, we will help women to learn new skills in different areas such as food processing, jewelry making, pottery, metalwork, roofing materials, natural oils for the cosmetic industry, and dressmaking to an international standard so that they can export their products. We want women to establish businesses that can go on from generation to generation. At the moment, I am looking at other ways of helping younger people who have high rates of unemployment. The answer to a prayer in this case is Professor Gundidza of the University of Zimbabwe Pharmacy Department. He is one of those most knowledgeable about the many medicinal plants and oils in our part of the world. Historically, it has been Europeans who came to Africa to learn about our medicinal plants, collecting them to take back to their countries, where they grew them in greenhouses and laboratories for their pharmaceutical businesses—benefiting from our natural resources. Africans have hardly profited.

One of the skills training courses that we would like to set up is a program featuring herbal, medicinal, and oil plants. This program would reach out to many urban and rural women and youths in the growing, or simply the gathering, of herbal and oil-producing plants, and it will encourage planting so that these natural resources are not depleted.

What can you tell us about the latest chapter with respect to your dream?

MAPONDERA: Finally, through the patience, determination, commitment of 10 years, and financial assistance from the Italian government, the dream of the vocational skills training center will soon be a reality. I am told by the Italian Embassy that the project is ready for tender, and we should soon be informed of which company will win the tender.

Of your many endeavors, on behalf of women in particular, what stands out as your most important or interesting accomplishment?

MAPONDERA: What I regard as my most important accomplishment has been the change of attitudes by women toward themselves—the idea of a woman venturing into her own business and making her own money through her own efforts.

I started talking to individuals or large groups of women, citing myself as a model of what a woman can do. I am not a rich woman, but I am comfortable. My lectures started changing women's attitudes.

The banks had regarded all women, let alone grassroots women, as unbankable. The establishment of ZWFT opened women's eyes and prepared them with the necessary skills and plans to apply for loans. It is such a joy to meet women who get loans and who are on their way to neighboring countries to buy merchandise for their shops or for selling at flea markets in Zimbabwe. Some even boast of what they are able to do or acquire. There is such a great demand for our services countrywide.

It is with respect to your achievements in gender issues that I understand you have been honored in special ways. Please tell us something about that.

MAPONDERA: I have many gifts in my home that women have made themselves. Then in 1989, I got the International Biography Center Award in appreciation of my services. In 1997, I was presented with the Dudley Products Trophy in recognition of my service in relation to the development and the advancement of Zimbabwean women.

Also, I have received a Lifetime Achievement Award for outstanding international service from the Inter-University Consortium for International Social Development at its 1998 Symposium in Cairo.

What are the personal interests and pursuits that you engage in or that you wish that you had time for?

MAPONDERA: I would like to fill the gaps left by other development NGOs, particularly in remote rural areas. These people are calling themselves "the forgotten people" of the nation. This is sad, especially when one remembers that it was people in these remote areas bordering with neighboring countries who bore the brunt of the liberation struggle. They suffered at the hands of both the Rhodesian army and the freedom fighters. Now, after 18 years of independence, little to no development has taken place in these areas.

Are there any concluding comments that you would like to make?

MAPONDERA: I would like to conclude with words written by my mother on her last Christmas gifts in 1981 (she died in April 1982). She had witnessed my trials and my tribulations which I had overcome, and she quoted Isaiah 40:31, "But they that wait upon the Lord shall renew their strength, they shall mount up with wings like eagles, they shall run and not be weary, and they shall walk and not faint."

MEHER NANAVATTY

B orn in 1917, Meher Nanavatty graduated with honors from St. Xavier's College, Bombay University, in 1942 and later from the Tata Institute of Social Science in Bombay (now Mumbai). He worked in community development projects early in his career. He earned his master's degree in Social Welfare Administration at the School of Applied Social Sciences at Western Reserve University in Cleveland (now Case Western Reserve University) in 1950. After returning to India, he joined the Faculty of Social Work, University of Baroda, and then the Delhi Municipal Corporation as director of social education and later as chief education officer.

Mr. Nanavatty returned to academic life as head of the Fieldwork Department of the Delhi School of Social Work in 1954. About five years later, he joined the Indian government as director of social education in the Indian Ministry of Community Development, later becoming adviser on social welfare to the Government of India. He was then seconded to the UN Commission for Asia and Pacific in Bangkok as regional adviser, Social Development Division, where he consulted for seven years, in 15 countries. In 1978, he was appointed social welfare expert with the UN Social Welfare and Development Center for Asia and the Pacific, headquartered in Manila, and he served as visiting professor on social development at the Asia Social Institute in Manila until his retirement in 1980. He has since been a consultant with the Baroda Citizens Council and other welfare-related organizations in Delhi. Mr. Nanavatty has written extensively for journals and has co-authored two recent books. He is the recipient of local, national, and international recognition. He is married and is a father and grandfather and lives in New Delhi.

BILLUPS: *You entered the profession at a very important period in the sociopolitical history of modern India. What can you tell us about that period?*

NANAVATTY: I graduated in 1942 from the University of Bombay. In 1942, Gandhi declared the Quit India Movement, urging the British to leave. I was influenced by this nationalist movement. Coming from an upper-middle-class family, I was torn between a pro-British atmosphere at home and a nationalist influence at school, and increasingly drawn toward the movement for independence.

This was when social work education was born in India. The first school of social work, Sir Dorab Tata School of Social Work, started in India in 1936–1937 under the leadership of Dr. Clifford Manshardt, a community-based neighborhood man, not a social worker in our sense of today's clinically oriented professionals. The early background of the Tata School of Social Work reflected the transition from the British to the Gandhian way of life. The faculty emphasized the dynamics of the independence movement. This was the background in which my concept of social work was formed.

This was also a period of conflict regarding higher education for social work. Most of our graduate students had gone to England, but when I was ready for higher education we were being drawn to America. The American influence engulfed the country as the British influence diminished, but this conflict between the Western and the Gandhian concept of social work remained unresolved.

What attracted you to social work?

NANAVATTY: Initially, I was a biology student from St. Xavier's College in Bombay. When I graduated with honors, I was inclined to continue in microbiology, but I read an advertisement, "Wanted: Volunteers for Community Service among the Parsees." I'm a Parsee, so I went to see the person in charge. I met Dr. Behram Mehta, who was a professor of social work at Sir Dorab Tata School of Social Work. I was impressed by his devotion, and I offered to work under him three evenings a week in conjunction with his fortnightly talks to youths on leadership. He appointed me an "efficiency officer" to supervise the playground activities as a volunteer in an honorary capacity. It gave me an opportunity to learn more about young people from ages five to 21 and to understand the problems not only of their lives but also of their low-income families.

After a year, when the post of superintendent of the colony fell vacant, I was asked by Dr. Mehta to take it up. I went from voluntary to paid work as superintendent of a neighborhood residential colony. I was to study each family and find out their needs, including the educational needs of the children and the employment needs of the adults, most of whom were considered unemployable. They were ill-equipped to compete in an open-market economy. At the same time, they had to be helped, so Professor Mehta started a small-scale industry for them. The factory (Artytoys), produced educational toys. Each worker was paid a minimum stipend of 200 rupees per month. Tata Charities supplemented the costs of production. The industry brought a work culture in a residential colony. Dr. Mehta eventually arranged for my fellowship at the Tata School of Social Work.

Did you ever seek employment in the field of biology?

NANAVATTY: No, by that time I was already admitted to the Tata School, so I said goodbye to biology. There is discussion among some of us as to whether science students or art students are better prepared for social work. At present, schools of social work in India admit both, but experience has shown that science students, perhaps because of their experience in laboratory work, tend to be more analytical. After I graduated from the Tata School, I joined the Parsee Charity Organization. Professor P. A. Wadia, head of the group, had a plan to coordinate the Parsee charitable trusts, and he wanted me, along with other graduates from the Tata School, to take up this work. We were to coordinate 18 Parsee charity trusts into one organization, the Liaison Committee for Charity Organization. We launched the program to investigate family cases of need and recommend the amounts to be given by a charity to a family, to eliminate duplication.

The question became how to merge Professor Wadia's approach to charity organization with Dr. Mehta's approach to neighborhood and community development. Each worker was allotted a neighborhood in which to study, and work with families with respect to charity requirements, education, vocational training, employment, and other needs. The investigator thus became a family counselor and was also identified with evening activities at the community service center. Thus, we moved from being charity investigators to community development workers. Our emphasis changed to community-based services that emphasized the people's self-reliance and training in leadership, along with the acquisition of an ideological base for social development. I continued with this work for four years. It was satisfying, but exhausting.

Could you tell us something about your social work educational experiences?

NANAVATTY: Dr. Kumarappa, then head of the Tata School, attended an international conference on social work in Canada where Dr. Leonard Mayo, dean of the School of Applied Social Science (SASS) at Western Reserve University [now Case Western Reserve], offered a fellowship, asking Dr. Kumarappa to send a student to [Western Reserve]. Dr. Kumarappa asked me to arrange for travel and stay. I obtained loans from various trusts and traveled by boat to New York and by land to Cleveland.

Once in Cleveland, I stayed at the Students Cooperative (or Student Co-op) and worked in a restaurant in the evenings. Then the school advertised for local families to host foreign students. The Hickox family offered me and my wife a free place to stay.

I took group work and community organization, as my special studies. I remember two experiences in class vividly. One was the case history of a hobo. Our teacher was leading the discussion, trying to solve the problem of the hobo as a caseworker would through counseling. For some time I listened, and then I just could not contain myself. I said, "Madam, I feel we are on the wrong side. This hobo is a part of a larger social problem, not an individual problem. Society makes him a hobo. Therefore, our treatment should relate to the society rather than this man." That really disturbed many students: Is Meher a leftist? I mean, they didn't verbalize it but really questioned me. Fortunately, the teacher was mature enough to say, "We will need to do both. Unless we help to structurally adjust the economic and social and political system, individuals will continue to suffer." In other words, social work should include counseling and social action. The debate between the two "sides" continues. As I see it, the concept of social development tries to resolve this conflict.

A somewhat similar conflict prevails in India. We have a course on labor welfare and personnel management in some schools of social work in which social workers are seen as employed personnel officers who have to look more after the interest of management than labor. When I was teaching at the Delhi School of Social Work, I tried to place a very mature student for a three-month block of time in fieldwork in an industry. On the first day, the manager asked me whether the student would ensure the interest of management with a minimum emphasis on labor welfare and if the student would avoid mixing too freely with labor and advocating their interests. I argued that the student needed a free hand to work with both groups. But the question of whether students are to be agents of management or are to work for the welfare of the person remains an issue even today.

During my first-year fieldwork placement at Western Reserve, I worked for the Central Area Council in a geographical area inhabited mostly by African Americans. It was a satisfying experience; the people responded favorably to me as an Indian coming from the land of Gandhi. This experience also taught me additional ways to work with minority groups in a deprived neighborhood. The second-year placement was at the Cleveland Welfare Federation, where I learned more about how to coordinate the activities of voluntary agencies.

At the school, Professor Grace Coyle was my inspiration. Grace Coyle always used to say, "Meher, when you go back to India you don't need to carry out our program. You need to carry the principles of social work, applying them to your people's and your society's unique needs."

Before leaving Cleveland, I asked Dr. Coyle for an opportunity to study the Social Security system in America. She arranged contacts for me with some alumni in Washington, DC. My wife and I stayed with Paul Cherney and his family for one month, while I took advantage of this special learning opportunity. We are friends with the Cherneys to this day.

After your return to India your professional career turned to social work education and municipal and national government. Tell us something about those responsibilities.

NANAVATTY: On my return, I decided not to go back to community charity and development work, but to enter the larger field of social welfare. But first my classmate and colleague at the Tata School, Dr. Perin Vakharia, who had become dean of the School of Social Work at Baroda University, offered me the post of reader [associate professor]. I taught group work and community organization.

My first experience of teaching group work was so different from what I experienced in the United States. Some of my students objected: "This is all a Western concept. There is no group work to speak of in India." I pointed out that we had religious groups, labor groups, neighborhood groups, and community groups. Many of these could be venues for social work practice. Still the first reaction was negative. To them, with their nationalistic sentiment, any ideas from outside were considered unacceptable. Unfortunately, at that time we did not have teaching records on indigenous groups and community practice for course studies, and that was our weakness. It was my regret, because recorded firsthand practice experiences could have been a helpful teaching tool. However, gradually I convinced the students of the importance of group work and community organization, and they began to take hold of the practice concepts and principles.

Unfortunately, my stay at Baroda was quite short. I found limited opportunity for simultaneous work in the community, so I decided on a change. I wrote to Dr. M. S. Gore, my friend and colleague at the Tata School, who was head of the Delhi School of Social Work, asking if he could help find an opening for me. Soon I received a telegram: "Reach Delhi Friday. Interview Monday." Because we trust each other, I took a train. When I reached Delhi, he met me at the railway station, and I asked him, "Madhav, what is this job? You never mentioned the job." He said, "Don't worry. It is director of social education in the municipality, the city administration." And I said, "What is social education? I have never heard of it." He said, "Don't worry. I have asked my librarian to collect all the relevant literature for you by tomorrow, Saturday. Sunday you read, and Monday you go for the interview."

I went for the interview, and whom do I see on the selection committee but Dr. Zakir Hussain, who later became vice president of the country. He was then an adult education scholar and a university vice chancellor. At the interview, I was asked how my foreign education would be used in India: "You know this is a municipality and not a central government, so you will have to come down to the realities of the life of the people." I assured him that I would do my best as I came to realize that social education and social group work and community development were not all that far removed from one another. I was selected for the post.

The city was divided into neighborhoods, and my own experience with community work helped me to develop neighborhood centers in all the localities. Adult education with social values emphasized civic responsibility and, hence, civic education. I used to put great emphasis on discussion among groups of people regarding their day-to-day problems, cost of living, poverty, and indebtedness. This helped me to secure broad cooperation from many people who were economically deprived. Emphasis was also placed on developing fellowship among people of all faiths (Hindus, Muslims, and other communities) and also on cultural programs—music, dance, songs, and so on. A strong community spirit developed.

In the early stages of the program, literacy teaching was primarily geared to learning letters and forming sentences, but people were neither interested nor motivated in adult literacy classes that employed this approach to learning. So we undertook a new approach with discussions focused on the subjects of most interest to the people, such as prices of commodities and costs of living in general, their indebtedness, and the areas of their life in which they experienced exploitation. In addition to learning to read and to write, they became conscious of their civic rights as voters and of their claims on municipal services, education for their children, and health centers for their families. We were successful in developing a sense of belonging to the neighborhood through our adult education and cultural activities.

You then moved on to other challenges. Tell us about what happened next.

NANAVATTY: After four years of working with the municipal corporation, I joined the Delhi School faculty, where we reorganized student field instruction. I insisted that all faculty members, in addition to other duties, were to spend at least four hours a week in the field, supervising and guiding students. We held monthly meetings in which faculty members would report. Then we would discuss field problems and relate these to classroom teaching. This was a learning experience for all of us. It really did create a new, higher standard of student fieldwork, instruction, and learning. Perhaps more importantly, it also made the teachers more sensitive to community issues.

My experience in rural areas provided an opportunity for social action. In one village of farmers, the land belonged to a Hindu landlord who initially cooperated with the farmers and their families. However, one night a village leader came to my house and said, "Police have occupied our fields, and we have been told to get out." The next morning we found that the owner had sold his land to the government without informing the farmers, their families, or the fieldworkers. The government wanted the land for a radio broadcasting station. We did not know what to do. The School of Social Work could not take direct action because it was getting a grant from the government."

We enlisted another agency to file a suit against the landlord on behalf of the farmers. The next day all the local leaders went to court to stop the eviction. Ultimately, the justice system ordered the police to vacate the field and allow the farmers to occupy the land until completion of the harvesting season. The court also ordered compensation to farmers and asked the government to provide employment for them. This was a great learning experiences for students and teachers in organizing social action.

I can go back to teaching any time. It remains my first love, but unfortunately with the passage of time, I worry that the sense of protest and social action for civic rights is being lost in today's social work.

Could you share your thoughts on some of the other critical issues in social work education?

NANAVATTY: Social work education in India can be viewed from two perspectives. One is the beginning of the Tata School of Social Sciences, which was the first school of social work in India. Fortunately, the first director, Dr. Manshardt, had worked in neighborhood slum areas with "antisocial elements." He had visited the residents and studied their lives. He was a practical man and stressed that social work should be rooted in community life. Thus, from the very beginning social work education in India was community based; 50 percent of social work education was field practice, and it was given proportionate weight in examinations. However, as schools of social work have gained university affiliation, this emphasis on student practice in the field has suffered.

A second problem relates to the conflict between generic and specialized social work education. Most schools combine and compromise on this issue. They offer generic training in the first year and special subject training in the second.

The third problem relates to limited emphasis on national culture and overemphasis on Western teaching. Only a selected number of teachers, such as Dr. Gore and Professor Pathak, have studied Indian culture in depth, but suitable literature on the subject for social work has yet to be developed. In a globally interrelated world we need to understand the local and national, as well as the international, aspects of social work. A fourth issue is the need for minimum standards of social work education and field practice under the supervision and monitoring of a national council of social work education and practice.

After your early experiences in social work education and in local government, you served at the national level as well.

NANAVATTY: Social work education without practice remains inadequate. During my four years at the Delhi School, I thought that some of my field experiences were drying up and that I should go back to practice, so when I received an opportunity to join the staff of the Ministry of Community Development, I jumped at it.

In the beginning, I concentrated on adult education, because that was my experience with the Delhi Municipal Corporation. Gradually, I was asked to look after women's welfare as well as the total social welfare program under community development. Fortunately the minister, Mr. S. K. Dey, who was an engineer by profession, was broad minded, and I must say I enjoyed working with him. He was a warm, friendly administrator who loved fieldwork.

Because of this man with a vision, I was able to get schools of social work involved in the training of staff members for social education responsibilities (although the Ministry generally thought of them as extension workers, primarily operating through service activities programs). While I wished for a more integrated community organization to help achieve integrated community development across the nation, social work was not powerful enough to influence policy or practice. Nevertheless, my working with the Ministry was a valuable experience. I obtained an ongoing picture of the country, its people, and their problems and prospects. We as advisers in agriculture, animal husbandry, social education, social welfare, and small-scale industry were told to visit each state together for a week once a year. On return to the capital, we would write our reports and submit them to the secretary of the Ministry for administrative approval. On the following day, all heads of the state departments, with the chief secretary of the state in the chair, and the secretary and all the advisers of the Ministry of Community Development would come together to review the reports. The next day, we would rewrite our reports on the basis of the discussion and submit the agreed conclusions to the state government. This was a valuable, unique, and enriching experience.

There were other advisery and consulting responsibilities that you carried out as well.

NANAVATTY: Yes, after serving the Ministry of Community Development for seven years, the secretary of the Department of Social Welfare asked me to serve as adviser on social welfare for the government of India. In this capacity, we established a small committee, with a senior member of Parliament as chairman, to examine child welfare services in India. This committee consisted of officers and consultants dealing with maternity and child health services, welfare of handicapped children, nursery school education, and so on. After months of deliberation, a report was published promoting integrated services of child nutrition, maternity and child health, child care at home, and preschool education, instead of various ministries looking after these services separately. With the passage of time, the program was accepted as the Integrated Child Development Services program implemented by the state governments.

As an adviser, I joined various delegations to foreign countries. I went to Manila to attend the UN-sponsored Conference of the State Ministers of Social Welfare. The United Nation wanted to establish a regional training center for social welfare. While inaugurating the conference, President Ferdinand Marcos of the Philippines assured the audience that his country would be willing to sponsor the proposed training center, but at that time the Philippine Islands were more under American influence than most Asian countries, so the rest of the delegates did not favor setting up the center in Manila. The resolution adopted resolved to have the center in the region, without naming the country. Subsequently, after consulting member countries through diplomatic channels, the UN Social Development Division decided to locate the center in Manila.

For much of your professional career you were posted with United Nations offices in Asian countries. What can you tell us about those responsibilities?

NANAVATTY: As India had an extensive program of family planning, a representative of the country was considered a likely prospect for Regional Adviser to the UN Economic Commission for Asia and the Far East (ECAFE). I was appointed. My first assignment was in Papua New Guinea. Because this country was primarily inhabited by the tribals, traditional practices of birth control prevailed. They used natural resources—herbs, leaves, seeds, fruits, and the like for controlling births.

During my visit, a number of anthropologists from various countries were studying the socioeconomic aspects, in addition to the cultural manifestations of the residents' lives. These studies helped me in understanding family planning practices. I visited the interior regions for two weeks and studied the social customs related not only to family planning and birth control but also to family welfare in general.

After my study of the program in this and some of the other most underdeveloped countries of the region, a regional seminar on social welfare aspects of family planning was held in Bangkok. The purpose was to acquaint state officials, including directors of health and welfare, with the concepts and findings of the new programs.

During the seven years that I served as regional adviser, I attended many country missions. Every year I used to get four to five invitations from governments. I would visit these countries for four to six weeks and study their problems relating to family planning and allied subjects. A few distinctive site-visit experiences illustrated the importance of gaining awareness of local sociocultural practices. For example, Burma was a Communist country that did not make reference to "family planning." The program of family welfare and activities of family planning were closely related to the support and guidance of the Buddhist monks as well as the prevailing socialist system of mothers' and children's services. In Burma, they preferred to refer to family planning as simply part of "family welfare." Family relationships were strong, so we helped them build a family planning approach, using their term while educating grandmothers, parents, and young girls on limiting the size of the family.

While in Burma I was teamed with an English-speaking demographer who was educated in Russia. We traveled the countryside together for 15 or 20 days and became friends. I inquired how Russia promoted birth control. He said the number one method in Russia was full employment. Everyone worked, including women, and that in itself contributed to family planning, because when a woman leaves the home and works she is aware of the need to control the number of births. Second, there was complete nursery school education for all children, so the mothers were not required to look after children at home. In addition, complete health services including maternity and child care helped to limit the size of the family. Besides this, sex education was given to all youths and married couples. Many of these measures were being tried in Burma, much as they were by other Communist governments at the time. In the Philippines, the most important birth control measure was sex education among youth. The country is predominantly Catholic, and abstinence was encouraged in addition to other family planning measures. A Commission on Population had also been established.

In Thailand, the Buddhist temple and its monks greatly influenced the life of people in the villages. The good offices of the monks were used to spread the word about family planning. Modern programs of family planning through contraceptives played a role as well, especially in urban areas.

During my assignment to Iran before the Islamic Revolution, I learned that the country had a recent history of relatively advanced sociocultural development, and the receptivity of Iranians to change was relatively good. While in Iran, I advised on promotion of family planning activities through trade unions. Under the Trade Union Act, there was a provision for maternity and child welfare services that could be effectively harnessed in promoting family planning activities among trade union members, especially women.

In Afghanistan, groups of families lived together in one compound. The programs of family planning were most readily advanced in the compounds through the influence of the head of the Jirgha (the social organization of families living together, functioning under the head of a local tribal group). In addition, I came across an interesting example of the acceptance of peace workers in promoting family planning programs. A German couple who spoke the Afghani language had readily gained acceptance from the people because of their informal, friendly approach. They were not only allowed to go into the Jhirga but also to participate directly in maternity and child health services and in the promotion of family planning. In Sri Lanka, two measures proved effective in controlling family size. One was to facilitate universal education in high school and college, and the other was to provide institutional facilities for delivery through trained midwifery and post-delivery residential care and education for mothers. Much of the challenge was to help nurture culturally sensitive change in the values, norms, and practices of improved health care and of childbirth rather than to focus merely on the methodology of birth control alone. With this approach, people gradually began to accept change. An integrated approach might call for promoting measures that provided a threshold of family planning: (1) raising the status of women in family and society, including advancing universal literacy and education of girls; (2) raising the age of marriage; (3) expanding maternity and child health services, including institutional delivery services for limiting infant mortality; (4) extending family life education for all young people before marriage; and (5) making contraceptives readily available in the community.

During all of these missions, we made efforts to visit centers of health education. Also, my interest in social work education was fully harnessed in my visiting schools of social work in different countries and in my efforts to encourage relating social work education to education for family planning, while assisting with improving course syllabi, training, and education.

After your years with the United Nations office in Bangkok, what was your next assignment?

NANAVATTY: After seven years of work in the UN Economic and Social Commission for Asia and the Pacific (ESCAP, earlier abbreviated as ECAFE), I decided to shift to research, study, and training in social development. From Bangkok, I went to Manila. I worked at the Social Welfare and Development Center for Asia and the Pacific (SWADCAP) for two years. I organized a number of regional workshops on youth development, sex education awareness among youths, population education, and community development.

I remember two workshops most vividly. The first related to social aspects of health services, especially in rural areas. State directors of health and social welfare were invited. For the first few days, the officials discussed the prevailing traditional health services in rural areas, including faith healing and herbal treatments. For the remaining period, these directors of health were placed in the homes of rural families. The support of rural missionaries was invaluable in this process. Although at first they resisted living with rural families, the medical practitioners later appreciated the experience of being exposed to rural health practices so intimately.

A second program was a retreat for professional social work educators and practitioners to learn the structural analysis of social work. A professor from the University of the Philippines and some progressive members of the clergy enabled the participants to examine the subject closely. After a week of analysis, they realized that traditional social work and social work education were establishment-oriented and were not enabling the most deprived people to become self-reliant to lift themselves out of poverty. In other words, they needed real social development. Schools of social work were urged to undertake a similar structural analysis of social work and social work education with their faculty. This was the most enlightening and satisfying experience of my life.

In addition to your professional responsibilities, I understand that you have been active in a number of voluntary organizations.

NANAVATTY: Because I was in an important position in the government, I was able to serve as a government representative as well as in an individual capacity on various voluntary bodies. Since I had worked in adult education, I still had contacts in the field, and we had an all-India Adult Education Association with which I was active. Dr. Zakir Hussain was chairman of the association. As an educator, he was able to promote national policy on adult education through neighborhood councils as the base for people's participation. In the 1960s, the adult education movement was at its peak in India and was quite powerful. Sadly, after Dr. Hussain's demise, political support was lost. In the absence of good leadership, adult education workers felt disheartened and lost interest.

The second voluntary organization I was closely associated with was the Indian Association of Trained Social Workers. In the mid-1960s, I became its chairman. We promoted minimum standards for social work education in the country. We held a number of meetings and seminars, but in the absence of active support from professional social workers and the government we could not achieve all we would have liked. During my chairmanship I had the opportunity to negotiate with the chair of the National Association of Social Workers (NASW) in the United States to enter into an agreement for corresponding memberships between the two associations. Some of our members who later settled in the United States made use of this arrangement.

My third area of interest was the Indian Council of Social Welfare. In the late 1940s and early 1950s, two of my colleagues at the Tata School, Dr. Gore and Mr. Chatterjee, were very active in the formation of the Council. I was supportive. It was a highly effective body in the 1950s and 1960s. It successfully pressured the government to form the Department of Social Welfare.

The ICSW also promoted two schools of social work, one in Madras under the Guild of Services, the other at Hyderabad. Earlier, a school of social work had been established by the YWCA at Delhi.

And your role in the International Council of Social Welfare?

NANAVATTY: After retiring from my government and UN positions, I revived my interest in the Indian Council of Social Welfare. I became a member of the executive committee, and later the president appointed me as adviser to the Council. At that time, the Indian Council took active interest in the International Council of

Social Welfare, to which I was nominated as the Indian representative. I was a member of the executive committee of the International Council for about three years.

The ICSW was Western-oriented in its composition, so there was always a conflict of interest between developing and developed countries. I remember one meeting in Washington in 1992 when there was sharp, contrasting opinion about giving greater representation to developing countries. Interestingly enough, others from the West agreed with my views. They supported programs in the Asian and African regions and pursued greater representation of developing countries on the board.

Tell us more about your responsibilities as an officer, board member, or adviser in international professional societies and organizations.

NANAVATTY: From the very beginning I had an interest in professional organizations. In the late 1960s, I was working with the Ministry of Welfare. Litza Alexandrika of Greece, the organizing secretary of the International Federation of Social Workers (IFSW), asked if I would be interested in helping her organize a regional meeting in Bangkok. I did. At the meeting it was decided to formalize a regional unit under the leadership of Ms. Teresita Silva of the Philippines. Since then the federation has become a force to be reckoned with.

My association with the Inter-University Consortium for International Social Development (IUCISD) is relatively recent. I got interested in the consortium in the early 1990s. Its membership is relatively small, participation is meaningful, and deliberation professional. The very informal functioning and intimate atmosphere made me take greater interest. I was happy to contribute to the Indian Association of Schools of Social Work, becoming the consortium's first national association serving as an organizational member.

Your articles published in the Indian Journal of Social Work *and elsewhere during the 1990s carry through some interesting themes concerning social work and community, regional, and global development. Would you care to comment?*

NANAVATTY: In recent years I have started writing on various aspects of social work as related to social development. If I had adopted the practice of maintaining written records of my work with people and community earlier, it would have provided valuable teaching material.

Having received repeated requests from friends like Hans Nagpal and P. D. Kulkarni, I have recently co-edited two books. Both are compilations of papers prepared over the years; both reflect connections between social work and social work education and social development. The first of these, *Social Issues in Development,* covers development-oriented welfare, social work intervention in a market economy, the effect of globalization on poverty alleviation, analysis of the UN World Summit Social Development reports, and social change and social action.

Our second book, *NGOs in the Changing Scenario,* includes chapters on volunteerism and NGOs, prevailing myths and the realities of voluntary action, and the role of voluntary social work in revitalizing civic society. It also has a chapter on professional social work education in developing countries, integrating indigenous with modern trends. Although these papers reflect prevailing trends of social work in different years, their common theme is the importance of the interrelationship between and among individual, group, and community.

In your writings, you mentioned some distinctions between social work in Western countries and in developing countries such as India.

NANAVATTY:Yes, I recall writing on the subject in *NGOs in the Changing Scenario.* Since then, the influence of the universalized market economy on the world scene, including developing countries, is having a pronounced impact. Your question requires examination from several angles: adoption of the system of professional social work education in India, efforts at indigenization, emergence of three models of social work education, and the all-pervasive influence of the universalized market economy on social work education.

The development of professions is a phenomenon of an industrial civilization. As specialized services are required, systems of professional education have emerged. The professional education of social workers is no exception, although it has emerged very late compared with other key professions. India as a developing country tried to adopt the system of professional social work education established earlier in the West, following first a British and then an American model.

Fortunately, however, the initiator of social work education at the professional level, Dr. Manshardt, emphasized field-based services and a community-based approach in social work education at the Tata Institute. To meet the emerging requirements of industrial labor, courses on labor welfare and personnel management have been introduced, along with the courses in child and family welfare, rural development, and medical and psychiatric social work introduced in the 1940s and 1950s.

There emerged the urge to indigenize social work education to fit more closely with India's circumstances. Since independence, social work has tried to relate to national development programs (including the nation's five-year plans and the community development movement in both rural and urban areas) as well as to the promotion of voluntary social welfare agencies through grants-in-aid. Indigenization and the need to balance traditional social work methods with modern trends of development varies in emphasis from school to school.

With the passage of time, it was realized that the development process promoted in the country did not yield sufficient benefits at the ground level. Access to basic services of education, nutrition, health, and welfare did not sufficiently reach those who were marginalized, who constituted more than 50 percent of the population. The restless youth of the country, highly sensitive to the need for change, began to feel concerned with the slowness of development. They took to social action for change, including protest, agitation, and even revolt.

These young people's movements further influenced social work education. Three models emerged: generic social work, specialization of fields of service, and social action for social change. It is increasingly (if sometimes only gradually) being realized that the traditional approach of counseling and adjustment of people to the prevailing system could not remain the mainstay of social work education in India. There needs to be an emphasis on change in policy development, accompanied by change in administration. This may yet become the major distinction between social work education in India and in developed countries.

I now come to the last stage of my analysis: A universalized market economy has overtaken the world economy. With its spread, even state boundaries are obliterated. Economic systems are being merged into one another, resulting in the economic dependence of developing countries on the developed countries. New forms of economic colonialism have emerged, affecting state governance. Under this influence, the process of development is measured mainly in economic terms, spreading a consumerist, materialistic culture. Social aspects of life are being neglected or given low priority. Marginalized people throughout the world are adversely affected. The ideals of equitable distribution of resources and the overall quality of life have suffered.

Social work educators in both developed and developing countries need to work together as never before, to enable their students to learn of the emerging deprivation of resources for marginalized people throughout the world. Equal distribution of resources, and social justice, need to be emphasized in education across all borders. A course on international social work should be offered to students in both developed and developing countries to help unify understanding of social work everywhere. Some efforts are being made in this regard—for example, by The Ohio University College of Social Work in the United States, which is taking students to Sri Lanka and India.

Finally, education for social action and change has to be emphasized in all countries. Education must include ways to help empower people to overcome hazards of life. This could form the main content of social work students' study.

Among your volunteer activities, I understand that there is another that we haven't discussed. What has been your experience with the United Way?

NANAVATTY: The first three years, United Way International and UNICEF combined to support the initial expenses, later fundraising expenses were borne by the Baroda Citizens Council. In America, the United Way primarily raises funds through payroll deductions. However, in India there has been no such tradition; so in the first year the United Way of Baroda (UWB) raised funds through religious discourses, attended by large numbers. Subsequently, this practice was given up because of high administrative expenses.

As an alternative fundraiser, we organized annual cultural programs, for which the state of Gujarat in western India is famous. We found that in a continuous seven days of cultural programs during the festival season, we could collect nearly 1,500,000 rupees (approximately US $40,000), after deducting around 50,000 rupees as organizational expenses. Two-thirds of the net collection was shared with 35 to 40 voluntary agencies in Baroda. The United Way became financially functional.

Earlier, our emphasis on community development led to the formation of the Baroda Citizens Council, which has been active in some 15 slum areas of Baroda. Given our successful experience with projects in these 15 areas and with fundraising, we have since combined United Way Baroda with the Baroda Citizens Council into one organization.

We were interested in spreading the United Way idea, but the local people have not yet thought beyond Baroda. We have, through individual efforts, continued to get other cities, like Pune and Bangalore, interested in starting a United Way movement, but progress has been very slow.

What about some of the awards and honors that you have received?

NANAVATTY: I have received a number of awards, including (1) special appreciation of my services at the International Council on Social Welfare by Asia and Pacific Regional Conference at Kuala Lumpur, Malaysia in 1989; (2) special appreciation of services rendered to the Baroda Citizens Council jointly with the United Way Baroda, 1981–1990; (3) special recognition at the Tata Institute of Social Sciences, Bombay, on the occasion of the Diamond Jubilee of the Institute, along with senior alumni of the class of 1945, in appreciation and recognition for making a pioneering contribution to the profession of social work in India; and (4) a special award for outstanding international service from the Inter-University Consortium for International Social Development at its 10th Biennial International Symposium, Cairo, Egypt, in 1998.

As you reflect on your professional career, is there anything you think that you or the profession might have done differently?

NANAVATTY: The overall emphasis in social work should be on community development. The emerging emphasis on human resource development should be blended with community development. This does not mean we should neglect studies in casework.

Besides this, I would like to suggest three choices to students of social work in place of the existing syllabus. The first choice would be generic social work education, with emphasis placed equally on all fields of social work and methods of social work practice. The second alternative would be a specialized stream of social work education. After the first year of generic training, the second year would be devoted to a study of a specific field of social work, like child welfare, women's welfare, medical and psychiatric social work, or labor welfare and personnel management. (This alternative is widely offered today.) The third alternative would be to learn the methodology of social action and social change.

Aside from these suggestions for social work education, what do you see for the profession and for social agencies in India?

NANAVATTY: Many voluntary agencies have had a proud history of serving the welfare needs of women, children, seniors, and people with disabilities. Not only that, they succeeded in establishing an Indian Council of Social Welfare in the 1950s and became an effective force in pressuring the central government to establish a separate Department of Social Welfare in India. Most of these agencies were community-based, functioning with the participation of the people. However, over time, many of these agencies became dependent on government financial assistance, in the process losing their roots in the local communities. Added to this, many international organizations offered financial assistance for development and welfare activities in a big way in the 1970s.

Both of these developments, in the absence of any regulation by either the government or the profession, have resulted in a lack of openness about the use of funds and in unplanned development and increasing dependence on grant-giving agencies. The whole area of welfare and development was debased.

A regulatory body is needed, either of the government, the Council of Welfare and Developmental Agencies, or both to introduce rules for giving and taking grants, ensuring ethics of work, transparency of accounts, and accountability in the use of fund development.

Looking back over your career, do you have any other thoughts that you would care to share with future generations of social workers or current colleagues?

NANAVATTY: I would encourage students to make a career decision in favor of social work and to take professional training in social work. The profession provides possibilities for analyzing oneself and one's responsibilities in the context of the realities of life. It provides an ideological base of service as well as opportunities for work for social action and for social change. The challenges the profession offers and the sense of satisfaction it provides are unique.

JONA M. ROSENFELD

Born in Germany in 1922, Jona Rosenfeld immigrated at age 10 to Jerusalem with his parents. After high school, he joined a kibbutz and served in the Coastal Watch. From 1946 to 1948, he studied at the London School of Economics (LSE), earning certificates in colonial social science and mental health (with professional training at the Tavistock Institute and Maudsley Hospital).

When he returned to Israel, he worked as a mental health officer with the Israel Defense Forces as well as with health, mental health, and child guidance services, completing his bachelor's degree at Hebrew University in 1954. He then studied for his master's degree and doctorate in social work administration at the University of Chicago (1955–1961). Returning to Israel, Dr. Rosenfeld joined the Paul Baerwald School of Social Work at the Hebrew University, and over time became its first professor and served as its director. He has also lectured at universities in Africa, Europe, and North America.

Dr. Rosenfeld was a pioneer in conducting action research and developing innovative learning projects gleaned from effective practices with Holocaust refugees, as well as with individuals, families, and groups experiencing extreme poverty and exclusion. His aim has been to improve social policies, organizational structures, and practices. He continues to be engaged in research, teaching, and practice, principally through the JDC–Brookdale Institute and its Center for Children and Youth, where he heads the Unit on Learning from Success in the Social Services. He has served as expert adviser, member, chair, and activist of several public and professional committees on health, welfare, and education issues and has written extensively. For his accomplishments, Dr. Rosenfeld has received the Israel Prize for Research in Social Work. He is married and has two daughters.

BILLUPS: *Could you please tell us something about your early childhood years?*

ROSENFELD: I was born into a well-situated Jewish family in a relatively small town called Karlsruhe in southern Germany. Three of my grandparents were from there; all were observant Jews, well-versed in German culture.

My paternal grandmother came from a family with quite a few cultured and prominent people. Many impressive women belonged to the clan. Among them was the well-known psychoanalyst Freida Fromm-Reichmann, one of the first psychoanalysts to treat people with psychosis. Another is Dr. Helene Simon, who left her orthodox Jewish home at the turn of the century to study at the London School of Economics with Beatrice and Sidney Webb. She wrote a book about Robert Owen, the Fabians, and other utopian socialists. This was the intellectual heritage and ambience of my childhood.

My father's paternal family were growers and merchants of cattle for centuries. He went on to study law and, at an early age, became a Zionist. This was quite unusual in this small town with few Jews. How unusual it was became evident to me one day when I walked with him in the streets of Jerusalem and he pointed to somebody across the street and said, "There is Dr. S. When I married your mother, he came to your grandfather and told him he shouldn't allow his daughter to marry me because I was a Zionist."

My father didn't like being a lawyer—I think he was really a potential social worker. When I was a schoolboy in Palestine and he was the head of the German Immigrants' Association, I remember him patiently advising newcomers on how to find their way in this land. He was quite a romantic. He played cello and my mother played the piano. Both sang, read a lot, and were passionately interested in psychoanalysis; both had undergone personal analysis, which was quite rare in that day and age. My father knew Greek, Latin, French, and Hebrew. He was an idealist and a realist. Because of his Zionism, so many of our family left Nazi Germany in time. Much of what he was has shaped my life.

My mother was an extremely colorful and interesting woman. Though she had not finished high school, she was well-educated, highly literate, musical, and of the world. Her father's family, Ettlinger, came from a nearby village named Ettlingen, inhabited for centuries by families who were orthodox Jews, some of them rabbis. Her mother's family had come from a rich Russian family, and it was said that we had lost all of our money because of the Russian Revolution.

This is my heritage. It consists of literate people who were idealists, social minded, deeply involved in their community, and also quite daring, as is reflected in both my parents giving up religious observance. All these four families were interconnected, played an important part in our lives, and contributed to an atmosphere of familial togetherness.

I was the youngest of three brothers. We were all members of a Zionist youth movement, which was quite unusual. My brothers went to non-Jewish schools throughout their school years; I only went to a non-Jewish school during my first year. In 1929, my father changed occupations, and we moved to Berlin, and I went to a Zionist school.

Berlin was a big city that felt cold and desolate. We left it after four years when the Nazis came to power. On the eve of the boycott day, my father left Germany, after the February 1933 torchlight parade where the Nazis sang, "When there will be Jewish blood on our spears, life is going to be better." That I had seen from our fifth-floor veranda and it left an indelible impression, an impression of having met evil. On that Saturday evening we took my father to the railway station on his way to Holland.

My brother had gone there to live on a kibbutz, and my middle brother, then 16 years old, went on his own to Holland to train how to become a farmer. For both of them, to leave their well-situated, middle-class family was a tremendous change. Hitler's rise to power gave them the impetus to pursue Zionism because they believed in the importance of Jewish youth becoming productive, devoting themselves to developing the country rather than pursuing other careers. This was what my brothers did.

I had stayed behind with my mother in Berlin, where we packed some of our belongings into a wooden container that was then shipped to Palestine. I remember how I hated to leave so much behind, even though I knew that my father and my brothers certainly thought it was an opportunity to get out and to get to a place where one could finally live as one wanted.

It was important for my parents that one be faithful to oneself. To be faithful to oneself meant to live as a Jew, and if you are a Jew, to be a Zionist, and not to assimilate. All of these were aspects of one's integrity, of being genuine and authentic.

We left Germany by way of Switzerland and then, on September 15, 1933, arrived in Haifa. I was 10 years old, and it was rough. It was a strange land, and I didn't fully understand why we had come there.

What were some of the highlights of your school years in Palestine?

ROSENFELD: In Germany we lived *mainly* among Jews, but here it was *totally* among Jews. At school the children were told to be nice to us newcomers, but during the first year making fun of foreign German boys was the rule. During the second year the school became a continuation of the Berlin school, with the headmistress from my Zionist school in Berlin. There were a lot of German-Jewish boys and girls there, so I felt more at home. What seems important is that I was able to read German all my life, though later I read mainly English and much less Hebrew. I read a lot of German literature and took literature courses, which few others did. I might not have done this, but I was searching to feel at home in a strange environment.

I had fantastic teachers. That was very important to me and also for my later life as a teacher. First of all, they were knowledgeable. Second, they liked to teach. And many of them were very nice people. I was not an excellent student, but I liked what I learned. I learned a lot from the Bible, not from a religious point of view so much as from a literary perspective, which I came to like very much. I did quite well in mathematics, but it was the humanities that interested me. At home we had a large library, including books on psychoanalysis. I read much psychoanalysis in my youth, some of it prematurely.

Many people, especially relatives, came to visit us. Some were uprooted newcomers who came to stay with us for awhile. Our house was a kind of center for newcomers from Germany. It was a friendly place. As in Germany, there were musical evenings. This helped to counterbalance my feeling a bit of an outsider at school.

When I finished high school in 1941, the war was on, and I had to decide what to do. I joined the kibbutz of my brother in a marvelous place near the Lake of Galilee called Ginossar. Once again I felt like a displaced person. I was the one with the most education. The others were very intelligent, but most of them had not had much schooling. I had some friends there. I was quite good at manual work, and for a time I wanted to become a carpenter. Being there was a kind of time-out, because during the war you couldn't go and study. One was afraid the Germans might invade.

In retrospect, I got a lot out of being on this kibbutz. It was my first exposure to the world and life in a humane collective society. I became a librarian to maintain my intellectual interests. I taught some literature, and some nights I walked for an hour and a half to and from the kibbutz to take courses in Tiberias. Though there was no radio, there were concerts and a gramophone in the kibbutz.

Staying in the kibbutz meant doing some kind of national service, and I was sent to join the Coastal Watch. Our task was to defend the country against any invasion from the sea. We lived in primitive conditions and I felt quite strange among the people there. I used the time to study for the London matriculation by correspondence. I also studied for three months in an intensive seminar organized by the kibbutz movement to train to be an emissary to Jews who survived the Holocaust in Europe and to bring them to Palestine. I decided not to go to Europe because I didn't think this kind of underground work suited me, but I learned many things in that seminar.

And about this time your journey in social work started.

ROSENFELD: It started one Saturday when I was walking in the German colony of Jerusalem and passing the British Council, just a hundred meters from where we live now. I walked in and said, "I would like to go to England to study. Do you have a stipend?" They said, "What would you like to study?" I said, "I would like to study English literature." They said, "Sorry, we do not have a stipend for English literature, but we happen to have one for colonial social science." Three weeks later I was on a plane to go to the London School of Economics and Political Science (LSE) to study for a certificate in Colonial Social Science. I had no idea what it was. That was one stroke of great luck.

So, off to England for study. What do you care to share of that experience?

ROSENFELD: The war had been very frightening. During that time Churchill was my one hero. Whenever he spoke on the radio, I was not only fascinated, but also reassured. He has remained all these years the one man whom I admire most, which partly explains my affinities for England.

It was totally fortuitous and tremendous luck that I got this stipend for tuition. My parents paid for the rest of it. I came to the London School of Economics, about which I didn't know anything, and joined my class somewhat late. There were fellow students from the Caribbean islands, Aden, Kenya, and Mauritius, as well as an Arab from Palestine. They were a select group of people who came there to train for introducing welfare into the colonies, which was what the British Labor government wanted.

The London School of Economics had just moved from Cambridge back to London. In Cambridge, the teachers had been underemployed; at long last they had students who wanted to learn. They were eager and fantastic teachers. There was Arthur Lewis, for instance, an economist, who later became vice chancellor of the University of the West Indies. I remember once when he talked about the British empire he said, "You know, in another five to ten years all there will remain will be England's green pastures, no empire, no nothing. This will all fade away." We were shocked. We thought that the British empire would last forever.

I liked it so much I stayed for a third year, on my own initiative, to become a psychiatric social worker. Again at the London School of Economics, I took what was called the Mental Health Course and, once again, I had excellent teachers. My clinical training was in two marvelous places, the Maudsley Hospital and the Tavistock Clinic, both famous for their teachers. Some of them were quite well-known, like Aubrey Lewis, professor of psychiatry at the Maudsley Hospital, and John Bowlby, the child psychiatrist and psychoanalyst, at the Tavistock Clinic. This clinical training was really excellent.

To make London home for almost three years was an event in itself. The first half-year I just walked through London and looked at shop windows. Then there was the theater and ballet. Teaching at LSE, there were Harold Laski, a socialist, professor, and, for a time, head of the Labor party, as well as Friedrich von Hayek, the conservative economist, and Karl Popper. It was not so much what I learned from them that was important as it was the atmosphere of societal renewal and idealism.

What followed your study at the London School?

ROSENFELD: Toward the end of my stay, the War of Independence broke out in Israel. I had become active in Zionist activities as a member of the council of the Jewish/Palestinian student organization. I prepared to return to Israel. There, with the guidance of Gerald Caplan, a child psychiatrist and public mental health specialist who later became a professor at Harvard, we set up a psychiatric unit in the Israeli Army. It was fantastic.

I came back to Israel in August of 1948, and, under Dr. Caplan's leadership, we recruited to set up a modern psychiatric unit in the army. As I used to say, I became the first mental health officer in the Israel Army since the destruction of the second Temple. I participated in setting up mental health services as my first social work responsibility—all this in the middle of the war. It was terrible to see young people suffering from battle neuroses and trauma. Never in my life did I learn so well or so much in such a short period of time.

I worked for the Israeli Army for one and a half formative years. I remember the names of many of the patients, and I felt that I was most useful to people—soldiers—in dire straits. The soldiers not only had lived through the terrible occurrences of battle, but many of them had come from the Holocaust, and it was a repetition of trauma. I had a tremendous opportunity for doing good as part of the struggle for the establishment of the Jewish state.

My boss, Gerald Caplan, was an excellent teacher. He and our team were very inquisitive, curious, entrepreneurial, adventurous, and committed both to the soldiers and to our new society. It was really a marvelous setting. I could not have wished for a better first job as a social worker. I remember how worried I was about being a novice and going back to a country at war. My tutor at LSE had noticed this and asked me, "Why are you worried?" I said, "Look, I know that I shall have to do something I have never done before. I'm afraid that I won't have the intuition." She said, "Intuition is a master of experience." So I went back reassured that I could get the experience, and that's what I did.

From 1950 to 1955, I had the good fortune of aiding in establishing the first Child's Guidance Clinic in Israel, and probably in the Middle East. The Hadassah Lasker Mental Health and Child Guidance Clinic, initially headed by Gerald Caplan and then by Fred Stone, was staffed by very able and dedicated colleagues, including social workers. We worked under the best of conditions for budding professionals. We had a well-equipped office, qualified staff, regular case conferences, lectures from famous professionals from all over the world who flocked to Israel and wanted to contribute. We also had fantastic supervisors, first a supervisor from England, Elizabeth Irvine, then one from Washington, DC, named Pauline Miller-Shereshefsky. Her husband, J. Leon Shereshefsky, who had been with the Manhattan Project, had come to Israel for idealistic reasons. Both would remain close friends of mine. I learned a lot from her, as from other colleagues, as well as from the patients and from the kinds of work I did.

Of the three areas I worked in, my most unusual work was in the marvelous well-baby clinics established for Jews and Arabs in 1917 by Hadassah, an American Jewish women's association. Our idea was that it was important to work with families of young children before problems emerged. I went one day a week to a poor neighborhood, working both with mothers who had difficulties with parenthood and with the nurses who served them. I had supervision from psychoanalysts to learn how to work with these mothers and their infants, in addition to working with nurses to become equipped to work with these families, which I had never done before.

The second area was a very moving one: participating in the integration of children and adolescents who had come to Israel after the war. We were retained by an organization called Youth Aliyah, an organization that brought children from the Holocaust as well as others from the countries of Asia. We were three social workers working with 13,000 children with tremendous problems. We had the vision to invent something, which I wrote up in my first two papers, one with a fellow social worker, Joseph Neipris, the other with Caplan.

Since we did not have enough staff to work with so many children and youths in need, we helped the staff in charge of these youths to be caring to the children, not to be afraid to hear their stories—especially of those who had come from Europe, and to give them space. They had the tendency not to want to hear what they had to tell because it was too cruel and upsetting. What we did was really not that sophisticated. It was to help them tell the story, talk about it, and not hide it.

I remember many of their stories, but I shall only mention my first boy patient, whom I am still in touch with. Offering therapy to him and others was the third component of our work. He, as a four-year-old boy, had been living with his parents underground in Poland—literally under the ground. One day his parents departed to get food for him, the Poles turned them over to the Germans, and they never came back. What this four-year-old had to come to terms with was a frightening legacy. The relatives with whom he survived were not nice to him. He ran away and came to Youth Aliyah, where he was referred for therapy because of his misery. Through him I learned for the first time what the Holocaust was all about. Some of what I learned then about how to work with victims of the Holocaust I published with Dr. Margaret Brand in what is one of the first articles on this subject, "A Mother Whose Child Wouldn't Eat."

During this period you continued with your formal education and entered into university teaching as well. Could you speak to this period of your career?

ROSENFELD: At this time I began to study for a bachelor's degree at the Hebrew University. I had obtained certificates at the London School of Economics. Now I wanted a degree. I studied sociology and education, again with some excellent teachers, among them S. N. Eisenstadt and Joseph Ben David, both well-known sociologists.

I then started to teach in the Department of Sociology at the Hebrew University. I taught mainly interviewing, which was a totally new skill in that department. Some of the people I taught were very gifted, and some of them became famous.

What happened next?

ROSENFELD: That brings me to 1955. My employer at the time was the Hadassah Medical Organization, sponsored by the Hadassah Women's Organization of America, which had done a lot for the health services of Israel. After I had worked for them for five years, they offered me a scholarship to study for a doctorate in the United States and to set up their hospital social services on my return. I applied to Columbia University and to the University of Chicago.

I went to Chicago after stopping over and working in England for a few months. There I met Richard Titmuss. He and I hit it off well, and he asked me to be his assistant at the London School of Economics. It was very tempting. But I went to the States for two reasons. First, S. N. Eisenstadt thought that since I had already been to England, I should go to America and see another world. Second, I had read J. D. Salinger's *Catcher in the Rye,* and I wanted to get to know the world of Holden Caulfield.

I went to America in 1955 and stayed in Chicago for six years. It was a long period for studying, but I needed it as a kind of intellectual and professional moratorium. Living in Israel, in Palestine, was very hectic. My studies before were always in between or in some way before or after; I had never had the opportunity to devote myself to study and research.

When I came to the School of Social Service Administration (SSA) in the first year, I felt utterly out of place. I saw myself as a clinician, interested in psychotherapy, psychoanalysis, and only in applying my clinical acumen to excluded populations.

The best thing about Chicago was that the teachers were not only good, they were also extremely tolerant. They let me do my thing. For instance, I could not agree with the problem-solving approach, but those who taught it were such marvelous teachers and people—Charlotte Towle and Helen Perlman.... Then there was Alton Linford, the dean, and Mary MacDonald. They didn't always understand who I was, but what I appreciated most was that they were always curious to find out. Certainly for a long time I did not understand who they were, but they gave me room for whatever I needed.

I had one idea that was more important to me than anything else. Social work meant working with people with whom we don't know how to work. This was my main interest, not to work with people who had "motivation, capacity, and opportunity." It was up to us to give the people the opportunity to get what they needed. I can say that today much better than at the time; still, I said it then, and I think they respected me for it.

What I wanted to do was to find out the difference between those who continued using psychiatric services and those who did not, without attributing it to their socio-demographic characteristics. I wanted to look at their help-taking expectations. I assumed that those who were able to come to therapy and stay had previous help-taking experiences that fit what they were offered. Hence we had to learn about the help-taking experiences or expectations of the noncontinuer to be able to adapt ourselves to what they could use. To do this has just really been the main thing that has preoccupied me throughout my professional life.

I called my thesis "The Strangeness Between the Helper and the Client." I did an analysis of help-taking incidence of matched pairs of continuers and noncontinuers with psychiatric services. I traveled throughout Chicago, interviewing people in their homes, asking them to tell me "times in your life when you were helped, or not helped, excluding psychiatric help." I did a content analysis about who their helpers were, what the problems were, and what help they had been offered, and then compared the responses of the continuers and the noncontinuers. I came up with the idea that the responses of the latter group set the stage for social work.

The main thing I liked, and from which I benefited and learned, was how to allow my theories and opinions to be undermined by what "clients" experienced. It was not easy. I've become better at it in the last few years, but it was really pattern-setting for being respectful of clients, as of students and their ideas, and for helping them to become who they wanted to become.

That I could take courses with Edward Shils, Bruno Bettelheim, and Everett Hughes made these really important years for me. My gratitude to the University of Chicago has stayed with me.

Following the years in Chicago, you returned to Israel.

ROSENFELD: I came back to Israel and was hired by the new Paul Baerwald School of Social Work at the Hebrew University of Jerusalem. They had to buy me out from my contract with the Hadassah.

Eileen Blackey, an outstanding social worker from the States, headed the faculty. She was not Jewish. During the war she went with Eisenhower to Europe and worked with UNRA. She told the story of how she went to the cellars of Warsaw to look for documents where the Nazis had recorded how they had taken blond children from Poland to train them in what was called "Hitler Heime," in which they tried to breed a new race of Aryans. They had taken the children away from their parents, and Blackey initiated efforts to return these children to their parents. This totally floored me, and affirmed me in my seeing social work as the profession which acts in unusual ways for the benefit of people whose well-being depended on us. It struck me that we should do what those who had saved Jews during the war had done.

I came to the Paul Baerwald School of Social Work, founded by the Joint Distribution Committee, and again I was fortunate to come to a place where something was being created. We had an enthusiastic, collegial group. There was a kind of pioneer atmosphere, a sense of mission, and a sense of having to establish this most important profession in Israel. We were always politically involved, be it in social policy or in national professional issues.

For instance, the elections of the union of social workers were according to political parties and not based on professional issues. Two days before the election, we and some of our students and others paid for an ad in the newspaper telling social workers not to vote because you cannot vote according to parties when your professional organization has to fend for both social workers and clients.

The second director of the school was Yisrael Katz, an Israeli who had studied in America at Case Western Reserve as a student of Herman Stein. He had a lot of political acumen. (He later became minister of labor and social affairs.) This was a skill I did not have, and he carried us along in social policy issues. That's how we at the school became activists. I gradually moved more and more into this wider field of action. My teaching reflected this.

When I began, I didn't teach social casework. I taught about deviance, the introduction to social welfare, and the relationship between social science theory and social work. I always had my hand in working with the supervisors of students in the field.

I started out in charge of the human growth and development sequence. I later became head of the master's program and head of the committee that set up the program. Eventually, I became head of the school and one of the first social work professors in Israel.

Students were always very important to me, yet I was known as being rather demanding. It was very important to me to always have links to other departments in the university. My aim was never to be isolated in the School of Social Work.

During all these years, I was active in the International Association of Schools of Social Work (IASSW), twice as an elected member of its board. I went to many of the IASSW Conferences and made a career out of becoming a social work teacher and grooming others for that career.

I think I made it possible for social work not to be psychotherapy—not in spite of the fact that I was a caseworker, but because of it. I thought that we had to find our own domain. That's what I wrote about. All the years I worked in psychotherapy, I thought that, as some people play the piano and others the cello, some are psychotherapists and others social workers. These are parallel careers that influence each other. I always acknowledged that I was a psychotherapist, but when I taught social work method courses I was very careful not to turn it into training for psychotherapy. One can benefit from what psychotherapy, psychoanalysis, and dynamic psychology can teach, but I did not think that's what we should train for in social work.

Your time in academia has included visiting professorships in countries other than your own. Could you tell us something about those experiences?

ROSENFELD: I have always been in touch with the International Association of Schools of Social Work (IASSW). I was always deeply moved by meeting social work leaders from different countries. I admired their struggle to be teachers under what were often impossible conditions, and I learned a lot from them. I was intrigued by using indigenous material for teaching rather than importing it from elsewhere, yet I was also quite aware that doing that may put one at the risk of not availing oneself of what is the best.

It was fascinating to see social work enter the Communist bloc, for instance, China. I had met a Chinese sociologist who groomed himself in Hong Kong and learned how to introduce social work into China. He told me, "In China in the past, before there was social work, we were engaged in interpreting the collective to the individual. Now we are trying to interpret the individual to the collective." I also had the opportunity to admire the struggle of social work in South America. There, they were engaged in the struggle between radicalism as introduced by Paulo Freire versus serving the interests of the individual, the issue being how the collective considers its own needs without becoming obsessed with them.

My first research was sponsored by the U.S. Department of Health Education and Welfare. My late colleague, Lotte Salzberger, and I conducted a study on the relationship between the need of socially deprived populations and the provision of services. It was the first study on poverty in Israel. I got connected with people from the School of Social Work at Columbia University, like Alfred Kahn and Mitch Ginsberg. They repeatedly came to Israel, and I went to Columbia for two years (from 1978 to 1980). There I learned how to teach casework. I also taught a doctoral course on which I based much of what I have done since.

While at Columbia, I did a study with the Jewish Children and Family Society about people whose homes had burned down. I explored how some of them fared better after their homes had burned down than before. I interviewed them, at times in slums, trying to find out what the secret of their doing better was. It turned out that those who did better had had someone who had treated them nicely in their childhood and that they, themselves, had mutually caring relationships with their children. This study set the stage for all my subsequent work on learning from success.

I also lectured at the University of Witwatersrand in Johannesburg, addressed the conference of social workers in Ghana, and had, and still have, many contacts with the Alice Salomon School of Social Work in Berlin, where I was a visiting professor and where I have recently become an honorary professor.

What would you say have been other highlights of your professional work?

ROSENFELD: As a mental health officer, I helped to shape the important work in the Israeli army. What was important to me was not just that we might help the Israeli army to win battles. It was also that the army might provide people from deprived backgrounds not just with the opportunity to do military service, but also to serve their society and, thus, to increase their social mobility.

I presented these thoughts in my 1980 Teller Lecture at the School of Social Service Administration at the University of Chicago. "Serving the Individual or the Collective: Lessons from the Wars of Israel" was published in English and Hebrew. I described what the army could do to make it possible for people of deprived backgrounds to serve their nation and be served by it. The number of children in residential care is higher in Israel than in any other country. In contrast with some of my American colleagues, I always thought that this is a desirable and effective way in which this society serves its children and youth. I always have tried to make sure that residential care remained socially acceptable and of good quality so that it could benefit children and youths from deprived backgrounds, not for recruiting children from poor families to support political or religious causes.

Another facet of my work has been as one of the founders of the National Council of the Child. This is a kind of citizen's committee set up to create public concern for the needs and rights of children and youths. It has functioned as a watchdog and has had a remarkable impact in contributing to legislation and reforms in the field. Its activities resulted in the Knesset (Israel's Parliament) setting up a permanent committee on the rights of children.

I am a member of a committee on poverty trying to give people the opportunity to hear about, ferret out, and disseminate useful programs for families living in poverty.

My work on public committees is to draw attention—to provide visibility and to give a voice to those underprivileged, underserved, and socially deprived groups that society does not know how to serve. For example, in the 1960s there was an interest in youths who were on the periphery of society, a group no one thought existed. I headed a committee of citizens and teachers and students from the school of social work to provide services and opportunities to these youth.

This social workers' action committee joined forces with social workers in welfare offices in Jerusalem who had no budget or mandate to serve these youths and their families. Some of the social workers who joined us were dismissed for a while; we fought for them to be reinstated. Our work contributed to separating the provision of social benefit from the delivery of social services, and it established a tradition of the social work profession fighting for its clients, i.e., not seeing itself responsible for the well-being of society as an abstraction or just for its own salaries.

I may have overdone it at times, but I thought my role in the education for the profession was to provide professionals and their organizations with knowledge and opportunities to discover and serve new groups of potential clients. What was most important for me was to help social workers be proud through discovering and effectively serving those who were least well-attended to, playing a role in enabling their society to put into action its humanizing commitment toward those people who were least well-served.

Perhaps my most important article is "The Domain and Expertise of Social Work: A Conceptualization." I state there that the nobility of social work is to serve people and their needs that society and other professions have not attended to. So I consider the profession's major expertise to be the "invention of intervention."

An area where I made a difference was our study of socially deprived families in Israel. In the course of this study I coined the phrase "incongruence between needs and provisions," the former referring to the "client" and the latter to the network of " services."

This work got me in touch with the ATD Fourth World Movement, with which I have worked ever since and to which I owe so much. I learned through them how to drop any patronizing and overprofessional stance and to adopt a stance of joining or working in partnership, learning directly from families who are living in extreme poverty and exclusion. The movement is working in many countries worldwide. I hope we shall be able to establish some work in this country, perhaps for and with both Palestinian and Israeli families.

Please share some highlights in your work with the International Association of Schools of Social Work.

ROSENFELD: One highlight is a paper I wrote for the IASSW conference in Puerto Rico 20 years ago, in which I talked about the particular and universal in social work. What is universal about social work is that, wherever we are, we are to serve those who are the least well-served. The particular is that we do so by adapting to the context in which we work; therefore, we cannot transfer expertise from place to place and learn from the knowledge that is in the field in the different societies in which social work functions.

The paper I gave in Puerto Rico may reveal why I served so long on the board of IASSW. I really was interested in how our profession serves societies and people in different lands, and I tried to be of use to people from unfamiliar countries. For me, the only thing was to be in tune with what I consider the heart of social work, which is to help people and colleagues in countries where it is hard to do this work, rather than congratulating ourselves on what we do when it is relatively easy.

During my visits to Ghana and Zimbabwe, I felt passionate about providing colleagues with any support they needed to do their work, not to teach them, but to help them become what they are. I think IASSW has had some successes in this area during the last 10 or 20 years, but 20 to 30 years ago that was an uphill struggle, because there was that tremendous wish to dominate.

This might explain my reaction to questions about some aspects of recent attempts to introduce social work into countries that had been under Communist rule. I thought that, rather than just coming and teaching them what to do, we might try to find out what we can learn from what they had done right, not because I wanted to uphold Communism, but because they had done things we had not done, in the field of education and in opportunities for women, for example. Enabling ourselves to contribute to those who are least well-served and to develop the expertise necessary to serve them: That's what connected me with IASSW, as did my friendship with so many who served it, like Katherine Kendall, Robin Huws-Jones, and Ralph Garber.

Have there been professional concerns and themes that you haven't mentioned? Any changes in your thinking that you could share?

ROSENFELD: I have become very interested in finding ways of learning with and from people working in the field, trying to extract how they are working successfully and how to learn with them and from them—how they work with those I call "the inaptly served." I have been deeply influenced by my late and deeply beloved colleague from the Massachusetts Institute of Technology, Donald Schön. He wrote about the "reflective practitioner"; the idea is that you learn by reflecting about what you do. He coined the metaphor that in the past, people from the vineyards went to the people on the top of the mountain to learn from them, and that it's about time the people from the top of the mountain went down into the vineyards and learned with and from them.

In recent years, I have become engaged in "reflective practice" (another term for it I learned recently is "cooperative inquiry"). That means partly learning from those who do well and partly learning with them, as well as those with whom they work. We have written about such practices in a book, *Out from Under.* There we took eight Israeli practitioners who work with families and with children with whom others didn't know how to work. We asked them to write up the story of how they were working with families. The findings are markedly different from what we teach in schools of social work.

This has led me to my current interests in documenting effective practice and seeing how it can have an impact on policy, organizational structure, teaching, and research. What might be considered universal is that we do not go from policy to practice, from organizational structure, research, and teaching to practice, but the other way around. The pathway is to use effective practice as a catalyst for improving policies, organizational structures, research, and training. This is where I am now.

I am now engaged in an inquiry with a group of colleagues in Jerusalem and England in "the neglected area" of child neglect. Here we try to find out how one can effectively work with these families, and what the implications of these practices are for shaping the organizational structure. We also explore what is required to provide the social workers with what they need so that they can treat their clients well. It means to address and care for what Olive Stevenson calls "the pain of the worker," which cannot be done within a hierarchical structure but needs a kind of a "collegiate system." I'm passionately interested in how to create systems in which people can have support and opportunity for reflection.

During the past eight years, I have worked with nurses in well-baby clinics because I believe that universal services provide the best entry and opportunity for people who are underprivileged. These service settings are not stigmatized; they are accessible, and everyone can address their concerns. We are now trying to introduce this work into the whole public health system by training people from inside the system. We are trying to transform the well-baby clinics into a major source of support and services for families with young children by enabling nurses to become partners of the families with whom they work.

I much prefer partnership to empowerment, which I consider a militant, patronizing, even "male" word; I do not bestow power on you, but join you. Partnership, or, rather, joined work with stakeholders, seems to me to enable social workers to change the course of their work.

Following John Dewey, I just learned there's something called "interaction" and "transaction." In contrast with interactions between billiard balls, which remain unchanged, there are transactions where both participants are transformed. Our business, then, is to transform not just social work but also social institutions through contact with clients—that is, transactions where each has contributed to the change in the other. This means that however poor families may be, they can have an impact. Families rarely if ever have the sense of contributing to changing social services. Our book on this theme (with Bruno Tardieu), *Artisans of Democracy: How Ordinary People, Families in Extreme Poverty, and Social Institutions Become Allies to Overcome Social Exclusion*, has shown how, through getting to know poor families, employer-employee relationships within the organizations with which ATD worked have changed substantially.

You have received a number of awards, most recently a highly prestigious award for research in social work.

ROSENFELD: Yes, I was the first to receive the Israeli Prize in research in social work. The significance of this award is that what our generation of social workers did is taken seriously. It acknowledges that what my colleagues, some of whom have been my students, and I have done has had an impact. It is a recognition of the profession and a recognition for our having worked in unexplored areas, like the army, with its personnel and families of the merchant marine, another area of my studies — that is populations about whom nobody or few had thought about. This refers as much to

Arab refugees as to those Israelis who had to return from the Sinai to Israel 20 years after the Six Day War. I have always worked with people who had lived through the Holocaust, whose trauma had to be worked through.

This pertains also to what I am currently doing at the Brookdale Research Institute, where we have set up a Center for Children and Youth and where I established a small unit, the Unit of Learning from Success in the Social Services.

Let me say something about my interest of working with Arab populations living in poverty. If you look at the Arabs living in poverty and Jews living in poverty, it is their poverty that they have in common. I have the idea that when you look at the things that they have in common, and not just the differences, you enable them to join forces.

As a member of the Fourth World Movement, I went to visit all kinds of poor families in Europe and in Israel, Jews and Arabs, Bedouin families living in caves in the Negev or poor Palestinian families in the old city of Jerusalem. What all of them have in common is that they have something to contribute that is rarely explored. At the end of the visit with a Palestinian woman, Mme Alwyne de Vos van Steenwijk, the International President of ATD, asked whether our hostess had a message for other families living in poverty in the rest of the world. The woman didn't believe that is what she had been asked. "A message?" "Yes." And after a while she said, "Yes, I've got a message. Tell them what I am telling my children every morning. 'Always hope, never give up, and struggle for tomorrow.'" I am now planning a symposium in which poor Arab families and poor Jewish families will tell their stories to the world and to each other.

You were invited to give the keynote address at a recent joint congress of the International Association of Schools of Social Work and the International Council on Social Welfare in Jerusalem. Could you share with us any thoughts about your presentation?

ROSENFELD: I accepted it on short notice, and it was a very hard task. It took me some time to decide on the topic, but I liked the one I chose.

The Congress was about peace and social justice. I decided not to talk about peace because it was too difficult in this day and age to talk about peace here in Israel if you wanted to remain loyal to your country. So I thought I should call my lecture "Exclusion and Social Justice: From Impasse to Reciprocity." What I meant by that was that we have to focus not on abstractions like equality, welfare, or social development, but on something that clearly points to what happens in the course of the interactions, or, rather, potential transactions between people and social institutions to those who are socially excluded, who do not know how to use social institutions and whom social institutions serve ineptly.

My lecture refers to moving even beyond from what Adam Smith called sympathy and compassion. The latter he had thoughtfully called "the fellow feeling for the other's pain". However, I believe that to do the job of social work, compassion is not enough. What is really necessary is "generosity," which I have defined as the "fellow feeling for the other's pleasure." If we are good social workers, we will be different people after we work with our clients than we were before, not just professionally, but also in how we treat our children and our neighbors. That's also what I mean by reciprocity, where each is the other's beneficiary and benefactor.

On reflection, is there anything concerning your professional career that you might have done differently?

ROSENFELD: When I was first a teacher, I think I was too harsh. It is alright to be a demanding teacher, but the art of teaching is that you talk *with* your students; you don't talk *at* them.

I think I didn't always make use of the quality of the students we had. There is a tender balance between keeping up the standards and being considerate. I wasn't so aware of this 30 years ago. I'm glad that I'm aware of it today.

Have you continued to be active politically?

ROSENFELD: Yes, I have been active with organizations that deal with such public services as the conflicts between Arabs and Jews and between religious and non-religious people. We try to create dialogue among these groups and with the members of the Knesset. We are trying to write a covenant about the relationship between the religious and the nonreligious members of the Knesset.

I have been active also in the Federation of Social Workers, heading and appearing before public committees, signing petitions, and working with most of the ever-changing heads of the Ministry of Labor and Social Affairs, the ministers or the director general. I have always been engaged in what happens around me.

What words might you have for current members of the social work profession or for students yet to enter social work?

ROSENFELD: Don't be doctrinaire. What you have to do is to mobilize, to discover, to invent, to search for what will work, and the origin of this knowledge is not just in books, but in people themselves.

It's all about learning, cooperative inquiry, about making others partners in one's search of knowledge. This is not only worthwhile and effective—it also keeps you alive. A good professional is a constant traveler. You are like a hippie, like a wandering scholar. Don't become a specialist in one area. This doesn't mean you need consider yourself a weak generalist, someone ignorant about many areas. The world changes so fast; it is important that you change with the world. You won't catch up with everything, but what you can do is be attuned to what happens.

Another thing I would say is that you have your hand in many, if not all, aspects of the society in which you live. Don't use your profession to do your thing, but try to find out what is going on around you, what the context is in which you operate.

I would also say it is important to be politically involved—not necessarily in politics, but so that you don't ignore what is going on. When Yitzhak Rabin was murdered, we social workers set up a special meeting to try to understand what we could learn about violence in this society. We "used" the murder of Rabin not just to preach or teach, but also to learn from what is going on.

Don't be content with anything that is shabby—not in teaching, nor in learning, nor in the profession. Another way of being a good social worker is to put in writing what you are doing, to disseminate what you believe is worthwhile—not your theories but your real achievements, those that may continue to inspire you and inspire others. Without minimizing the intellectual aspect, a lot of social work is inspiration and a passion for and fascination with action. The knowledge is in the field and it is up to us of the schools to help our colleagues to extricate, formulate, and disseminate it.

RICHARD SPLANE

Born in 1916, Richard Splane studied economics, history, and social work at the London School of Economics, McMaster University, and the University of Toronto. He earned a bachelor's degree in economics and history, master's degrees in history and social work, and a doctorate in social work. His early life included pioneer farming in northern Alberta and service as a pilot in the Royal Canadian Air Force in World War II.

As a public official in the Canadian Department of National Health and Welfare, Dr. Splane led the development of social welfare programs. As Assistant Deputy Minister for Social Allowances and Services, he represented Canada internationally, including on the board of UNICEF.

In 1972, Dr. Splane became a professor of social policy and administration at the University of Alberta. From 1972 to 1984, he taught at the University of British Columbia, while continuing in international work. He promoted links among the International Council on Social Welfare (ICSW), the International Federation of Social Workers (IFSW), and the International Association of Social Workers (IASSW). With others, he organized the first North American Regional Seminar of the IASSW linked to the Habitat Forum in Vancouver in 1976.

Dr. Splane has served as president of a number of provincial, national, and international social development organizations. He has written extensively about national and international development for professional publications and for the popular press. He has received three honorary doctorates and several distinguished service awards and other citations. He is married and lives in Vancouver, British Columbia, with his wife, Dr. Verna Splane, who has collaborated with him on a major work on senior nurses in government.

BILLUPS: *Could you tell us something of your early life experiences that may have contributed to your later choice of career?*

SPLANE: I was born in Calgary in 1916. While in the Canadian army, my father, was gassed. While he returned home in apparently good health, he died of throat cancer within two years.

My mother was left with six children. I was the youngest. Allyn, the oldest, left school at 14 and, like many Calgarians, worked for the Canadian Pacific Railway. Leaving school in one's early teens was common then. This was the course followed by my other two brothers and my sister Claribel, who made it through grade 10, the entrance level for nursing training.

Although I had learned to read before starting school and had made good use of the Calgary Public Library, I was not happy at school and had the shattering experience of being failed in grade four.

I was happy, therefore, when my brother Allyn bought, sight unseen, a pioneer farm in northern Alberta. We left the city and became a farm family. I adapted to it rapidly and enjoyed having my own horse, my own rifle, a set of traps, and a lasso.

I also enjoyed school and skipped a grade, making up for my earlier failure. I walked nearly four miles to school when it was too cold to leave my horse in the schoolyard all day. My enjoyment of school waned with the quality of teaching. In my early high school years I failed French and only scraped by in mathematics. As family circumstances changed, my mother decided that she and I should return to Calgary, where I attended my last year and a half of high school. Crescent Heights High was one of the best schools in the province. Its principal, William Aberhart, later became premier of Alberta.

We had a summer cottage near McLaurin Beach Gull Lake, a well-organized Baptist summer camp, where I thrived—becoming sports director and discovering my role models. These were five or six vital young people from established Baptist families who were returning in the summer from McMaster University or its satellite, Brandon College. I wanted to follow in their footsteps.

My mother was manager of the dining hall at McLaurin Beach. She was the sister of two widely admired missionaries, Dr. Jessie Allyn, M.D., and Miss Laura Allyn, R.N. Renowned for establishing a hospital and nursing school in the Godavari district of India, they enjoyed the almost reverential esteem that Baptists in those years extended to their missionaries in foreign fields. Their lives and travels and the pen pal relationship I had with one of their wards attracted me to international endeavors.

By the end of high school, I had seen the harsh effects of the Great Depression of the 1930s on the lives of farm and city people alike. I eagerly followed the debates on how to deal with the economic, social, and political problems of the times. For some years I was a young conservative.

Lack of money ruled out going directly from high school to university. I took the one-year teacher's training course at the Calgary Normal School. I made the debating team that won the city championship for the first time and was surprised to be elected president of my class in the second term.

There was an oversupply of teachers, most having what we graduating teachers lacked: teaching experience. I nonetheless was hired for a two-year period in a relatively prosperous district in central Alberta. I boarded with people who subscribed to left-of-center periodicals, which rapidly eroded my conservative faith.

What can you tell us about your further education?

SPLANE: While teaching, I finished the subjects needed for Alberta High School graduation and applied for admission to McMaster (university), where my role models had been. It had a program sequence called "Political Economy and History" that seemed to be the ideal combination for my course major.

My savings from two years of teaching at $750 per year were not enough to pay for university, but my mother offered to move to the city of my choice. Thus, I lived at home in Hamilton while at McMaster, from 1937 to 1940.

In addition to my studies and playing soccer, I made the interuniversity debating team and also was admitted to the invitation-only International Relations Club.

What else during your McMaster years was important for your later career?

SPLANE: I hitchhiked to the 1939 World's Fair in New York twice, once in the spring and again in the late summer. The fair and New York left indelible impressions on me.

Even more important was what I gained from my summer jobs, notably my work in 1938 and again in 1939 as a laborer-teacher with Frontier College. This was a highly renowned adult education organization. Its program was designed to provide education and socialization for workers (mostly new immigrants) in mining, lumbering, and railway-building camps throughout Canada, especially in remote areas. Mature college students and graduates spent the summers working as laborers side by side with other workers during the day and providing education and maintaining a small library in the evenings and on weekends, and arranging sporting and other activities.

In 1938, I worked at a gold mine north of Lake Superior. It was dangerous, demanding, and challenging. I developed a lasting respect for mining and miners.

In 1939, I was a laborer-teacher on a railway extra gang near Windsor in southern Ontario. The job was not considered high-status employment among most students, but I greatly valued my Frontier College experiences.

The beginning of the 1939 fall term coincided with the outbreak of World War II. I joined the Canadian Officers Training Corps (COTC). I also wanted to make at least a start in graduate studies toward a master's degree in history before being called into active service. I was able to follow that course.

Where did your plans take you after McMaster?

SPLANE: Acting on the recommendation of one of my professors, I applied for admission to the Department of History at the University of Toronto, renowned for its eminent historians. How long I could work toward my degree depended on when

I would be called into military service. That did not happen until 1943, however, and I had three years of stimulating study and social life in Toronto.

After a year of both undergraduate and graduate history courses, I was searching for a thesis topic when I had the good fortune to be invited to discuss my need with Professor Frank Underhill. For the next several years, interrupted by my Air Force period, I worked, with some direction from him, on a topic about politics in Ontario in the decade after Canadian federation, 1867 to 1878. Professor Underhill was a controversial figure, enjoying strong support from those with liberal and progressive views, but anathema to those on the right.

When the call came to become an active member of the Royal Canadian Air Force (RCAF) and I began the training sequence, there was a period of uncertainty about whether at the advanced age of 27 I was "pilot material." The decision was positive, and I proceeded through the various stages, receiving my wings at an air station near Weyburn, a small town in Saskatchewan.

Did you see active service?

SPLANE: Yes, I was lucky enough to spend many months in advanced training at an airfield just four miles north of Stratford-upon-Avon. There I enjoyed the first of four seasons at the Shakespeare Memorial Theatre. That experience was only one of the delights of my years in England. I became an instant and, as time would prove, lifelong Anglophile.

Various postings and fairly frequent leaves gave me an opportunity to see much of the British Isles and enjoy many aspects of its life. London, bomb-damaged though it was, held unending appeal, and although it was nominally out of bounds during the German rocket bombings, I went there as often as I could.

I became a pilot engineer, second pilot in the RCAF's renowned 427 Squadron based in Yorkshire. The war in Europe was over, but 427 was to be one of two Canadian occupation squadrons, and I was able to stay in England well into 1946.

I began to feel less committed to a teaching career in history. Rather, I felt attracted to what I had seen of social work in meeting my fiancée's friends, men as well as women while at university. I managed exploratory visits to some British schools of social work and social administration. The only one that attracted me was the Social Science and Administration Program at the London School of Economics (LSE).

I then had three goals to achieve: The first was to gain permission to be "demobbed" from the RCAF in Britain; the second was to be admitted to LSE, in competition with countless others; and the third was to persuade Marion to obtain passage to England to marry me and face the privations of postwar London.

All three objectives were attained. Not only was I able to leave the Air Force and attain civilian status in England, but I was entitled to rehabilitation maintenance for the duration of my course. Marion was soon able to get transatlantic travel.

Eileen (later Dame Eileen) Younghusband was the chair of the LSE selection committee. When, after being grilled on whether I would be able to cope with the course, I claimed familiarity with the works of the Webbs, Coles, and Hammond. I was welcomed to the program. I may have received conclusive help from the letter of support that had been sent by Professor Underhill—well known at LSE. My linkage with Eileen Younghusband happily did not end there.

LSE was an exciting place to be in 1946–1947. The school had been founded by Bernard Shaw, Sydney and Beatrice Webb, and other members of the socialist Fabian Society. It was in its element with the victory of Labour in the general election of 1945. Many of its faculty had been appointed to public service positions, and the new rulers of the country were frequently seen in the halls and seminar rooms of the one building (other than the library) that was LSE. My tutor and emerging friend, an Oxonian just released from army service, was John Spenser, later to come to the University of Toronto for a few years before being called to the first Chair in Social Administration at Edinburgh.

On your return to Canada, did your career follow the course you set at LSE?

SPLANE: Yes, but I was determined first to take my uncompleted history thesis out of the storage vault and finish it.

Meanwhile, Marion had been asked to rescue the troubled Children's Aid Society of Cornwall, Ontario. She agreed, subject to my being able to join her and perform the administrative responsibilities that she handled well but did not enjoy. Thus, I was launched into my social work career. I had a good sampling of all aspects of child welfare in an Ontario children's aid society, which mixed nongovernmental and governmental elements.

Starting in 1945, under the federal family allowance program, every child received an allowance, paid to the mother, whatever the family structure. The payments were made for all children from birth through schooling years without any test of means, need, or income. They made an enormous difference. But they were not, nor were they intended to be, the major means of family support. I carried with me the hope that I might someday be able to help bring into being an adequate system of social assistance.

Were you able to advance your career in that direction?

SPLANE: Yes, but that occurred through many seemingly unrelated stages. I was able to establish contact with one of North America's best prepared and most experienced social welfare leaders, Harry Cassidy. A senior executive in the government of British Columbia, in 1939 he became the founding dean of the School of Social Work at the University of California in Berkeley. In 1946, he was appointed director of the School of Social Work at the University of Toronto.

We had him come to Cornwall to conduct a weekend social welfare workshop. There I told him that I planned at some point to enter doctoral studies at Toronto in history with a dissertation on the development of social welfare in the province of Ontario. Dr. Cassidy strongly advised against that plan, stating that my LSE certificate would depreciate in value over time and that I should enroll at the School of Social

Work. I could, he stated, complete a master of social work degree in one academic year and enter the doctoral program in social work that he was pushing through the academic structures. I would thereby become a charter candidate.

I was admitted to the school without undergoing any admissions process—simply on Dr. Cassidy's dictate. I found most of the courses worthwhile. The exception was casework, which was shrouded by a certain mystique and driven by two rival theories: diagnostic (Freudian) and functional (Rankian) approaches. This did not unduly affect me at the MSW stage, where I enjoyed and profited from the other courses, as well as my field placements in public welfare settings. My thesis was on a publicly administered child welfare program.

Moving through the doctoral program was a harrowing 10-year experience. As agreed, I appeared at the school in the fall of 1951 to enroll in the program, only to learn that it did not exist. I learned later that it was opposed by a commanding academic figure, who, it was said, would have blocked it as long as Harry Cassidy was promoting it. Harry Cassidy, however, had died during the summer at the early age of 51, to the grief of countless admirers. My situation at the school was quite different without his presence. The university's memorial service, however, gave such dramatic evidence of the greatness of Harry Cassidy that his wish to see a doctoral program established could no longer be blocked, especially as shepherded by his successor, Charles H. (Chick) Hendry.

I will not dwell on the obstacles I faced as the first doctoral candidate in any Canadian school of social work. In 1960, the defense of my dissertation and its hardcover publication as a "landmark study of immense value" represented a happy conclusion to a stressful process. The book, *Social Welfare in Ontario, 1791–1893*, "the preeminent work in the field," ensured a welcome to a later career in academia.

Did the completion of your MSW and DSW pave the way for desirable employment?

SPLANE: It did, in what I regarded as the ideal setting for a public welfare career: the Department of National Health and Welfare.

In 1952, the department was in its eighth year and had already built a reputation for a high level of accomplishment. Following the advent in 1942 of Britain's famous Beveridge report, a documentary prelude to the creation of a welfare state, the Canadian government had begun its own postwar planning represented by the Marsh and Haegerty reports on social welfare and health. It then developed what came to be known as the Green Book Proposals for a nationwide system of income support and health and social services. Some were to be wholly federal programs, but others involved shared costs with the provinces, where the administration had to be at the provincial level.

Health and Welfare Canada, as the department begun in 1944 was generally called, had two distinct parts, a health side and a welfare side, each headed by its own deputy minister, an official comparable to the permanent secretary in the United Kingdom. The government was able to recruit, for the health side, Dr. Brock Chisholm, who later became the first director general of the World Health

Organization; and for the welfare side, Dr. George Davidson, who became a key figure in my own career.

The Research Division, headed by Dr. Joseph Willard served both the health and welfare divisions. I was delighted when Dr. Willard offered me a position in the research division where I worked from 1952 to 1960.

With what research endeavors were you involved?

SPLANE: The division's research covered a wide spectrum of the social problems faced by Canadians, on which little basic work had been done. I valued the work in the health field on the prerequisites of national health insurance that later became the most valued component of the Canadian welfare state.

My major research then shifted from health to welfare. There had been no systematic collection of data on child welfare. The information that did exist was found in a variety of agencies and institutions, some under religious auspices, some under public programs ill-defined and, in most provinces, indifferently regarded. Getting a handle on it required communication, including travel to provincial capitals and individual agencies.

When Canada was about to start a new social welfare endeavor, it sought models and information from both the United Kingdom and the United States. In the United States, Canada looked to individual states and to the nation's capital. Canada and the provinces had been doing this, as my master's thesis had illustrated, since as early as the 1830s—always with good results.

In keeping with that tradition, I arranged a visit to the Children's Bureau in Washington. The visit marked the beginning of what was to become a central part of my total social welfare experience—meeting, becoming associated with, and forming friendships with Americans, including Dr. Martha Elliot and her predecessor, Katharine Lenroot.

Did your years in the Research Division offer other opportunities?

SPLANE: The opportunities to make direct contact with those working in policy and practice across Canada and in the United States proved to be of immeasurable value. Marion and I were active in the Canadian Association of Social Workers (CASW); by the mid-1950s I was on the CASW Board and served as treasurer. Marion's associations were very broad. While we were in Toronto, she played a key role in the family and child welfare component of the Toronto Welfare Council. When it was known that we were going to be living in Ottawa, she was asked to take on a difficult, but promising, assignment: the executive position in one of the oldest (and for years most prestigious) agency in the city, the Protestant Children's Village. It needed to be converted from a quasi-orphanage into an institution for emotionally disturbed children. In succeeding in that endeavor, Marion became part of what was then a continent-wide movement for the creation of a new type of service for older children who were beyond the control of regular child welfare programs.

When Marion turned that endeavor over to others, she was recruited over the next several years to various roles in the Canadian Welfare Council (CWC). The CWC, later the Canadian Council on Social Development, was a unique nongovernmental organization with no parallel in the United States. Until the 1970s, it embraced virtually the entire range of the human services in Canada and had strong linkages with international organizations like the International Council on Social Welfare (ICSW) and International Social Service (ISS).

Its founding director, Charlotte Whitton, later the first woman mayor of a Canadian city (Ottawa), had been succeeded by Dr. George Davidson (before his appointment to Health and Welfare Canada) and then two outstanding leaders, R.E.G. (Dick) Davis and Reuben Baetz. Dick Davis was skilled in recruiting the best talent available in Canada and from abroad. During his regime, the council's staff was reputed to know everybody in social welfare across Canada, what things were wrong in the various social systems, and what measures were needed to remedy them.

What other influences were important in your Ottawa years?

SPLANE: Not long after my return from Toronto, I was delighted to be appointed to the position of executive assistant to Dr. George Davidson, the Deputy Minister of National Welfare. Dr. Davidson had an ideal background for the roles he was called upon to fill. He was born in Nova Scotia, and his schooling was in British Columbia, where he was identified early as a brilliant student, winning the Governor General's medal at matriculation, starring at the University of British Columbia, and proceeding on scholarship to Harvard. On his return to British Columbia, he became a rapid convert to social welfare, working for a time under the direction of Harry Cassidy in the department of the provincial secretary and later succeeding to the department's most senior welfare position. That, however, was after a three-year period in the nongovernmental sector with joint appointments as executive director of the Vancouver Council of Social Agencies and its Welfare Federation, where he made great strides in bringing the city's social services to new levels of effectiveness.

Being in day-to-day contact with a person of great intelligence, charm, and practicality was a rare privilege. In addition to being tutored on the administration of the welfare side of the department, I gained a glimpse of international social affairs at the highest level.

Canada in the late 1940s, '50s, and '60s was highly regarded in world affairs as a middle power unencumbered with the stigma of being a colonial power. Accordingly, many of its most able citizens were recruited to undertake highly significant international assignments. John Humphrey was a major author of the Universal Declaration of Human Rights; Brock Chisholm was the first director general of the World Health Organization; the minister of external affairs, Lester B. Pearson, who some years later became prime minister, was awarded the Nobel Peace Prize for his contribution to resolving the Suez Canal crisis.

What was the nature of your appointment to Dr. Davidson's office?

SPLANE: My appointment initially was as acting executive assistant, because the outstanding person who had filled the position with distinction for several years, Adelaide Sinclair, was on indefinite loan to the United Nations.

The Unemployment Assistance Program was administered by the provinces but could come into effect in a province only after the province had signed an agreement under which the province would agree to a number of important standards. In return, the federal government would meet half the costs of assistance granted to persons who were unemployed and in need. The legislation was of crucial significance in the evolution of Canada's social programs, but it had been written and enacted quickly and contained limitations that would become increasingly evident over time.

Coincidentally, soon after I was assigned responsibility, the situation changed dramatically. Provinces that had stayed out decided to come in. Of crucial importance was the signing-in of Quebec. Its government was ideologically opposed to federal–provincial social welfare programs because of the influence the national government would then have on matters deemed under the exclusive jurisdiction of the provinces. Quebec was especially resistant, because for practical reasons the province would have to remove the administration of social programs from the church, which had played a dominant role in both health and welfare matters since the province's origin.

What was your specific responsibility?

SPLANE: I was in charge of the program as director of unemployment assistance. For the next five years, from 1961 to 1966, the greater part of my life was centered on it. It proved to be the ideal vehicle for the establishment of a broader program, free of the flaws in the existing legislation and capable of embracing three earlier programs: Old Age Assistance, Blind Persons Allowances, and Disabled Persons Allowances.

What made my position far more promising and challenging was that the two deputy ministers to whom I successively reported, Dr. Davidson and Dr. Willard, encouraged me to devote as much skill and energy to developing a program that would replace unemployment assistance as to the administration of the existing legislation.

Against these positive factors were numerous negative ones. Federal finance sought to derail what would clearly be an even more costly measure. Officials in some provincial treasuries shared their concern, because, as well as bringing in many millions of new federal dollars, the measure would also encourage the creation of new or expanded provincial programs.

Did the more comprehensive program come to pass?

SPLANE: It did with the return of the Liberal Party in 1963. It was Liberal governments from 1940 to 1957 that had enacted the earlier welfare state programs, and it was the Liberal Party's promise of taking further social welfare initiatives that contributed to its new mandate.

The Canada Assistance Plan (CAP) emerged as one of these initiatives. The rediscovery of poverty in Canada was comparable to the phenomenon in the United States identified with what Daniel Patrick Moynahan had described as "the impetus for a massive government assault on poverty within the Kennedy and Johnson administrations." The development and enactment of what became the CAP was heralded as the foremost advance in public assistance and social services in the country's history and an outstanding example of cooperative federalism. A half dozen books and countless articles have been written about it.

Did your concentrated work on the Canada Assistance Plan rule out other professional activities?

SPLANE: To some extent that was the case, but in 1961 and again in 1964, I represented Canada on UNICEF's executive board. Being at a high-level meeting at the United Nations in New York in 1961 was in itself a mind-expanding event. The Cold War intruded on the process, and Canada could not always support the positions taken by the United States. We were also embarrassed by our inability to give official support to Sweden's family-planning proposals, because until 1971 the practice of family planning was proscribed in Canada's criminal code.

In 1964, for the first time in its history, UNICEF decided to meet away from New York at the regional UN center for Asia in Bangkok. An associated decision was to have the executive board members, in groups of six, visit projects of UNICEF, the World Health Organization (WHO), and the Food and Agriculture Organization (FAO) in Asian centers before the Bangkok meeting. By this means we would have direct knowledge of the work of UNICEF in the field. The group I was with began in New Delhi and viewed projects there and in Agra, Lucknow, Banaras, and Calcutta before flying to Bangkok.

We had a greater understanding of what we heard from the directors of the six UNICEF regions, and our deliberations benefited from our enhanced understanding. Perhaps more important than the work were the friendships I formed with UN and UNICEF staff and with executive board members. Among the former were Adelaide Sinclair, Martha Branscombe, Phyllis Burns, Aida Gindy, and John Charnow. Members of the national delegations included Zena Harman (Israel); Fred Delli Quadri (United States); and several from the Commonwealth, Africa, and Asia.

Along with these outside involvements, my responsibilities in Health and Welfare Canada increased from the mid-1960s, and my title changed first to director general and then to assistant deputy minister. Among the additional programs that came under my directions were the national welfare grants, family planning, and the Experimental Guaranteed Income Security Program.

What can you tell us about your other international involvements while you were with the federal government?

SPLANE: In 1970 at Manila in the Philippines and in 1972 at The Hague in the Netherlands, I attended the conferences of the International Council on Social

Welfare (ICSW), the International Federation of Social Workers (IFSW), and the International Association of Schools of Social Work (IASSW).

In Manila I was principally involved with ICSW. At that time, an important component of its biennial program was the Pre-Conference Working Party. As the one selected from Canada, I worked with the other members of the working party to develop the paper that would be the keynote address. It was the first biennial conference I had been able to attend since the one in Toronto in 1954, and it convinced me that I should strengthen my resolve to miss no more of them. I made numerous new friends, among them John Lawrence of Austrailia, who was the final editor and presenter of the keynote address, and Yuichi Nakamura, dean of a school of social work in Tokyo.

What career opportunities presented themselves as you prepared to leave the government?

SPLANE: I wanted to have opportunities to advance social policy as a teacher, researcher, and advocate. Accordingly, I was pleased first to be offered a visiting professorship at the University of Alberta for the academic year 1972–73 and to receive an appointment as a fully tenured professor in the School of Social Work, University of British Columbia, in 1973. I was pleased that my visiting professor position was in a program known as Health Services Administration. This was in harmony with my advocacy of close linkages between the fields of health and welfare.

In 1971, I married Verna Huffman, a long-time friend of Marion's and mine. After Marion's death after a short illness in 1970, our friendship blossomed into love. Verna had joined Health and Welfare somewhat earlier than I and had risen to the most senior nursing position in the department. She also reported directly to her deputy minister and was thus able to influence not only broad measures relating to the role of nursing in health policy, but also the day-to-day decisions touching on resources and personnel that over time have a cumulative impact on policy.

Verna had been given educational leave to obtain a bachelor's degree in nursing from Columbia University and a master's in public health from the University of Michigan. Of equal importance for her later career both during and after her tenure in the federal government were lengthy secondments to WHO to consult on nursing and public health to governments in the Caribbean and in North Africa.

In this first of two new settings, the University of Alberta, I understand that your international involvement continued.

SPLANE: While in Edmonton, I was pleased to be asked to travel to New York to help plan a UN expert group and later to serve as a member of the Expert Group on Social Welfare Policy and Planning. The 10 members of the group were drawn from all continents and possessed a wealth of relevant knowledge and experience. I greatly enjoyed being a part of a highly worthwhile endeavor.

Then you went on to the University of British Columbia (UBC)?

SPLANE: After moving to Vancouver in 1973, we were relieved to find that being on the West Coast did not cut us off from national and international associations. Within a few months, Verna was elected vice president of the International Council of Nurses and later to the boards of International Social Service and the Canadian Red Cross, which required frequent travel. Having become a social work educator, I took a lively interest in how social work education had advanced nationally and internationally. Orientation at the national level was readily available; George Hougham, who had recruited me to the UBC School, had just completed a term as president of the Canadian Association of Schools of Social Work (CASSW). Although there were then only 12 schools that were members, the organization had a small office and a part-time executive director. It would soon manage to engage, first in a research role and then as executive director, Marguerite Mathieu, who was to become one of the foremost leaders in social work education nationally and internationally.

My experience in teaching social policy and administration came easily, and I soon put down roots. One substantial linkage was with the profession of social work. I became an active member of the British Columbia Association of Social Workers (BCASW). In 1978, I became its president and was then elected for two successive years, 1979–1981, to the Canadian Association of Social Workers (CASW) of which I had been national treasurer in earlier years.

Was it at about this time that you had an opportunity to become involved in the work of the International Association of Schools of Social Work (IASSW)?

SPLANE: What thrust me into the center of the activities of IASSW was a telephone call from the president of CASSW, "Gif" Gifford. He said that, to his great regret, he could not attend the IASSW seminar and executive board meeting in Nairobi and asked if I would sit in for him—an assignment I was pleased to take on.

It was there that I came to be a close colleague of Dr. Katherine Kendall, founder and executive head of IASSW. She induced me to become coordinator of the first North American Regional Seminar to be sponsored by IASSW, bringing together social work educators from Canada and the United States. It proved to be an enormous undertaking, but I had the warm support of George Hougham and many others in Canada and the United States. Its papers and proceedings were published in a highly regarded book, *People and Places*.

The seminar was part of Habitat, the Conference on Human Settlements sponsored by the Untied Nations, which ran for two weeks. The IASSW seminar was to be held during the concluding week, conceivably leaving the opening week free for another social welfare event. Dorothy Lally, a key figure in the international work of the U.S. Department of Health, Education and Welfare, proposed an event that would embrace the whole of social welfare to complement the one planned for social work educators.

My UBC colleague, Mary Hill, who headed the School's Continuing Education Programs, agreed to be coordinator of what became the Symposium on Social Welfare and Human Settlements, and I opted for the role of program chairperson. Helvi Sipila

(United Nations) agreed to be the keynote speaker. The symposium program and pro-ceedings were published and sold for a modest fee by the UBC School of Social Work. The friendships and linkages I formed during this event proved, as had those of the seminar, to be significant in my later roles in the human services.

Where did your strong connections with the international social welfare field take you following the Habitat seminar?

SPLANE: I was on the board of the Social Planning and Research Division of the United Way of Vancouver and became president of the Social Policy and Research Council of British Columbia (SPARC).

While president of CASW, I made presentations to two Royal Commissions, one on social development and the other on the Canadian constitution. The constitution was substantially amended in 1982, most importantly through its inclusion of a char-ter of rights and freedoms. My principal plea was for a change in the division of pow-ers between the federal and provincial governments, arguing that they should have equal powers respecting social programs, thereby removing the exclusive powers that the provinces had in the earlier constitution.

More important than being able to express my views as a spokesperson for CASW was my membership on the boards of two high-level social policy organizations. One was the National Council of Welfare that is advisory to the office of the Minister of Health and Welfare. Through its media presentations and frequent publications, it made a powerful case for humane and rational economic and social policies.

Somewhat comparable was my participation in the work of the Canadian Council on Social Development (CCSD), the organization on which I commented favorably while it had its former name, the Canadian Welfare Council. CCSD continued to be a strong voice for social development, basing its forceful advocacy on soundly based research. I became vice president for British Columbia and the Yukon Territory.

What opportunities did you have to pursue your interest in linking social work, social work education, and the broad field of social welfare?

SPLANE: The interest I developed in maintaining the close linkages of IFSW, IASSW, and ICSW (the three sister organizations) had many roots. The most basic was that I had membership in the Canadian component of each of them and associ-ate membership in the international body when that option was available.

A significant step in moving me toward my commitment to the continued bond-ing of the three organizations came somewhat indirectly when I was first elected to the Board of ICSW in 1974. Dorothy Lally approached me to vote against a proposal of the charismatic British representative that ICSW should hold its international conferences every three years rather than biennially. I learned that, among other dis-advantages, this would have a devastating effect on the finances of the organization. No less important was my discovery that neither IFSW nor IASSW had been con-sulted on this proposal, and each would be seriously affected by it.

The triennial proposal, though tentatively adopted by the ICSW Board in the 1974 meeting, needed final confirmation at the next biennial, and I joined others in seeing that that would not happen. I collaborated especially with ICSW board members who had strong linkages with one or both of the two sister organizations. Sybil Francis of Jamaica was a notable example. My course of action was taken in spite of the views of some Canadian colleagues, whose friendship with the British leader was the basis of their support for him. In a vote at the ICSW Board meeting at Puerto Rico in 1976, the proposal was defeated, my negative vote canceling the affirmative one of the other Canadian and ICSW president at the time, Reuben Baetz.

What concerned me was that there seemed to be no ongoing structure for tripartite consultations by the three organizations. On no authority but my own judgment, I undertook to set up a luncheon meeting for the presidents and secretaries general of the three organizations: Reuben Baetz and Kate Katski for ICSW, Robin Huws Jones and Katherine Kendall for IASSW, and Mary Windsor for IFSW (the secretary general, Andrew Apostal, had returned to Geneva). I did not presume to sit in at the luncheon, but I had made the point that there was a continuing need for collaboration. The next biennial conference, 1978, was held in Israel and was notable for the honors paid to two secretaries general who had decided to retire: Kate Katski from ICSW and Katherine Kendall from IASSW. Each person seemed to have the creative energy to serve at least to the end of the century, and in a variety of different roles, that is what they have proceeded to do. Andrew Apostal in partnership with his wife Ellen continued to serve as the executives of IFSW until 1997. Katherine Kendall was succeeded by Marguerite Mathieu, and I believed I could count on IFSW and IASSW to support tripartite collaboration. I was less certain of Kate Katski's successor as secretary general of ICSW, Ingrid Gelinek, but she was an Austrian, and ICSW and IASSW had moved their headquarters to Vienna, to which city the key social component of the United Nations had been relocated.

My conviction that the three organizations should work closely extended to the continued existence of the journal *International Social Work*, which had enjoyed their informal support from its beginnings. The journal had been sustained through the devotion of many volunteers and for some years was published in India, where costs were less and where many volunteers strove valiantly to keep it functioning. Always underfunded, however, it seemed on the point of collapse when Sage Publications offered to take on its publication, provided there was a guarantee of support by the three sister organizations.

IASSW (due especially to the leadership of Terry Hokenstad) and IFSW, readily agreed, but Ingrid Gelinek of ICSW adamantly opposed the idea. I introduced a motion to the ICSW board and it was seconded by a member from a developing country to support the journal. It passed with no significant opposition, and the tripartite proposal was adopted.

Identifying persons with leadership potential and promoting their election or appointment to the boards of the three sister organizations became one of my major causes. In the early 1970s, Mary Catherine Jennings telephoned to ask me to stand for election to the IFSW Board. I suggested someone else, Gayle Gilchrist James. She was a person with limitless potential, the key member of Alberta's social work association, and the person who had followed me as president of CASW, working closely in that role with her friend and fellow Albertan, the executive director of CASW, Gweneth Gowanlock.

I mentioned earlier that I had encouraged Norbert Préfontaine to attend the ICSW biennial conference in 1970 and that he had taken an immediate interest in how it functioned. In the following years, he assumed various roles on the governing bodies of the organization and became the ICSW president in 1984.

In 1978, I sought out Ralph Garber, who had returned to Canada as dean of the Faculty of Social Work, University of Toronto, after serving at the same level in three schools of social work in the United States. He said that his career had reached a point where he could become active internationally. Moreover, he would not discourage my stated intention of promoting his participation in the affairs of IASSW. In the course of time, I found it possible for him to come onto the IASSW board as treasurer. His rise to the IASSW presidency was not delayed long, and he was destined to serve magnificently.

During a period of a month or so when Norbert Préfontaine's, Gayle Gilchrist James's, and Ralph Garber's terms as president happened to overlap, I had the satisfaction of seeing three Canadians whom I had recruited simultaneously heading the three social welfare organizations and performing with great distinction.

I carried and formalized the tripartite concept into the plans for the sister organizations to hold their conferences in Canada in 1984. ICSW Canada was the leader and, on the initiative of Norbert Préfontaine, we secured the services of a gifted organizer and fundraiser, Pierre Dionne. I realized that his skills could be extended to the two other organizations. I proposed the creation of a new umbrella organization: International Conferences on Social Development (ICSD). Its main virtue was that a great deal of conference planning and fundraising could be done by one planning body, rather than three. In the early 1980s, ICSD came into being. I became the first president, and Pierre Dionne became the executive director. Each of the three organizations had comparable representation on the board. Among the advantages Canada gained from the creation of ICSD was the bargaining power it gave for all aspects of conference planning. It worked remarkably well through the Montreal Conference of 1984, and the approach was adopted by Japan for its 1986 conference planning. Japanese officials credited it with bringing various social work groups into a single social work body that could be recognized by IFSW and join ICSW Japan and the Japanese Association of Schools of Social Work in the tripartite body that planned and executed the conference.

ICSD is alive in Canada and has served for the collaboration of other agencies in conferences on the family and homelessness. Pierre Dionne is now its president. In only two or three of the biennial years after 1984 have the three organizations followed the tripartite model, but some joint planning continues, especially between IFSW and IASSW in the joint conference of the two organizations in 2000.

SPLANE: Yes. Quite early I became concerned about the threat to IASSW, particularly in respect to attendance at the biennial conferences, posed by a new organization, the Inter-University Consortium for Social Development (IUCISD). It began recruiting members—almost entirely social work educators—to conferences held just before or after those of IASSW. They had attractive conference themes and some prominent keynote speakers. I knew and respected a number of their leaders—all social work educators—and took the position that if they held their conferences at noncompetitive times I would join them. They have changed their conference dates to years that do not compete or conflict with IASSW symposia.

At the same time, I worked to remedy a weakness in IASSW conference planning, namely its failure for many years to adopt the call-for-papers approach—papers that would be peer reviewed and would have importance for social work educators in receiving conference attendance funding and providing an additional item on their curriculum vitae. The other cause I espoused was that of creating a North American Region in IASSW. For a long time, Canadian schools of social work were accredited by the Council on Social Work Education (CSWE) of the United States. Even after the advent of CASSW, no action was taken. Until the 1950s, all Canadians wanting doctoral standing attended U.S. schools, and many continued to seek doctorates at Chicago, Columbia, Brandeis, and other American venues into the 1990s. The Habitat Seminar in 1976 stood as the only time the term "North American Region of IASSW" had any meaning.

What had to be confronted was that every jurisdiction south of the United States was deemed to be in the Latin American Region. Whether it made sense for non–Spanish-speaking countries in the Caribbean seemed not to have been given much thought.

I set out to have a North American Region recognized by IASSW. With the collaboration of Terry Hokenstad and the head of CASSW, that proposal was acted upon, and I became the first representative of the North American Region of IASSW to sit on the IASSW board. I devoted as much thought and energy to winning the agreement of the leaders of the Latin American region to give countries in the Caribbean the right to opt out of their region and into the North American fold. Although I approached the undertaking with considerable anxiety, the matter was dealt with amicably, and we were able to establish a constitution for the North American Region.

I understand that there have been other international involvements.

SPLANE: Yes. I had found that it was possible to bring outstanding leaders to Canada from the United States and Britain if a suitable program and some financing could be arranged for them. Herman Stein, of Case Western Reserve University in Cleveland, for instance, came for a brief visit to Vancouver as a follow-up to Habitat. Bringing people from Britain required more planning, particularly if they were to visit centers across Canada. Three visits were notable: those of Mary Windsor, a London-based social worker and president of IFSW; Professor Robert Pinker of LSE, editor of the *Journal of Social Policy* and author of *Social Theory and Social Policy*, for presentations in Ottawa, Toronto, and Vancouver; and Professor Robert Leaper of the University of Exeter, editor of the journal, *Social Policy and Administration*, and a prominent leader in ICSW, for visits in five centers in Canada, including Vancouver, where he lectured at the renowned Vancouver Institute.

I supported, through various means, including attendance, the celebrations of the 50th anniversary of the United Nations, the World Summit for Social Development, and Habitat II.

The World Summit for Social Development, held in Copenhagen in March 1995, was the event that most clearly carried forward the objectives of ICSW and its sister organizations. Dirk Jarré, president of ICSW addressed the meeting on behalf of nongovernmental organizations. The summit confronted the issue of poverty more thoroughly and courageously than ever before, proclaiming that poverty could be eliminated by early in the next century and setting specific target dates for this important objective.

Because of our devoted work for Habitat in 1976, Verna and I felt it important to participate in Habitat II, billed as the United Nation's Second Conference on Human Settlements. I carried to the conference a paper that I had urged the headquarters of the World Federalist Movement to develop. Entitled "Habitat II and Reform of the United Nations," it made the case for the creation of the kind of UN system that is capable of implementing the global policies enunciated in the succession of world conferences dating from the early 1970s.

An international organization with which Verna and I both have had a long association is International Social Service (ISS). From its headquarters in Geneva, it links social agencies in more than half the countries in the world in dealing with the social problems of individuals and families that require solution in more than one country. The early work of ISS in Canada was handled for many years by the Canadian Welfare Council; I had a part in it because Marion managed it for a time. Later, when the ISS Canada Committee asked me to join it, I suggested instead that they recruit Verna Huffman, then principal nursing officer in Health and Welfare Canada. Under her direction, ISS Canada became a national branch of the organization, and she was elected to the executive committee of the ISS International Council. In 1997, I was asked to become a patron of ISS Canada. I thereby share an additional interest with Verna, who continues as an honorary member of the ISS Council.

An organization with a more overarching approach to global affairs is the World Federalist Movement. It is an organization (whose president is Sir Peter Ustinov) that espouses the distant goal of universal world governance; meanwhile, it describes itself as a movement for a just world order through a strengthened United Nations. It promotes every responsible measure designed to prevent war and conflict, like the elimination of land mines, the adoption by all countries of the law of the sea, and the international criminal court that seeks to bring to trial those guilty of gross crimes against humanity. From 1993 to 1998, I served as president of the Vancouver Branch of World Federalists of Canada, organizing public meetings on issues of world peace.

How do your experiences affect your present work and plans for the future?

SPLANE: I retain an interest in the three sister international organizations. I am pleased that IASSW and IFSW are proceeding with plans for their biennial conferences in Montreal in the year 2000; I am disturbed that a rift has developed in ICSW but am hopeful that it will be resolved.

My major work is, as it has been in the recent past, writing. Two books published in recent years are *Chief Nursing Officers in National Ministries of Health*, published by the University of California, San Francisco, the product of an eight-year study that Verna and I did together, travelling to 50 countries to gather data; and *Seventy-five Years of Community Service to Canada: Canadian Council on Social Development 1920–1995* (1996). The former was well-received and a factor in our receiving honorary doctorates from the University of British Columbia. I steer away from writing for learned journals, which reach a limited audience and seem to have little effect on policy. Instead, three or four times a year I write letters on some current issue to Canada's national newspaper, *The Globe and Mail*, where they are usually published.

My main writing, however, constitutes a major and long-term endeavor, the title of which is *George Davidson: Public Policy Mandarin*. I hope to have it published early in 2002.

What reflections do you have on the international aspects of your career as a social worker, social work educator, social policy administrator, social welfare historian and human rights advocate?

SPLANE: The term "international" is now often superseded by the term "global." I would normally have welcomed the terms "global" and "globalization" as in harmony with what we have been striving for in the organizations that have had the advancement of human rights and human well-being as their defining objectives. The achievement of those objectives is, however, in increasing peril from what is virtually the corporate ownership of globalization, engineered by self-serving, profit-oriented, neoconservative ideologues. We are faced in the new century with having to win back what we had once attained and to move forward with skill and determination to realize the values proclaimed in the Universal Declaration of Human Rights.

FAITHFUL ANGELS

HERMAN D. STEIN

Born in 1917, Herman Stein earned a bachelor of social science degree from The City College of New York and master's and doctoral degrees in social work from Columbia University, where he was appointed to the faculty in 1945. In 1947, he became director of the Welfare Department of the American Joint Distribution Committee's Paris headquarters, planning and advising on Jewish refugee needs in Europe and North Africa. He rejoined the faculty at Columbia in 1950, where he initiated courses on the application of social and behavioral science to social work and on international social work, and was director of the Research Center. After 1950, he was consultant to the UN Division of Social Development.

In 1962, Dr. Stein took a year's advisory assignment in community development with United Nations Children's Fund (UNICEF) in what was then Tanganyika (now part of Tanzania). In the subsequent 23 years working with the organization part-time and full-time, he became senior adviser to two executive directors. He also directed UNICEF Senior Inter-regional Staff Seminars for 10 years and advised on the UNICEF program and organization in headquarters and developing countries.

Dr. Stein was appointed dean of the School of Applied Social Sciences at Western Reserve University in 1964, was university provost and vice president of Case Western Reserve University from 1968 through 1972, and was reappointed provost from 1986 to 1988. He was president of the Council on Social Work Education from 1966 to 1969 and president of the International Association of Schools of Social Work from 1968 to 1976. He also was a fellow at the Center for Advanced Study of the Behavioral Sciences at Stanford University in 1973–1974 and 1978–1979. His honors are many, among them the University Medal, the highest award presented by Case Western Reserve University. Dr. Stein has five books and more than 100 published papers to his credit and has lectured all over the world. He is married and has three children and five grandchildren.

BILLUPS: *Could you tell us something about the years before your formal training for the social work profession?*

STEIN: I was born in the Bronx, in New York City, of immigrant parents, the youngest of five children in a lower-middle-class family. I went to a public elementary school until my parents sent me to a yeshiva, a Jewish parochial school, for the last four years of elementary school. In public high school, although shy, I soon found myself elected president of the academic and service societies.

In my third year, I was chosen by the faculty to represent the high school in the competition for a unique academic award that Columbia University offered to only one high school student in New York City. The aspiring students were to take a series of examinations over a two-year period. Each high school in the five New York boroughs could select one candidate. The prize was admission and free tuition to Columbia, plus a sizeable annual stipend. In the midst of the Depression, this was a huge award.

I came through the first year's examinations quite well and was looking forward to the second year because my prime subjects were coming up, in English and social studies. However, about a month before the scheduled examinations, I had an accident in a school relay race. A friend of mine won the prize.

I lost the opportunity to compete in the competition and I needed physical therapy for many years, but the real price I paid was that I was not permitted to join the military when the draft came up because of that hip injury. A few years later, in 1943, I took leave from the family agency where I was working to undertake a research task in the induction station at Grand Central in Manhattan, under the auspices of the War Manpower Rehabilitation Administration. I thought I might get familiar enough with the process and the people there that I could be accepted into the military, but when they looked at my X-rays I was turned down again. I tried joining the Red Cross but was told I was overqualified. I volunteered as a medical field agent with the Selective Service System and later became a supervisor of volunteers. This work was essentially to help young men cope with problems that may have arisen when they were classified 4-F, meaning rejected.

When, where, and how did your professional interests emerge?

STEIN: My interest in social research was stimulated by my major in sociology. In college I undertook a number of independent research projects. When I graduated from The City College of New York, I was invited to join the Department of Government and Sociology as an instructor with the title of director of the Social Research Laboratory. However, by that time I had been accepted to the New York School of Social Work (now the Columbia University School of Social Work).

I had also become interested in social work through my brother's experience as a student in the Graduate School of Jewish Social Work, the experience of other peo-

FAITHFUL ANGELS

ple I had met in the field, and through reading. Also, one of my part-time jobs was in the Bronx Young Men's and Women's Hebrew Association, leading two groups and supervising the recreation area three nights a week. Social work beckoned as a satisfying career.

I was a family caseworker until 1945, when I was invited to join the faculty at the New York School of Social Work to teach social research methods and supervise the master's thesis program. I enjoyed teaching and leaned toward academic pursuits. I took advantage of my free tuition at Columbia University to audit and enroll in courses, studying with Robert Merton, Paul Lazarsfeld, Robert MacIver, Seymour Lipset, and C. Wright Mills.

I also audited courses in anthropology and economics. This period of studying and teaching, followed by my experiences in Europe and North Africa from 1947 to 1950, formed the basis of my interest in developing the first sociocultural courses at what became the Columbia University School of Social Work. I had left the school in 1947 to work with the American Joint Distribution Committee (AJDC) in Europe as deputy director of budget and research, but soon organized the first Welfare Department at the Paris headquarters. This was a combination of administrative work, planning, and consulting with AJDC staff in various parts of Europe. The AJDC was dealing with the survivors of the Holocaust in displaced persons camps and refugee programs, and with heartrending, chaotic conditions in many shattered Jewish communities. My work also took me to North Africa frequently on problems facing the indigenous Jewish communities, but I also was able to observe the conditions of life of the Arab populations and the impact of French colonialism.

The director of administration at the AJDC Paris headquarters had been a senior management consultant in New York. We had numerous conversations about management issues and problems of productivity, efficiency, personnel selection, training, and morale. When I returned to New York, he invited me to lunch one day. I discovered a third person there, someone for whom this consultant had previously worked. My friend left the two of us alone, noting only that this individual was president of a manufacturing company and would like to talk to me about doing some work with him. I had no experience whatsoever in manufacturing companies and was not an organization consultant. But I finally agreed to try it for two months.

It turned out to be a fascinating and productive experience for me. I continued to consult with this company for about 10 years.

During these years, I delved into organizational theory and management literature. Subsequently, I did short-term organizational consultation elsewhere and led planning exercises for several social agencies. This organizational study and practical experience during the 1950s led to my teaching courses in administration and developing a doctoral course on management and organizational theory.

I was due for a sabbatical in 1962–1963 and was preparing for a year of research when I received a call from UNICEF, asking whether I would be an adviser to the Planning Commission of the newly independent government of Tanganyika. Apparently the UN Division of Social Affairs recommended me; I had been working with the UN informally since returning from Europe in 1950. Thus began a 23-

year consulting association with UNICEF. For most of those years, my title was Senior Adviser to the Executive Director.

In 1963, I agreed to become dean of the School of Applied Social Sciences at Western Reserve University. Among my pursuits were infusing an international perspective into social work education, relating to other disciplines and professions, and raising admission standards and the intellectual quality of the curriculum. I changed staffing, curriculum, and relationships within the university and the community. These successes led to my appointment as provost of social and behavioral sciences when Western Reserve University and Case Institute of Technology were federating in 1967, and then to my appointment as university provost and vice president of what became known as Case Western Reserve University (CWRU).

The years of 1967–1971 were turbulent on many campuses and certainly on our own. After a change in the presidency, I took leave and was considering new opportunities when I was invited to return to CWRU as University Professor (a designation of high academic status held by only one other faculty member, a Nobel Laureate), which would permit me to take leave without pay whenever I wished. I was also fortunate to have been invited to spend 1974–1975 and 1978–1979 at the Center for the Advanced Study of the Behavioral Sciences at Stanford. One year was devoted to the study of social development, the other to studies in administration. Several years between 1962–1983 I devoted full-time to UNICEF, with intermittent doctoral teaching.

I also organized a public lecture series at CWRU called Global Currents, which I directed for five years. For the critical years of 1986–1988, I became University Provost again. At age 70, I concluded my career as a university administrator and turned my attention to my family and other interests.

I understand that you were tempted to undertake a different career entirely—in the theater. Is this true? And did that interest connect at all with your other activities?

STEIN: Yes, it's true. I had been interested in acting ever since I was a child. In my early teens, I read Stanislavsky and anything else serious I could find. In the spring of 1937, I was seen acting in a school production by the director of theater productions for various vacation resorts, and was invited to join a company he was organizing for the following summer. Although I had been considering research that summer at the invitation of the chairman of the Sociology Department, I agreed to join the group and soon found myself launched into a professional theater company headed by Danny Kaye. I did acting for two more seasons. It was magnificent theater training and a very enjoyable, rewarding experience.

My theater experience helped me in teaching, particularly in establishing audience contact when lecturing to large groups or presiding. I was also occasionally stimulated to write and present humorous sketches at social work meetings. When I taught at the Smith College School of Social Work, I helped in the production of shows the students put on, and I wrote dialogue and enjoyed a great collaboration with Katherine Kendall and others who wrote and produced takeoffs on social work education for the annual meetings of the Council on Social Work Education.

FAITHFUL ANGELS

As a professional practitioner, what were your principal responsibilities and the highlights that you recall most vividly?

STEIN: I began my professional social work career, after fieldwork in a family agency and a psychiatric hospital, as a caseworker in a highly reputed family agency. I gained understanding of the helping process, learning to listen carefully and be patient and nonjudgmental.

After two years, I was asked to be the resident psychiatric casework consultant to the counselors in a summer camp run by the agency for children with psychological and emotional problems. I learned how dramatic changes can take place in children over a relatively short period, and what the results can be if these changes were reinforced after the summer. I wrote detailed reports on each child for the use of caseworkers in the agencies that referred the children and was gratified to receive words of praise and encouragement from the social workers. I wrote "The Caseworker in a Children's Camp," which was sent to *The Family*, the major social work journal in the country at the time, and it won first prize in a casework article contest that I did not know I had entered.

My work in Europe and North Africa with the AJDC was a different kind of practice. As deputy director of budget and research, during my first seven or eight months, I helped to estimate the need for food, clothing, health care, and other supplements that the AJDC could provide to Holocaust survivors in displaced persons' camps in Germany and Austria, and for refugee children throughout Europe.

When I then established the Welfare Department at Paris headquarters, my function was essentially consultative, to work with the directors in the field on planning their programs. This brought me to every country in Western Europe. I got firsthand reactions to how the war affected various populations and witnessed the enormous wreckage created by the invasions and the bombings. The horrors committed by the Nazis made a profound and lasting impression on me. The images continue to haunt me. The experiences strengthened my connection to the Jewish community.

In 1948, I promoted the idea, which was accepted by the AJDC, of forming a training center for social workers who would return to their communities in Europe. I recruited a former professor at the Columbia University School of Social Work, to help staff and devise a program for the school, to be named for philanthropist Paul Baerwald. Thus, the Paul Baerwald School of Social Work was established in Versailles. By the fall of 1949, the program was under way. By then, however, the Iron Curtain had been lowered over Eastern Europe, and there was no contact possible with anyone there. The number of candidates for social work jobs in Western Europe was relatively limited; after a few years, the decision was made to close the school and help fund a new one with the same name in the Hebrew University in Jerusalem.

When I directed the Tunisian program, much of my time went into reconciling different groups in the community, helping to mediate conflict between the Jewish community and the French civil authorities, bringing some dignity to the indigenous traditional relief program for impoverished people, and helping to develop more community self-reliance. All of my social work knowledge was put to the test by a different culture.

I don't know whether I can legitimately call my 23 part- and full-time years with UNICEF social work practice, except for my first year in Tanganyika (now Tanzania). There I worked very closely with C. D. Msuya, a young and gifted graduate of Makcrere, who was the first Tanganyikan director of community development, in thinking through, testing, and organizing his operation, and assisting him in providing training and supervision to his staff. Those were heady days for Tanganyika, just after independence. President Julius Nyerere was trying to develop a nation state out of 120 or so different ethnic groups. There was great a optimism and jubilation in many quarters. There was also a certain amount of chaotic effort. However, planning did get under way, and substantial external aid started to arrive. I returned to Tanganyika after it became Tanzania every year for about 12 years, each time being welcomed by C. D. Msuya, who became head of one ministry after another, including the Ministry of Finance, and at one point prime minister.

Most of my time with UNICEF between 1962 and 1984 was spent in consultation with UNICEF staff in the field, particularly in relation to their joint planning with governments, and in New York on organizational issues of policy, personnel, and strategy. For 10 years I was consultant and then director of the Senior Interregional Staff Seminar, which is still regarded as outstanding in its success.

Of your many consultant responsibilities, which do you think had the greatest impact on the lives of others or yourself? Any examples?

STEIN: Judging one's own personal impact is risky at best. I hope I made a significant impact as a teacher at Columbia, Smith, and CWRU. However, among my consultancies, which included the National Institute of Mental Health and many other agencies, I was privileged to serve the two extraordinary organizations that continue to touch the lives of millions: UNICEF and AJDC.

In UNICEF, I was deeply engaged in work in organizational policy, structure, and management and also in program direction. In 1964, UNICEF held an international conference in Bellagio, Italy, with many ministers from developing and industrialized countries present as well as outstanding economists and planners. The subject was "Planning for the Needs of Children in Developing Countries." This conference changed the course of UNICEF.

Until then, UNICEF staff in the field could make no decisions without getting approval from the World Health Organization (WHO), the Food & Agriculture Organization (FAO), and the United Nations Educational, Scientific and Cultural Organization (UNESCO). UNICEF staff members were also, in effect, blocked from meeting with ministers of government or other top-level officials because they had to work through the specialized agencies, whose staffs were predominantly in Paris, Rome, and Geneva.

As a result of the conference, UNICEF field staff was free to work directly with ministers of education, health, planning, agriculture, or finance, and get into planning for children with cooperating governments directly. Cooperation with specialized agencies continued and their resources were used, but UNICEF became much more nimble, flexible, and self-directing. The report of the Bellagio conference (which I edited) was translated into several languages.

Evaluation was another area of concern to me. I was instrumental in creating a department to see that evaluations were conducted. I also helped develop the instrument for internal audit.

Two top executives of the agency and I worked out a program for an annual three-week interregional senior staff seminar for advanced training, principally for people who showed promise of rising to higher executive positions. During the first two seminars, I was a resource consultant. I then directed the seminars for the next eight years, until I left my continuous association with UNICEF in 1984.

These staff seminars included didactic information related to UNICEF concerns—always using top-notch local specialists—but they also had the function of helping staff to develop their own questions and ideas and to debate the merits of agency policies or programs openly, without fear of retribution. Many of the staff had come from societies which frowned upon such argumentation. The staff also learned to work in teams and had rich experience sharing with people from cultures other than their own and getting a sense of different values and perspectives.

In program development, I was a proponent of the integrated child development approach. Concentrating on education without adequate attention to food production, nutrition, health care, environmental sanitation, or opening opportunities for girls and women would not be effective. I helped to initiate the first major child development project in India, with UNICEF support.

I was also a proponent—at first almost alone—of UNICEF giving attention to mental health resources. Probably as a result, I was asked to be a plenary session speaker at the World Congress of the International Federation of Mental Health in Manila.

In 1982, I prepared a summary of research I had undertaken, with a few part-time investigators I had recruited, on the commercial exploitation of children around the world. This study dealt not only with sexual exploitation and physical labor, but also the exploitation of children by tobacco companies, well before the U.S. government warning on cigarette health hazards. Much of my UNICEF consulting work was also devoted to issues such as lines of authority between headquarters, the regional directors' offices, and the country directors' offices.

I hope I also had an impact on the American Joint Distribution Committee, known throughout the Jewish world as "the JDC" or the "Joint." It was established in the United States during World War I primarily to aid Jews in distress in other lands through rescue activities, materials and cultural support, and community development. It also had a nonsectarian development program. The height of JDC's activity was immediately after World War II in giving support to the shattered remnants of the Jewish population in Europe.

My consultative work with the JDC began in 1954. I was asked to go to Israel to help negotiate the establishment of the Paul Baerwald School of Social Work at the

Hebrew University. It was to be the first university-based school of social work in Israel. Although there was resistance at first, the school was finally established.

My next JDC consultant relationship was in helping to change its organizational structure as part of a consultative team headed by the late Henry Zucker. For some years, I chaired the Professional Advisery Committee overseeing JDC programs and advising on policy in programs for Holocaust survivors throughout Eastern Europe, in nonsectarian development assistance, in community development in Latin America and welfare in Israel. From 1989 to 1991, I led a strategic planning review for the agency that resulted in substantial changes in structure, program directions, and relations with local federations. I continue to be involved with JDC from time to time.

I understand that you worked with several executive directors of UNICEF.

STEIN: I was privileged to work with the first three executive directors of UNICEF, Maurice Pate, Henry Labouisse, and James Grant. These three helped to instill in UNICEF a culture of common sense, productivity, and integrity.

Having been appointed University Professor, I could take leave without pay whenever I wished. In addition to my part-time work with UNICEF, I was therefore able to devote several years of full-time service to UNICEF until 1983. I was always impressed with the generally high caliber of the UNICEF staff. In those years I worked closely with the brilliant and hard-working senior deputy executive director, Dick Heyward.

I understand that your work with the UN Division of Social Development took place before your work with UNICEF.

STEIN: Yes. My connection with the Division of Social Development, sometimes called the Division of Social Affairs, took place soon after my return from Europe in 1950. The director of the social welfare section, Martha Branscombe, asked me to help with the latest survey of social work education internationally. Katherine Kendall had worked on the first, Dame Eileen Younghusband worked on the third, and I worked on the fourth or fifth. While I was there I was brought into policy discussions with Julia Henderson, who was director of the division, in considering the role that social work could and should play, if any, in social development. With the title of Senior Adviser to the Conference of Ministers of Social Welfare, I helped plan the largest international conference of its kind. I drafted many of the conclusions for the final report.

Given your ongoing ties to the Jewish community, could you tell us about some of the people who influenced your work there?

STEIN: Most of my work with the Jewish community has been with the JDC. The leaders who influenced me include Joseph Schwartz, the director for overseas operations during and after the Holocaust. He was an outstanding, creative, and courageous executive. One of his successors, Ralph Goldman, an old friend who still works with JDC as an emeritus director, also was an exceptional executive. For the past 10 years, the JDC has had another superb professional leader in Michael Schneider. The late Henry Zucker was a vital influence in developing the Cleveland Jewish Federation into one of the most efficient and effective agencies of its kind anywhere.

Are there any hazards that you can relate with respect to your UN and JDC work?

STEIN: There are health and traffic hazards in all countries, but more in the poor ones. I got malaria in Tanganyika even though I had taken all recommended precautions. On one of my visits to Tanzania, in 1974, I was hit by a car, and my right arm was fractured in several places. This prevented me from presiding over the Congress of the International Association of Schools of Social Work in Nairobi. Because there are no driving tests in most developing countries and few resources for traffic control, traffic accidents are more of a hazard in poor countries than might be thought. Psychological and political hazards are a different matter.

Back in the United States, you were an adviser and consultant in government agencies and with several universities.

STEIN: For a number of years while I was at Columbia, I served on training groups at the National Institute of Mental Health (NIMH), and for a period I was chairman of the Interdisciplinary Experimental and Special Training Review Committee. I conducted a number of site visits for NIMH around the country. At the Social Security Administration, I served on an advisory committee that, with the dawning age of computers, examined such issues as privacy of information. I served also on committees of the Health, Education and Welfare Administration, did a study for the Welfare Administration, and served on a subcommittee of the National Academy of Sciences.

Two universities asked me to evaluate their schools of social work. In both cases, the schools were on thin ice and the university administrations were seriously thinking of closing them. They needed and received reform and both schools survived.

One of the most interesting assignments was an evaluation of an innovative program by Five Schools, Inc., an association of five colleges in Massachusetts that included Smith, Hampshire, Amherst, Mt. Holyoke, and the University of Massachusetts. Scholars in very specialized fields would be engaged for three-year periods as Five College Fellows, based at one of the colleges but available to students in any of them. One of the people invited, for example, was a specialist in Irish literature and its connections to the European continent. Another was an authority on Sanskrit and dance in India.

I was delighted with the number of students I interviewed who would take courses that had no connection to their career path, simply because they were interested in learning and understood that the teachers were excellent.

Returning to your consultation with a manufacturing company, could you provide an illustration or two of what you did?

STEIN: The plant manager was irritated with a worker who was clearly an informal leader, bright and well-liked by his peers. The plant manager had offered him a foreman's job, which would mean that he would be on regular salary and not on an hourly wage. He refused. The young man, I found out, liked the people he was working with and did not want to be their boss. He also did not want to worry about anything in the plant when he went fishing or when he went home. Moreover, he was reasonably satisfied with the income he was getting and didn't expect it to go down because he was a productive worker. The notion that anybody should not have upward mobility strivings was incomprehensible to the plant manager, sort of un-American, but he finally relaxed and found someone else who was competent and who wanted to be a foreman.

One of the principles we tried to instill in the company with respect to the handling of personnel was that nobody should be promoted without some indication of what weakness that person might need to overcome in addition to the positives that led to promotion. In addition, nobody should be let go or demoted without written indication of the strengths the individual had despite his or her shortcomings.

This was not an easy principle to adopt. It became a little clearer when the shipping clerk in New York, who received the supplies from trucks and was supposed to write down exactly what came in, was about to be fired. This fellow had taken courses at the Institute of Design; he was at this job not only to earn some money, but also to find out a bit more about the industry, which designed and manufactured children's dresses. I asked the supervisor why he was firing him and he said, "His handwriting is terrible; you can't read his numbers; he makes all kinds of mistakes and it's embarrassing and very bad for the company. It wastes my time." He added, "He's also away from his desk so often." I asked, "Where does he go?" "He hangs out with the designers." I asked, "What does he do there?" "Oh, I don't know."

I went to the designers and asked them whether they knew anything about this young man. The head designer said, "He's always asking questions and making suggestions, and the suggestions are often very good ones." I said, "What kind of suggestions?" She said, "He suggests how we can get the same effect at lower cost with different kinds of material or different methods of stitching the garment." In this industry, that kind of talent was worth its weight in uranium. The shipping clerk was appointed as a liaison between the design area and production. He left the company a few years later and, I understand, has become a major figure in the industry.

Could you tell us something about your social work teaching?

STEIN: Some social science was taught in schools of social work but there was no history of it being adapted to the practice needs of the profession. The "so what?" question had to be answered. What if I know from stratification studies, for example, that this individual can be characterized as an upper-middle-class person? What difference, if any, does that make on how I work with him or her or the nature of our relationship or in any other way? The intent of the course I initiated was to draw on sociobehavioral science to see how it could be applied to the kinds of situations that social work students were facing in their fieldwork experiences and would face later in their practice. To make this course really effective, we also conducted seminars for the fieldwork advisers to bring them up to speed on what students were learning.

In addition, we developed seminars for senior faculty in social casework, group work, and community organization on the relevance of social science materials and current research in the sociobehavioral sciences.

The first course I taught in sociocultural aspects in social work turned out to be remarkably popular, and we needed more faculty. I persuaded Richard Cloward, a sociologist and social worker, to join me. Although his area of special interest was somewhat different than mine, we complemented each other very well. We eventually produced a textbook, *Social Perspectives on Behavior*, which was very well-received.

I also introduced a seminar in the curriculum, "Social Work on the International Scene," which today would be called international social work. At that time every student had to be enrolled in a seminar in their final semester. The objective of this one was to help students understand the elements in different societies that would give rise to various policies and programs of social welfare and styles of relationship between social workers and their clientele—in general, to place social work within the cultural, political, and economic map of a country. The seminar was not designed to make experts out of any students, but rather to help them to get an appreciation of the diversity not only in the ways social work operates but of the very functions of social welfare in different societies. At the same time, they were to get a perspective of how one would look at social welfare in the United States the same way, as if one were a foreigner.

I can't help but wonder if the innovativeness and legacy of this particular course might have had anything to do with the Columbia school offering generalist social work practice when it's not all that popular a concentration in most schools of social work.

STEIN: I don't know if there is that connection, but there were implications, particularly related to foreign students.

I was involved in a national program that dealt with the education of students from other lands. In the United States this was a very hot subject after World War II, when people from all over the world wanted to seek higher education in the United States, particularly students from Asia but also from European countries. As a result of my experience in other countries and the school's increasing sensitivity to cultural factors, I persuaded the admissions office at Columbia to set up guidelines for whom to accept and whom to reject from other countries. I discussed these factors similarly at Smith. When I became dean at Western Reserve, it was not difficult to introduce the same guidelines.

One was to exercise care about admitting students who came directly for professional training without any working experience in their own country. It was important that they not be seen as outsiders when they returned and that they had a sense of the practicalities of life and institutional patterns from direct experience so they knew what they were going back to. There were instances of tragedies befalling students, from developing countries in particular, who returned to their country, found no way of convincing anybody to do things the way they had learned in the United States, and became isolated and depressed.

It was also important to understand the learning curve of foreign students generally and the extent to which many become depressed by the end of their first year in the United States. This is particularly true when they are no longer regarded as a delightful and exotic foreigner but are seen as everyday folk, expected to be doing what everyone else is doing, yet find handicaps in language and in coping with living in America. Students from other countries who come to our schools need special handling and counseling by people who understand them and their problems of adjustment, whether or not they are familiar with the specific culture of the student.

One year, the IASSW sponsored a meeting I chaired at the International Center in Hawaii on social work values across the world. It was a challenging seminar because there were social work educational leaders from every part of the globe and different points of view. This was particularly so between the societies that emphasized individualism, individual growth and development, and success, and those that were extended family, community- or state-centered, where one's obligations to others took precedence over individual needs. Most salient were the differences between the societies where the nuclear family was predominant and those where extended family systems were in effect.

This was a good period for The International Association of Schools of Social Work (IASSW). During the eight years I was president, IASSW moved steadily into the Third World from its European base, and new issues arose as well as new opportunities. One of the issues that remained hot for years was whether or not to accept schools of social work in South Africa as members during apartheid. UNESCO was threatening to void IASSW's consultative relationship to it, thereby threatening IASSW's relationship to the whole UN system. It was agreed that I'd go to South Africa, officially as a guest lecturer but actually to explore the elements of this problem.

I was based in Cape Town and gave a few lectures at the school of social work there. I recall meeting with leading social work educators of varied political persuasions. I also met with two people who were under house arrest and who were not permitted to talk politics with me. They gave me, in an elliptical way, their views on whether it would be good for the anti-apartheid cause for the schools in South Africa to be related to the outside world through IASSW, which had a strong anti-apartheid platform, or bad because it would by implication give legitimacy to apartheid. I brought back an analysis of the pros and cons to the IASSW executive committee. We had a passionate discussion lasting two days, at the conclusion of which we decided on criteria that a school in South Africa would have to meet to be allowed to be a member of IASSW. UNESCO officials withdrew their threat. The IASSW continued to have problems with this issue over the years, but the end of apartheid has made such issues irrelevant. I feel fortunate to have been associated with the outstanding people I worked with in the IASSW and CSWE, especially Dame Eileen Younghusband and Katherine Kendall.

Perhaps you can elaborate a bit on some of the highlights of your experience with Western Reserve University and with the greater Cleveland area during the past 35 years.

STEIN: Three years after I was appointed dean at the School of Applied Social Services of Western Reserve University, there was movement by the boards of Case Institute of Technology and Western Reserve to federate. In 1967, I was asked to be Provost of Behavioral and Social Sciences when the federation was announced, and later I was appointed Provost of the new university. As Provost, I was in a leadership role in working with the faculty and President to guide the university in it's handling of the campus disturbances of the late '60s.

During my earlier years as dean, Mayor Carl Stokes, the first African American mayor of a large city, invited me to be one of his senior official advisors. Mayor Stokes asked me to be chairman of his Commission on the Crisis in Welfare in Cleveland and I accepted.

We organized a commission that included bankers, clergy, business people, leaders of all major professions, and welfare recipients. Many of the people who came to the meetings had never knowingly met a welfare recipient. Members of the commission interviewed the leaders in virtually every public sector of the city that affects poor people—education, health, public safety, and so on. The elite members of the commission were often flabbergasted at the knowledge they gained just through direct exposure. They had never considered what it meant for welfare families not to be able to buy what the children were told they must have to go to school, or their difficulty in getting to school at all. They had never seen the inside of a welfare office and what went on there. Even some of the members of the commission who were executives of private sector welfare agencies were unaware of what went on in the public agencies. Religious leaders who were members of the commission used the experience as themes for their sermons.

The commission's report, which I prepared, was received with acclaim and became the basis for a number of appearances that I made in churches and schools and at the Cleveland Forum, where I gave two lectures. There were other speeches and lots of press coverage, but the fact was that the city could do very little about welfare. Most of the responsibility was the state's. Our representation to Columbus, site of the Ohio state government, did not avail us much. The result was not much change in the actual conditions of welfare recipients, but a heightened understanding of the problems and some of the conditions of life of poor people in Cleveland by [local leaders].

Could you say something more about the Global Currents Lecture Series at Case Western Reserve University, and any other of your scholarly international involvement there or elsewhere?

STEIN: The lecture series was organized in the mid-1980s, after I returned from my work with UNICEF. We invited speakers to lecture on important issues, such as global warming or the impact of nationalism in the world. The lecturers were all prominent people. [They included] James Grant, executive director of UNICEF, a leading economist from Mexico, scientists from the laboratories dealing with a variety of environmental issues, and so forth. The series audiences started slowly but grew so that we attracted audiences of 500, including, of course, many students and faculty. Some of the critical world issues were brought to light before they attracted media attention. Tapes of the lectures were made available at cost to schools in the area.

Those first five years of Global Currents, I believe, helped give impetus to the move towards more international and global awareness throughout the university. This direction has been strong at CWRU this past decade, as it has been on many campuses in the country, and has grown in all professional schools. When I became Provost again, during a transition of presidents, in 1986–1988, I was able to help move the global perspective even further in the university.

As for other activities related to international themes, I suppose one can include my giving a two-day seminar annually for 10 years at the Harvard School of Public Health on planning for children in developing countries. At CWRU, I helped to initiate the Center for International Health, lectured in its orientation series, and thus became an adjunct professor of international health in the School of Medicine. The Club of Rome invited me to become an associate member, and for a number of years I participated in their meetings. Again, at this university I joined Professor Mihajlo Mesarovic in developing the first course on Global Issues. Professor Mesarovic is now senior adviser on education in global issues for UNESCO. This course highlighted an interactive computer program with a "what if?" scenario.

Turning to the social work profession once again, could you please share with us any general observations about international social work and the future?

STEIN: In the late 1940s and 1950s, some of us tried to have the term "international social work" confined to service with international agencies, such as those in the United Nations, or with agencies working internationally, such as CARE, Catholic Relief Services, the American Joint Distribution Committee, or International Social Service. We considered that a social worker going to another country to work or teach, valuable as it might be, was not doing international work, strictly speaking. However, over the course of time the term "international social work" lost any precise definition and seems now to refer to any relationship to social work outside of one's own country.

Every profession should be educating its members to have some understanding of how that profession is viewed and practiced in at least some other countries. If nothing else, it helps professionals to understand their own profession better in their own country.

Understanding other cultures is not something that can be done by fax or e-mail. It requires study, as it always has, despite the extraordinary developments in commu-

nications technology. Once there is knowledge of another culture, or at least awareness of how to learn about a different culture, communication technology becomes
precious. It can facilitate all kinds of collaborative work across national boundaries. I
think the future will see not only more but also new kinds of cross-national interaction in social work, as well as in other professions.

Many schools of social work are now involved with schools in countries outside
the United States. This is hopeful and healthy, particularly when the relationship
between the two is one of equal status. Some schools of social work also work
directly with agencies overseas, giving students the rich experience of working in
another society.

Our own school of social work at CWRU, for example, has a long-term commitment in Romania in child welfare and other areas. This, I think, is one of the most
important trends for professional education and service in the future. Interaction of
social workers across national boundaries is educational and culturally sensitizing for
all parties.

*Looking back, I imagine that there are both rewards and costs to a career as diverse and
rich as yours.*

STEIN: There are indeed. The rewards have been several—especially confronting
new challenges at different stages of one's life and summoning what talent one has
to meet them. Diversity has made life interesting. I have studied broadly, have met
some extraordinary people, made many friends, experienced a variety of cultures,
visited many countries, and enjoyed my teaching, consultation, and executive posts.
There was never a dull moment. I have witnessed deep and pervasive misery on a
vast scale as well as staunch courage and dignity in the face of deprivation and cru-
elty; and I have also been permitted to be a factor in significant organizational
efforts to help.

The downside of versatility and varied interests is that one does not sustain a
lifelong concentration on one principal focus and develop it to its fullest, or cap-
italize on the investment one makes in a given professional experience or research
undertaking. Although more than 100 papers of mine have been published and I've
edited or co-authored five books, much of my potential writing never got off the
ground because as soon as the spadework was done that would justify a book or a
published paper, I would report it and soon was off to something else.

The big cost, however, was not being able to be at home enough. I missed my
wife, Charmion, and our children for extended periods of time, and my family
missed me.

The moral, I suppose, is that you can't have everything. I have been fortunate to
be married to someone who supported and shared my interests, and I have tried to
support hers, but I recognize that she was carrying more of the burden than she
should have in raising our children. As time went on, however, my children also
became a source of support for everything I was doing, for which I have been and
continue to be grateful.

Of the many distinguished honors and awards you have received, are there some that you particularly value?

STEIN: Each award has its own unique significance, but the University Medal at Case Western Reserve University touched me very deeply. This is the highest honor the university can bestow, and only once before was the medal given to a faculty member. The fact that many emeriti faculty came to honor me and referred to my role in the University's dealing with disturbances of the late '60s, mean a lot to me.

The René Sand Award of the International Conference of Social Welfare is meaningful because it recognized my commitment to an international perspective in social welfare, in my work at UNICEF and other international agencies, and the connections I sought to help construct between social work and social development. The Katherine A. Kendall Award of the International Association of Schools of Social Work also holds special significance because of my long association with Katherine and because it was in effect recognition of the role I played in IASSW while I was president for eight years.

The most surprising recognition I received was the dedication to me of a fine book on medical ethics, *Drawing the Line*, written by a former philosophy professor at CWRU, Samuel Gorovitz, who was dean of students while I was Provost in the '60s. He became dean of arts and sciences at another university and we had not been in close communication for years when I received this totally unexpected tribute.

The awards from the Columbia University School of Social Work and the Smith College School of Social Work alumni touched me because they were from former students who valued my teaching of so many years ago. And, of course, I am gratified by the lectureship in international social welfare established in my name by the Mandel School of Applied Social Sciences at CWRU.

Finally, what can you venture by way of any predictions about the future?

STEIN: I don't have predictions, but I do have hopes. I hope social work engages more directly with the issues of the time where it has a professional contribution to make. I hope that it collaborates more with other disciplines in international as well as in domestic issues. For example, to connect with relevant professional bodies to examine such issues as social development and globalism, international health and the role of social work in private international agencies as well as in the UN system.

INDEX

Crisis intervention. *See* Emergencies

Cuban refugee families, 64

Cultural beliefs and attitudes, 84, 140

Cultural change, 31

Culture. *See also specific topics*

    underemphasized in social work education, 204

D

Daughter of Persia (Farman-Farmaian), 79, 94–95

Davidson, George, 242, 243

Decision making, 123

Dehli School of Social Work, 202, 203, 205

Delinquency, 118–120

Democracy, 123

Denmark, 119, 120, 125

Desai, Armaity S., 57

    administrative work, 66–71

    education, 57, 60–63

        influences of early, 59

        undergraduate experiences, 60

        at University of Chicago, 62–65

    entry into social work, 60–61

        factors that influenced, 58–59

    guidelines for current and future social workers, 76–77

    international activities, 73–74

    publications, 75

    return to India, 66

    scholarships and awards, 76

    special assignments, 71–73

    at Tata Institute, 60–62, 67–71

    and University Grants Commission, 74–75

Deutsches Volksverein, 42

Developing countries, 63, 76

    problems in, 30

    role of schools of social work in, 87

    training in social welfare, 105

    UNICEF and, 108

Dionne, Pierre, 249

Disabilities, 110, 157, 243

Disasters, 70, 87, 110

E

Earthquake of 1990, 110

Economic Social Commission for Asia and the Pacific (ESCAP), 26–27

Education. *See also* School; Social work programs and education

in family planning, 140
Indian higher, 73
primary, 69
sex, 207
for social action and change, 212
sociology, 59, 60, 82, 100, 160, 256, 258
Egypt. *See* Gindy, Aida
Elders, talking and working with, 129–130
Emergencies, national, 70, 87, 110
Empowerment, xvi, 29, 89, 188, 230
England, 220–221
Ethics, 173, 176
Exchange programs with Latin America, 148

F

Factories, 90
Faithful angels, xi–xii. *See also specific individuals*
    commonalities among, xiv–xvi
    family backgrounds, xiv–xv
    vs. "unfaithful angels," xi
Family planning, 12–13, 26, 27, 86, 88, 95–96, 100, 153
    culture, religion, and, 206–208
    encouraging popular education in, 140
    funding, 152
    IASSW and, 152, 153
    Nanavatty's work in, 206–208
Family Planning Project, 88
Family welfare, 206–207
Family Welfare Bureau, 167–168
Family(ies), 228
    centrality of, xiii–xiv, 112, 182
    Cuban refugee, 64
Farman-Farmaian, Sattareh, xvi, 79
    awards and honors, 95
    changing a governmental institution, 90–91
    education
        decision to obtain social work, 82
        graduate, 83–84
        undergraduate, and difficulty learning English, 83
        at University of Chicago, 84
    family, 79–81, 97
        influence of father, 79–81
    and graduates of TSS social work program, 89–90
    international social work leadership experiences, 96–97
    on Iran and future of social work profession in Iran, 95–96

Health care and health services, 88
   social aspects of, 208
Health issues, public, 39
Holocaust, 222. *See also* Nazi Germany
Holocaust survivors, 257, 259
Homelessness, 47, 67, 85–86, 123
Huffman, Vera, 245
Human rights, 77
Human rights violations, 32
Humanities, xv

I
India. *See also* Desai, Armaity S.; Nanavatty, Meher
   independence movement, 200
   Ministry of Community Development, 205
Indian Council of Social Welfare, 209
Indian higher education, 73
Indian Journal of Social Work, 75
Indigenization of social work education, 211
Industries, 90, 137, 264
Institute of Integrated Social Services (ISSI), 42
Inter-University Consortium for International Social Development (IUCISD),
   210, 250
Interdisciplinary approach and collaboration, 52–53, 159, 163
International Association of Schools of Social Work (IASSW), 50, 139–140, 248, 250
   awards presented by, 130–131
   conferences, 26, 50–51, 178, 249–250
   Farman-Farmaian on, 96
   focus on social and socioeconomic development, 152, 153, 159, 178
   history, 156
   involvement in
      Almanzor's, 26–28, 73
      Desai's, 73
      Jones's, 139, 140
      Kendall's, 26, 96, 139, 145, 149–152, 154, 156, 159–161, 178, 248
      Rosenfeld's, 226, 228–229
      Splane's, 246, 250
      Stein's, 266–267
   making it an international organization, 156
   positions held in, 26, 27, 50–51, 73, 128, 139–141, 149–152, 178, 228, 246
International Bureau for Children's Rights, 52
International Conferences on Social Development (ICSD), 249
International Council on Social Welfare (ICSW), 51, 52, 177, 178
   Cornely's involvement with, 51, 52
   Kendall's involvement with, 150–153, 174

L

M

and Zimbabwe Women Finance Trust, 192–195

Marxism, 49

McDowell, Mary Eliza, ix

Media, 15

Military, mental health work in, 221–222

Minorities, 76, 86

Missionaries, 10, 81

P

Palestine, 219–220, 231

Pan American Health Organization (PAHO/WHO), 12, 14

Parker, Norma, 169

Participation, 32, 89, 110. *See also* Empowerment

Peruvian School of Social Work, 2–6

Philippine School of Social Work (PSSW), 21, 23–26

Philippine Women's University (PWU), 23, 33

Philippines, 206–208, 244–245. *See also* Almanzor, Angelina C.

Politicized situations/arenas, working in, 49–50, 70, 92–95, 122–125.
　See also World War II

Population policy, 140. *See also* Family planning

Poverty, 47, 67, 69, 82, 84, 108, 231. *See also* "Fortress"

"Poverty, Social Welfare and the University" (Almanzor), 31

Powerful and powerless, the, 77, 84

Prison psychiatric clinic, 116–117

Private practice, 159

Professional conduct, 173

Professional Social Work in Australia, 168

Prostitution, 92

Psychiatric clinics, 116–117, 119, 221

Psychiatric services, 224

Psychotherapy and social work, 226

Pumphrey, Muriel, ix

Pumphrey, Ralph, ix

R

Racism, 190. *See also* South Africa, apartheid in

Red Cross Society (Red Crescent), 100, 101

"Reflective practitioner" and "reflective practice," 229

Refugee families, Cuban, 64

Refugees, 124–127

Regional Commission of the Victims of Barrages (CRAB), 43

Rehabilitation social work, 178

Religious beliefs, 84, 232. *See also* Catholic Church; Islamic law; Missionaries

Religious studies, 36, 37

Review of Social Work Education in India (Desai), 75

Riga Institution, 122

Rosenfeld, Jona M., xv–xvi, 217
　awards, 230–231
　in Chicago, 223–225
　childhood and family background, 218–219
　education, 219–221, 223–225
　in England, 220–221

University Grants Commission (UCG), 73, 74
  structure and responsibility, 75
University of Alberta, 245
University of British Columbia (UBC), 245–247
University of Chicago, 62–65
University of New South Wales, 169–170, 172
University of Stockholm, 116
University of Wales, 135–136